ART OF THE PRINTED BOOK

1455-1955

WITH AN ESSAY

BY JOSEPH BLUMENTHAL

PUBLISHED BY

THE PIERPONT MORGAN LIBRARY

NEW YORK · 1973

ART OF
THE PRINTED
BOOK
1455–1955

MASTERPIECES OF TYPOGRAPHY

THROUGH FIVE CENTURIES

FROM THE COLLECTIONS OF THE

PIERPONT MORGAN LIBRARY

NEW YORK

EXHIBITION

11 SEPTEMBER TO 2 DECEMBER · 1973

THE PIERPONT MORGAN LIBRARY

Copyright © 1973 by The Pierpont Morgan Library

29 EAST 36 STREET, NEW YORK, N.Y. 10016

Library of Congress Catalogue Card Number 73–82830

ISBN 87598–041–4

PRINTED IN THE UNITED STATES OF AMERICA

TABLE OF CONTENTS

PREFACE

IT IS altogether appropriate for The Pierpont Morgan Library to sponsor a work devoted to the *Art of the Printed Book, 1455–1955*. The Library is celebrated not only for unique and very rare volumes in its collections, but for the superlative condition and the beauty of its books. It is as much an art museum as a research library, and the books have been collected by bibliophiles who were connoisseurs. One can expect a large number of the copies to be sumptuously printed on vellum, and in many of the books the relationship of text and margin can be seen in an ideal state. The one hundred twelve books selected to illustrate the highest achievement in printing in the western world are therefore also frequently among the finest examples known.

These masterpieces of typography are presented not by someone who is primarily a scholar or librarian, but by a man who is one of the most distinguished typographers of our time, Joseph Blumenthal. For forty-five years at his Spiral Press in New York Mr. Blumenthal helped to create and then to lead a small world where the art of the printed book was stimulated, where a distinctive style of printing was produced, where craftsmanship and superior presswork were the rule, where elegance, artistry, and balance were bywords. He has made the selection of books, written the introductory essay, and designed the *Art of the Printed Book, 1455–1955*, which is itself a model of the excellence in typography created by Joseph Blumenthal. I trust that this book is also representative of the quality of publications from the Morgan Library in the past and for the future. At a time when libraries and museums seem less concerned about the typography of their publications, we have tried to maintain and, if possible, to improve the quality of our printing and our photographic reproductions.

The exceptionally fine reproductions here are from photographs prepared in the Library by Charles Passela and Frank C. Drouin, Jr., who worked far beyond the call of any duty. Mr. Blumenthal in his Foreword has made acknowledgment to many who have helped in producing this book. I should like to add my thanks to Frederick B. Adams, Jr., my predecessor at the Library, who first discussed the possibilities of this work with Mr. Blumenthal.

We have found that the resources of the Morgan Library provided all the books that were needed, with a few exceptions, and almost all of those are books printed in the last hundred years. The books which we lack we hope will in time be acquired for the Library, and, in fact, several books which we needed were found for the Library during the time that this work was in preparation.

All of the books illustrated here will be exhibited at the Library from the eleventh of September to the second of December 1973. The one hundred twelve books are the work of less than one hundred printers and designers. There are a few books printed after 1935, but essentially the two terminals in the history of the art of the printed book are Gutenberg's great Bible of c.1455 and the Oxford Lectern Bible of Bruce Rogers in 1935. Rogers' Bible, magnificently bound by Roger Powell in 1959, was the recent gift of John M. Crawford, Jr., in honor of the fiftieth anniversary (in February 1974) of the Library as a public institution, and Mr. Crawford also similarly gave the superb copy of the Eric Gill–Golden Cockerel Press *Four Gospels*, 1931, number three of twelve copies on vellum. Two notable examples of sixteenth-century printing had to be borrowed from the New York Public Library (no. 54) and the Beinecke Library of Yale University (no. 60). Books were also lent by Robert Elwell (nos. 106, 108, 109), Charles Ryskamp (no. 88), Stuart B. Schimmel (no. 114), Leonard B. Schlosser (no. 113), and by one of the trustees of the Library, Gordon N. Ray (nos. 97, 99, 103, 105). Four books (nos. 72, 83, 92, 112) were chosen from the Glazier Collection and three (nos. 74, 75, 90) from the Heineman Collection; both of these collections have been on deposit in the Morgan Library for a number of years. Without these loans, and without the assistance and encouragement from many friends, and, above all, without Joseph Blumenthal, the exhibition and the book would not have been possible.

CHARLES RYSKAMP, *Director*

viii

FOREWORD

AND ACKNOWLEDGMENTS

THE ARTS OF THE BOOK, in common with all human endeavor, have been achieved by men of conspicuous sensitivity and highly developed skills. The tools of trade have been available; the men who used them with esthetic success have been rare indeed. The essay which follows introduces the most significant designers and printers of the great printed books, and sketches the historical backgrounds and conditions under which these books were produced. Printing, even at its best, is not a studio art. When pursued as an articulated craft, the printed book must involve scholarship and the correlation of men and machines. The men who achieved artistry in their volumes worked within this framework, whether in presses established for livelihood, or by royal or private subsidy. Gutenberg's great gift to civilization was the invention of a hand mold that made possible the mass production of individual mechanical letters (movable type) and the development of a machine, hand-operated to be sure, but clearly a machine, which we know as the printing press.

I have selected somewhat more than a hundred books which seem to this typographic designer and printer to represent the peaks of elegance and accomplishment during the five hundred years to 1955. With only a very few exceptions, they come from the extensive collections of The Pierpont Morgan Library. The responsibility of choice is my own, knowing, alas, that no anthologist can please everyone. A historian of the book or another practitioner would not have made the same choices in detail; nevertheless, after consultation with respected colleagues, the collection as a whole seems thoroughly representative of the heritage of the book.

It was early decided to avoid a compendious volume and to reduce technical data to the minimum. These limitations will, at the least, provide the virtues of brevity for the general reader; professionals who wish to dig deeper will find here a selective bibliography from which most of the historical data in this essay have been drawn. There are no footnotes because if every reference were substantiated the footnotes might well have been longer than the text. The comments and judgments about the printers and the books are my own, fortified by the usual personal prejudices and by privileged friendships among so many of this century's distinguished men and women of the book. Among the many gratifications in this undertaking has been the privilege of access to the remarkable volumes in the Morgan Library and other repositories. I find it difficult to acknowledge the extent and the richness of the rewards for a contemporary printer who was allowed so many uncounted hours of leafing through and living with the rare books of the great printers of the past.

It is now a profound pleasure to make grateful acknowledgment to numerous people who have helped with advice and encouragement. I blush to think what the essay might have been without them. The text has had the good fortune to have been read by four distinguished scholars and historians of the book: John Dreyfus of London, Karl Kup, New York, Rollo Silver, Boston, and Alan Fern, Washington, D.C. Their comments and corrections have been incorporated into the essay to its great advantage. I am also deeply indebted for critical help to David R. Godine, James Hendrickson, Philip Grushkin, Herman Cohen, Mary Coxe Schlosser, Joseph M. Bernstein, and others along the way, especially to Leonard B. Schlosser who has been a source of support in many ways. Special thanks, too, are offered to Kenneth Nesheim and his staff at Yale's Beinecke Library who brought forth large selections of books from their remarkable stacks. Lewis M. Stark and Joseph T. Rankin, curators of special collections at The New York Public Library, have been very helpful. Data has been generously supplied by Dr. Giovanni Mardersteig, Verona, Brooke Crutchley, Printer to Cambridge University, Ruth Mortimer of the Houghton Library, and Norman H. Strouse. A desk in the Reading Room of the Morgan Library has been a congenial corner for the past year thanks to the friendly cooperation of Mrs. Evelyn Semler, Paul Needham, and Charles Henderson. At The Stinehour Press and The Meriden Gravure Company, friends of long standing have given their usual skillful devotion. The text was typed and retyped with surprising patience by Virginia Potter. The index has been prepared by Martha Garlin. And now, finally, must come grateful acknowledgment of the staunch support given to this undertaking by Charles Ryskamp, Director of The Pierpont Morgan Library, of whom it can really be said that without him this book would not have become a reality.

J. B.

LIST OF THE PLATES

FIFTEENTH CENTURY

SIXTEENTH CENTURY

SEVENTEENTH CENTURY

EIGHTEENTH CENTURY

NINETEENTH CENTURY

TWENTIETH CENTURY

PRINTERS' MARKS: We are grateful to Aldus Manutius for the Dolphin and Anchor on our cover, and to those other printers whose marks decorate these pages.

THE GREAT PRINTERS
AND THEIR BOOKS

THE ART OF THE BOOK unites two of man's most cherished goals. The preservation of knowledge is linked with presentation of the noblest poetry and prose in form consistent with the significance of the words. The Bible, Cicero, St. Augustine, Chaucer, Shakespeare, and their kind dominate this collection which has been brought together to exhibit the masterpieces of five centuries of the printed book. In 1439 Johann Gutenberg described the early efforts toward his epoch-making invention as "afentur und kunst"—adventure and art. And so it has been from primitive man's picture writing to cuneiform tablets and hieroglyphics, and finally to the appearance of our modern Latin alphabet—those twenty-six characters with which the printer fashions his books.

The characters which form our present alphabet evolved from crude syllabic forms which appeared along the shores of the Mediterranean perhaps a thousand years before the Christian era. Unlike pictographic writing and the multitude of abstruse ideographic symbols into which it finally evolved, these few new forms were, marvelously, symbols of *sounds* related to language. Man's capacity to write thus became limited only to man's capacity to think.

Greece adopted these syllabic forms from the Semitic aleph beth and refined them visually into the alpha beta. Subsequently in Rome, capital letter forms reached a high degree of sophistication and elegance. The stone inscriptions, notably the incised letters on the Trajan column, are still the preeminent models for our capital letters.

At the beginning of the Christian era, the alphabet consisted only of capital letters, called majuscules. By the fourth century a transitional alphabet had appeared with capital letters more easily and quickly written in rounded forms. Known as uncial, this form of writing became established in Europe. The minuscules (small letters) evolved during the next five hundred years in the monasteries of Europe in response to the persistent and increasing need for more rapid writing of Biblical and liturgical works for the medieval church. These were the Dark Ages in Europe; nevertheless, surviving manuscripts provide fortunate evidence that widely scattered monastic centers kept alight a torch for the development of the alphabet and the book. National characteristics arose. Among the most famous of the medieval illuminated manuscripts which survived the widespread destruction of monasteries are the Northumbrian *Lindesfarne Gospels* and the Irish *Book of Kells* from the seventh and eighth centuries. On a March day in 781 in Parma, Charlemagne, on his way to Rome, crossed paths with Alcuin, the Northumbrian scholar and religious teacher returning to his school and library in York. Charlemagne invited Alcuin to aid him in the spread of learning in Europe. Alcuin accepted and spent the next ten years at the court in Aachen.

Alcuin was charged with responsibility to produce a standard text for Scripture, to create schools, and to establish Latin as the classic spoken and written language of scholarship. In 796 Alcuin became abbot of St. Martin's at Tours where two hundred monks were said to be at work. Here in the scriptorium appeared the beautiful, free-flowing, alphabetical script known as the Carolingian minuscule. (It may have been inspired by Alcuin's handwriting.) This script which became the dominant book hand in Europe is the foundation of our modern alphabet, and no radical changes in form have since been made. This crowning achievement was an essential milestone on the way to the invention of movable type. However, another six hundred years of a developing society would be needed to set the stage for the introduction of printing.

From the year one thousand, population in Europe increased, communications opened, trade expanded, towns grew, new universities were established, literacy spread. All this brought vastly increased demands for the tools of learning. The thirst for education grew beyond the monasteries which had been the citadels of scholarship and the sources for written and illuminated manuscripts. Scriptoria were established with as many as fifty scribes. But means still had to be found to produce cheaper books, both secular and divine, in larger editions. When the answer came, the avalanche broke. During the last four decades of the fifteenth century, the newly invented "adventure and art" spread to every country in Europe, from Sweden to Sicily. During those forty years in a totally new craft, new craftsmen produced more than forty thousand editions, many millions of books, every piece of type picked out by hand, every page printed by hand, every book bound by hand. The dissemination of learning to the whole of society had begun.

GUTENBERG AND THE ADVENT OF PRINTING

The fifteenth century was the age of exploration, of Prince Henry the Navigator and Christopher Columbus. New horizons were also sighted in the world of scholarship. In 1455–1456 Johann Gensfleisch zum Gutenberg completed a magnificent, printed folio Bible in two volumes, 1284 pages, set in two columns of type, forty-two lines per column, in an edition of, probably, two hundred copies on paper and vellum (plate 1). This edition had been preceded in 1454 by Letters of Indulgence, set in type and printed in quantities for the Church. Thus were the beginnings made for book publishing and commercial printing in the city of Mainz on the Rhine, then one of the most important commercial centers in Germany.

This book, the first printed in Europe, is a work of art whose majestic craftsmanship has never been surpassed. Other technicians were also searching for ways to produce some form of mechanical, or "artificial," script. Several centers have claimed inventors, with Holland's Laurens Coster the leading, if somewhat shadowy, contender. However, it seems clear enough that only Gutenberg resolved and synthesized innumerable mechanical problems into an ingenious, workable method which has withstood the test of time. So much so that the various processes, manual operations, and the presses themselves became standard practice, with only minor changes, for the next three hundred and fifty years.

The heart of the invention of printing is the principle of movable type. As a goldsmith, Gutenberg was familiar with the cutting of punches, matrices, molds for casting, metal alloys, etc. For book printing this meant the capacity to put each letter of the alphabet on an individual tiny piece of metal. Gutenberg's font consisted of about two hundred and seventy different characters, including punctuation, ligatures, abbreviations, etc. These type characters were then set together by hand in unlimited combinations of words and pages, printed from, distributed after printing, and used again and again in subsequent work. The 42-line Bible contains approximately twenty-five hundred pieces of type on every page. Each of these bits of metal must be precision-made to align letter for letter, to be capable of locking for press, and to be of sufficient hardness to withstand many thousands of impressions, printed and reprinted. Gutenberg's presses, finally developed for sustained, heavy-duty printing, were no doubt modeled on the wine presses of this wine-growing region.

JOHANN
GUTENBERG
(c. 1397–1468)

The process of printing begins with letter design. Gutenberg's type is a faithful and beautiful rendering from the best German gothic manuscripts of the period. His artistry and his technical skills are clearly manifest in the type of his 42-line Bible. The manufacture of type began with the cutting of the letter on the head of a steel punch. This was struck into a matrix which was then inserted into a mold into which molten lead was poured from a ladle, and cast letter by letter until a sufficient quantity of type had been provided to begin composition. The finished type was then laid in wooden cases, the capital letters in the upper case, the small letters in the lower case. Gutenberg's compositors and pressmen probably set up and printed, say, twenty to forty pages of type. After the printing, page by page, the type was again distributed into the cases, the next twenty to forty pages were then set up and printed, and so continued in sequence to the final completion of 1284 pages. This remained the basic method of book composition until the development of stereotyping about 1800 and until the introduction of the Linotype machine in the last two decades of the nineteenth century. The inventors of the Linotype and Monotype machines found methods of setting type at great speed, but Gutenberg's principle of lead type was still involved. If the fifteenth-century inventor could have seen a Linotype machine in operation he surely would have been amazed, but he might also have been a bit proud

3

to recognize and acknowledge a direct lineal descendant. Not so before a modern electronic photocomposition machine or computer. These, together with offset printing, have been radical changes in the history of the printed word.

One must pay tribute to the vision and organizational brilliance which enabled Gutenberg to drive through to completion, over a fifteen-to-twenty-year period, long and extensive experimentation, building of plant, training of work force, and, finally,

about four years of disciplined, painstaking, controlled composition and printing. The prodigious costs would have taxed the resources of a Maecenas. They did indeed bankrupt Gutenberg. With his work at the high point of final realization, he was deprived of his triumph and his rewards.

The known facts of Gutenberg's life are relatively few. He was born before the year 1400 in Mainz of a patrician family. He left Mainz for political reasons about 1430 and settled temporarily in Strasbourg where a law suit in 1439 recorded that he was engaged in secret metallurgical experimentation dating back to 1436. He returned to Mainz between 1444 and 1448. These were the years in which Gutenberg must have been preoccupied with the many facets of the invention which later became his epoch-making contribution to the history of civilization.

There is ample evidence in existing Mainz archives that in 1450 and again in 1452 Gutenberg borrowed heavily from a financier named Johann Fust, who, with the second loan, invoked a partnership "in the production of books." Gutenberg was unable to repay the loans before he could finish and sell the Bibles then in work. Fust foreclosed in 1455 and evidently took possession of much of what Gutenberg had spent his life in building. Fust then took into partnership Gutenberg's most valued employee, Peter Schoeffer of Gernsheim, who later married Fust's daughter, and with these assets went on to become one of the great printers, and a successful publisher and bookseller.

Gutenberg's activities after completion of his great Bible are not known with certainty. It has been presumed by some scholars, without evidence convincing to the present writer, that Gutenberg had a directing hand in a 36-line Bible (plate 2) probably printed in Bamberg c. 1458–1459, and in a *Catholicon* (plate 3), an encyclopedic dictionary issued in 1460. Whether or not these are Gutenberg's work, the *Catholicon* is an early example of a step in the direction of less expensive printing, in smaller type, published for a larger market. Its florid colophon has seemed to more than one scholar to be Gutenberg's own inspired voice. Perhaps so. It reads:

> With the aid of the Most High, at whose will the tongues of children become eloquent and
> who often reveals to the lowly what he conceals from the wise, this noble book *Catholicon* has
> been printed and brought to completion without the help of reed, stylus, or pen but by the
> marvelous agreement, proportion, and harmony of punches and type, in the year of the
> Lord's incarnation, 1460, in the noble city of Mainz of the renowned German nation, which
> God's grace has seen fit to prefer and distinguish above all other nations of the earth with so

4

lofty a genius and such liberal gifts. Therefore all praise and honor to Thee, Holy Father, Son, and Holy Spirit, God in three persons; and thou, *Catholicon*, extol the glory of the Church and never cease praising the Holy Virgin. Thanks be to God.

Gutenberg's career may have come to an end early in the 1460's. It has been suggested that he became blind. In the sack of Mainz in 1462 he probably suffered personal losses along with so many other citizens. In 1465 he was awarded a pension from the Archbishop of Mainz which lasted until his death on the third of February in 1468. He was buried in the Franciscan church which was later demolished. Of Gutenberg's legacy to mankind, his great Bible, forty-seven copies in various states of preservation, have survived pillage, fire, and time.

As Fust's colleague, Peter Schoeffer, the former associate of Gutenberg, was responsible for three master-pieces of bookmaking. In 1457 Fust and Schoeffer issued a monumental Psalter, another in 1459 (plate 4), in 1462 a magnificent Bible in Latin (plate 5), and in 1465, a beautiful Cicero. The Psalter is famous as the first successful attempt to print elaborate two-color initials; it is the first book to bear a printed date; the first book to carry the printer's imprint and device, and a first colophon, which, translated, reads:

JOHANN
FUST
(c. 1400–1466)

PETER
SCHOEFFER
(c. 1425–1502/3)

> This book of the Psalms, decorated with beautiful capitals, and with an abundance of rubrics, has been fashioned thus by an ingenious invention of printing and stamping without use of a pen. And to the worship of God it has been diligently brought to completion by Johann Fust, a citizen of Mainz, and Peter Schoeffer of Gernsheim, in the year of our Lord 1457, on the eve of the Feast of the Assumption.

After a bloody contest for Mainz between two archbishops, the victor, Adolf of Nassau, expelled the citizens who had not supported him. This seems to have included most of the craftsmen who had learned the new art in the Gutenberg and Fust and Schoeffer workshops, and thereby hastened the spread of printing into the other cities of Germany and through all of Europe. After 1462 conditions in Mainz apparently prevented any Fust and Schoeffer work from appearing until 1465 when they completed their Cicero. The following year Fust died in Paris while on a journey to sell his books, having earned the distinction of being the first of an indomitable host of traveling book salesmen.

Peter Schoeffer continued to print, publish, and sell books, broadsheets, pamphlets, etc., until his death in 1502–1503. Indulgences and papal bulls printed for Pope Innocent VIII to raise money for his campaign against the Turks boomeranged a few decades later when Martin Luther found the printing press a ready and enormously effective medium in his own struggle with the established church.

THE SPREAD OF PRINTING: GERMANY

Printing spread like fire before the wind. Within five years of the appearance of the 42-line Bible, books appeared in Bamberg (Adolf Pfister) and in Strasbourg (Johann Mentelin) printed by men who had had some association with Gutenberg. Presses were then set up in Cologne in 1465, Augsburg in 1468, Nuremberg in 1470, Ulm in 1473, Leipzig in 1481, and by the end of the century presses were at work in some sixty German centers. Only a very few of these achieved distinction. Indeed, a bare handful of presses in the whole of Europe in the fifteenth century survived twenty years of operation. These early printers were, of necessity, also their own publishers and booksellers. They needed the ingenuity to design and cut type, to master the processes of printing, and to set up working presses. The market must have been very tempting to induce more than three hundred and fifty men to venture into the new business during the four remaining decades of the fifteenth century.

During the last quarter of the century, Germany's most important contributions were to the illustrated book. Augsburg was the center for artists who cut wood blocks for religious broadsheets and for playing cards. The abbot of the monastery of Saints Ulric and Afra in Augsburg which already housed a famous scriptorium invited

GÜNTHER ZAINER (fl. 1468–1478)

Günther Zainer, a scribe and illuminator who had been trained in the Mentelin workshop, to supervise a new press. Here the printers and the wood cutters joined their talents to produce books combining type and illustrations with decorative woodcut initials, all of which foretold the end of hand illumination and decoration. These books were in the vernacular with naive woodcuts made for popular appeal. Among notable Augsburg books is the *Spiegel des menschlichen Lebens*, 1475–1476 (plate 13). A copy in the Morgan Library, once in the collection of William Morris, has a note in his handwriting: "A vernacular edition of one of the most popular of medieval books . . . the best of the Augsburg picture books." Many of the German blocks were sold and resold. They appear in books printed in Basle, then Lyons, and elsewhere—a migration of wood blocks that was a rather common occurrence for some years. Forty

JOHANN ZAINER (fl. 1473–1500)

miles away, in Ulm, Johann Zainer, a kinsman of the Augsburg printer, also produced popular favorites among illustrated books, including a Boccaccio in 1473 (plate 12).

HEINRICH QUENTELL (d. 1501)

In Cologne, then the largest city in Germany, Heinrich Quentell completed c. 1478 an illustrated Bible in Low German (plate 14) which has been described as epoch-making due to the influence its woodcuts have had on Bible illustration for generations. Nuremberg was the chief mercantile city of Germany and a major market for central Europe. Because printing, successfully pursued, has been dependent on capital and a labor supply available only in the large centers of business, it is entirely logical that Nuremberg became the home of the largest printer-publisher-bookseller of the fifteenth century. Here Anton Koberger established a plant with twenty-four presses and a staff of one hundred compositors, pressmen, bookbinders, and traveling sales-

6

men. From his start in production in 1470–1471 to his death in 1513, Koberger issued more than two hundred titles sold throughout Europe, most of them large folios, including fifteen Bibles, patterned on familiar manuscript volumes. Although primarily an entrepreneur on a large scale, Koberger is nevertheless to be credited with considerable typographic achievement. The Nuremberg Chronicle, 1493 (plate 23), is a history of the world profusely illustrated with woodcuts by Michael Wolgemut (Dürer's one-time teacher) and Wilhelm Pleydenwurf. *The Apocalypse*, 1498, contains Albrecht Dürer's famous woodcuts, including the fabled Four Horsemen.

The letter forms in German manuscripts from the tenth to the fifteenth centuries evolved from the broad, flowing, Carolingian script into an angular condensed "gothic," which the first German printers naturally used as their models for type, and which was continued in common use in Germany into the twentieth century. Outside Germany, gothic type prevailed for religious and law books for about a hundred years. The reaction against gothic writing came from Italy during the first half of the fifteenth century and flowered there into a classic humanistic roman script—one of the glories of the human spirit—also derived from the Carolingian minuscule. This inspired calligraphy by Renaissance scribes then became the model for a burgeoning of great type design in Venice from 1469 to the end of the century.

On this subject of gothic vs. roman type, S. H. Steinberg in his admirable *Five Hundred Years of Printing* (London, 1966) states, "It was the penetration of western Europe by the spirit of humanism that brought about the victory of 'roman' and 'italic' types; and it was the resistance to the spirit of humanism that made the Germans, Russians, and Turks, cling to the isolationism of the Fraktur, Cyrillic, and Arabic types. The recent transition to the 'Latin' alphabet by the Germans and the Turks is a major step towards the unity of world civilization; just as the refusal of post-Lenin Russia to abandon the Cyrillic letter—nay, its progressive imposition on Soviet colonials—is a significant omen of the deep cleavage between East and West."

THE SPREAD OF PRINTING: LONDON, BRUGES, BASLE

William Caxton was a well-born Englishman who spent thirty years in the Low Countries as a prominent businessman and commercial diplomat. While attached to the Burgundian court in Bruges he translated the popular French *Recueil des Histoires de Troye* into English and became involved in its printing. Having learned the new art in Cologne in 1471–1472, he then set up a press in Bruges where, possibly in association with Colard Mansion, he produced six books. (Colard Mansion was a calligrapher who later set up his own press in Bruges where he printed and published a score of notable books.) In 1476 Caxton moved to Westminster to set up the first press on English soil.

7

The first dated book printed in England was issued by Caxton in 1477, *The Dictes or Sayengis of the Philosophres.* He followed this with a vigorous publishing program in English, including the first edition c. 1478 of Chaucer's *Canterbury Tales* (plate 15). The classics in Greek and Latin had to be imported from the Continent, as were Caxton's paper for printing and perhaps his type. Caxton died in 1491, having printed and published almost one hundred books, seventy-four of them in English, twenty-two in his own translations. Caxton cannot be called one of the great craftsman-printers, although he was, certainly, of immense importance to the history of the book in England. According to Colin Clair, "When English gradually assumed a definite literary form, largely through the influence of Chaucer, Caxton, by virtue of his new craft, and in his missionary zeal for disseminating works of literature, had as much influence as any man of his time in creating a fixed form for the language."

Caxton was succeeded by his foreman, Wynkyn de Worde, an Alsatian. Those

RICHARD
PYNSON
(d. 1530)

who followed were William Fawkes and Richard Pynson, both of French birth. Until the seventeenth century, English printers depended on the Continent for typographic direction and for the importation of the tools of their trade. Influential originality and a national British style did finally manifest themselves in the eighteenth century with the appearance of a Virgil in 1757 by John Baskerville in Birmingham.

JOHANN
FROBEN
(1460–1527)

The first press in Basle was established in 1467 by Bertold Ruppel, a former associate of Gutenberg. Several printers followed who eventually made this city the main center for the publication of works in Christian humanism. Chief among them were Johann Amerbach, who settled there in 1477, and Johann Froben, a Bavarian by birth who had attended the University of Basle and who started printing there about 1491. Froben's fame is due to his scholarly bookmaking and his collaboration with two of the most influential men of his time. He drew Erasmus to Basle, where the great humanist made his residence from 1521 to 1529 as Froben's friend, author, and editor. Among other books, Erasmus supervised Froben's complete edition of Aristotle and the New Testament in Greek for which Erasmus provided his own Latin translation, later used by Luther. Hans Holbein also came to Basle and lived there from 1515 to 1526, years in which, with woodcut illustrations, title-page borders (plate 37), decorative headpieces, and initial letters, he added luster to Froben's books.

THE SPREAD OF PRINTING: ITALY

Printing, which has been central to the growth of modern society, has been, from its first century, almost entirely the commercial product of men of business. A sustained enterprise requires the coordination of men and machines, editorial sagacity, and the capacity to find and retain a remunerative market. The men who made splendid printed books, especially during the first hundred years of the art, were artist-craftsmen who were also publishers and booksellers, participants in the culture of their times, pioneers and innovators in their work, professionals in their output. The endowment within one person of scholarship, craftsmanship, and worldly acumen is rare indeed, but were it not for the occasional appearance of such individuals there would be no esthetic of the printed book.

The first press in Italy was set up in 1465 by Conrad Sweynheym of Mainz and Arnold Pannartz of Cologne in the Benedictine monastery of Subiaco near Rome whose abbot was Cardinal Turrecremata, with a scriptorium staffed by German monks. Here the two printers produced a sturdy, excellent type, primarily roman but with marked germanic gothic characteristics. They printed four notable books: a lost Donatus grammar; a handsome *De Oratore* of Cicero, undated; Lactantius' *Opera*, 1465; and St. Augustine's *De Civitate Dei* (plates 6–7). The partners then moved their press to Rome late in 1467 where they cut a new type with greater dependence on contemporary rounded Italian calligraphy. After the output of some forty or more titles, they closed in 1473.

CONRAD SWEYNHEYM (d. 1477)

ARNOLD PANNARTZ (d. 1476)

One would have expected the city of Florence to be eager for the new craft of printing. On the contrary, the flamboyant Medicis, as well as other princely patrons in Italy, considered printing a degradation and would not, at first, allow printed books to enter their sacred libraries of magnificently written and illustrated manuscripts. Meanwhile Venice had become a great mercantile and trading center, strategically placed at the crossroads of Europe, the Levant, and the Indies. Its prosperity and the capital it could supply induced one hundred and fifty printers to set up presses between 1470 and 1500 where they produced — and overproduced — four thousand editions. With its affluence and architectural splendor, Venice became host to the printers who laid the foundation for the modern printed book.

The first printer in Venice was a German, Johann von Speyer who called himself Johannes de Spira. His first book was a folio Cicero, *Epistolae ad Familiares*, completed in 1469, typographically sophisticated and dignified. His type (plate 8), the first rendering free of archaism, was inspired directly by the beautiful contemporary

JOHANNES DE SPIRA (d. 1470)

Italian humanistic hands. It was innovative. De Spira received five years' protection against plagiarism, but his death in 1470 lifted the restriction and thus opened the way for one of the most important events in the history of bookmaking. In 1470 Nicolaus Jenson (who had, probably, designed de Spira's type) issued his Eusebius, *De Evangelica Praeparatione* (plates 10–11), printed in a magnificent typeface which has become the fountainhead for much of the type designed in the subsequent five hundred years.

Nicolaus Jenson, born in France about 1420, became master of the mint at Tours. According to legend, he was sent to Germany

NICOLAUS JENSON (c. 1420–1480)

9

around 1458 by the French King Charles VII, charged to bring back knowledge of the new art of printing for the benefit of France. Charles died in 1461, and it is supposed that Jenson did not wish to return to the Paris of Louis XI. In any event, we find Jenson in Venice where he became a printer and publisher of superb books, from 1470 to 1480, in roman, gothic, and greek types of the greatest distinction. The roman type in his Eusebius is invested with the mark of genius. His type has great clarity and liveliness, and at the same time an element of divine repose. The Jenson types are part of the same Renaissance glory that gave the world the supremely beautiful written letters of the humanistic scribes. Jenson died in Rome, having been called there by Pope Sixtus IV in 1475 where he honored Jenson and his work by creating him a Count Palatine.

ERHARD
RATDOLT
(1442–1528)

Erhard Ratdolt, another accomplished German printer who had been drawn to Venice, added to its reputation with a number of handsome books from 1476 to 1486, including the first edition of Euclid's *Elementa Geometriae* in 1482 (plate 18). He introduced decorative woodcut borders and initial letters, among other important contributions, both mechanical and artistic, including the first separate title page.

ALDUS
MANUTIUS
(1450–1515)

AL DVS

Aldus Manutius was one of the giants of the Renaissance and among its significant benefactors. He combined the gifts of scholarship and art with the capacities of a man of action. He was a tutor to princes who gave him financial support when, toward 1495, at forty-five years of age, he set up his press in Venice. His primary purpose was to print and publish the classics in Greek and Latin. Himself a man of learning, he drew a notable group of scholars to his workshop and to his home where Greek was the language of the household. Among his many associates were Pico della Mirandola, Thomas Linacre, and Erasmus whose *Adagia* he published.

Aldus was the first printer to break away completely from the ancient patterns of the medieval manuscript. He was the first printer with a major publishing program to insist on scholarly editing. He was the first printer to produce small books in relatively large editions which placed books within reach of a new generation of readers throughout Europe. His types — greek, roman, and italic — broke new ground and dominated European printing for two hundred years. The Aldine romans and italics are even now available on mechanical composing machines.

Aldus issued his monumental five-volume Aristotle (plate 28) from 1495 to 1498. Before his career ended, he had printed and published, often for the first time, the works of Aristophanes, Demosthenes, Euripides, Herodotus, Pindar, Plato, Plutarch, Sophocles, Thucydides, Xenophon, and others in Greek; and in Latin, works by Bembo, Dante, Petrarch, Pliny, Poliziano, Pontanus, Quintilian, Valerius Maximus, and the *Hypnerotomachia*.

In 1495–1496 Aldus issued a small quarto of sixty pages of the dialogue *De Aetna*

10

(plate 29) written by Pietro, later Cardinal, Bembo. The type is the work of Francesco da Bologna, surnamed Griffo, who designed and cut all the Aldine fonts. Griffo has never received adequate recognition for his enormous contributions to type design. His name has been overlooked and almost lost in the shadow of his great patron.

The letter design in *De Aetna* can well be considered the first modern type. Although the calligraphic background is manifest, Griffo departed further than Jenson from the then contemporary humanistic script. Griffo's type is less "artistic" than Jenson's, but also more workmanlike. It was Griffo's type which became the model for the great French type designers of the sixteenth century. In modern times, it has been cut as "Bembo" for machine composition.

Although Aldus' taste clearly inclined toward unadorned typography, and although his main interests and energies were expended in his widespread printing and publishing commitments, it is the more remarkable that he was responsible for one of the world's most beautiful illustrated books. In 1499 he completed the *Hypnerotomachia Poliphili* (plates 30–31) with a new typeface by Griffo, exquisite woodcuts by an unknown artist which blend perfectly with the type pages, and embellished with handsome floriated initials. The writing, "The Strife of Love in a Dream," is attributed to Francesco Colonna, a Dominican monk. It is a book of serene grace and charm, which further bespeaks the versatility of Aldus as printer and designer.

The Greek and Latin folios and quartos were expensive. Smaller, less costly books were wanted. With Griffo again as designer, Aldus brought out a new, small, condensed cursive type (based on contemporary cursive scripts) which permitted many more words on a small page. This was the origin of italic type, used by Aldus in a Virgil *Opera* (plate 32), in 1501 as the first of the Aldine octavo editions printed throughout in italic, but with the capital letters in roman. These books, with their device of the anchor and dolphin, spread over Europe and became the hallmark of scholarly, attractive, impeccable editions. They were the distant forebears of series of books such as Everyman's Library, The Modern Library, even the modern paperback.

Aldus died in 1515. With his death the importance of Italy as a seminal and dynamic force in printing came to an end. The course of typographic history next flows toward Paris and Lyons, where a new confluence of genius made the first half of the sixteenth century the golden age of French printing.

THE SPREAD OF PRINTING: FRANCE

Printing was introduced into France in 1470 under the scholarly roof of the Sorbonne in Paris when the rector, Johann Heynlin, born in the Rhineland, and the librarian, Guillaume Fichet, invited three German printers to set up a press in the university library. Here during the next three years these printers, Michael Freiburger, an educated friend of the rector, together with Ulrich Gering and Martin Kranz, "both workmen of the higher class," produced more than twenty books, mostly classical texts intended primarily for the university faculty and students, in a new roman type patterned after a type cut by Sweynheym and Pannartz in Italy. The publishing program was under the direction of Librarian Fichet who was, in his own words, "joyful about the new opportunity of using print to banish the plague of laboriously copied texts." The invention and spread of printing was welcomed by scholars, both for availability of books at lower costs, and because accurate and uniform texts were becoming possible. The multiplication of handwritten volumes involved copious errors by careless scribes. Petrarch, we are told, tried to establish correct texts by employing his own copyists, several of whom lived in his home. Chaucer's plea at the end of *Troilus and Criseyde*, "So preye I God that noone miswryte thee," must have been the fervent wish of medieval authors and readers.

In 1473 both Heynlin and Fichet had left the Sorbonne and France. The three German printers then installed themselves at the Sign of the Golden Sun on the Rue Saint Jacques, the street which then and later harbored French printers and booksellers. Here they produced books in gothic type, demanded by the clergy and still generally used for secular works. In 1477–1478 when Freiburger and Kranz returned to Germany, Ulrich Gering remained, cut new fonts in roman, worked until the end of the century, and earned the sobriquet "patriarch of French typography."

Meanwhile French-born printers entered and soon dominated the field. With the medieval illuminated manuscript still the model, these early books printed in Paris were characteristically and elegantly French. During the years 1476–1477 Pasquier Bonhomme printed the first book in Paris in the French language, *Croniques de France*, in a new, high-spirited, rather nervous, Gallic version of gothic type known as *lettre-bâtarde*. This type, derived from a contemporary French legal script, became the most commonly used form for books in the vernacular during the remaining years of the century.

JEAN DUPRÉ (fl. 1481–1504)

In 1481 Jean Dupré issued the first of the volumes with woodcuts which were to make Paris the headquarters for illustrated books. In these volumes we find the origins of the French *édition de luxe* which became a long tradition, often supported by the Monarchy, extending into the twentieth century, with illustrations by the most famous of French artists. In 1486 Jean Dupré as printer, with publisher Pierre Gérard, produced France's first typographic and illustrated masterpiece—the St. Augustine *La Cité de Dieu* (plate 20), printed in Abbeville. The most prolific publisher of the period, Antoine Vérard, came along in 1485 with the first of the many Books of Hours

PHILIPPE PIGOUCHET (fl. 1485–1515)

which he issued during a twenty-five-year career. Philippe Pigouchet produced handsomely illustrated *Horae* (plate 26) from 1485 to 1515. Before the turn of the century, sixty presses are said to have been at work in Paris, and forty in Lyons where international fairs attracted merchants from all Europe.

These decades were admirably summed up by the late A. W. Pollard of the British Museum: "It was in the Books of Hours that the genius of French printers first strik-

12

ingly evinced itself. For more than a century the decoration of manuscript *Horae* had invited all the skill of the finest illuminators of Europe, and it was in France alone that the attempt was successfully made to rival the glories of the scribe and painter by that of the printer and engraver. The names of Antoine Vérard, Philippe Pigouchet, and Simon Vostre as printers and publishers are inseparably connected with these Books of Hours, which for some quarter of a century from 1488 onward constitute the chief glories of the French press. More than 300 editions were issued altogether, in which some forty different printers had a share, Jean Dupré at the beginning of the series, and Geoffroy Tory, as late as 1525, being the most important after the three already named."

THE GOLDEN AGE OF PRINTING IN FRANCE

The dawn of a new century in France witnessed a great forward thrust in the history of the book. The French Renaissance, an expanding economy, and a king who indulged his love of the arts and who became a special friend to printing set the stage for a flowering of typographic genius. In 1515, the first year of his reign, François I invaded Italy. There he succumbed, not to Italian arms, but to Italian art and culture, and induced Italian architects and artists, including Andrea del Sarto, Benvenuto Cellini, and Leonardo da Vinci, to grace his court at Fontainebleau. The cultivated world of France capitulated to Italianate influences, not least the printers of Paris and Lyons who were already deep in debt to the work of Aldus Manutius. So respected was his reputation for impeccable editions among book buyers throughout the capitals of Europe that at least two printers in Lyons showed their flattery by counterfeiting the Aldine octavos, including the italic type and the mark of the dolphin and anchor. These piratical publications were the exceptions, of course. The leading French printers, who were scholars and humanists, built on the significance of Aldus, to which they added their own new competence and their Gallic inheritance.

The sixteenth century in France saw the physical book evolve into the form with which we are familiar today. The handwritten manuscript which had cast its long shadow over fifteenth-century printed books was history to these men of another time who were no longer forced to cope with the problems and hazards of a new craft. Their books indicate an easy familiarity with metal type; their planning and decoration show a new sense of design. They now manipulate type to achieve pleasing details in black-and-white rather than depend, as did their forebears, on impressive columns of type on vellum colorfully decorated by hand after printing. In the great new printed Bibles, in the impressive quarto classics, and in the smaller books, especially those from Geoffroy Tory, Simon de Colines, Robert Estienne, Michel de Vascosan, and Jean de Tournes, one can see the ancestors of our own contemporary typographers. Before mid-century the first evidence of specialization showed with the appearance of two independent type designers, among the most important in typographic history, Claude Garamond and Robert Granjon, from whom printers could buy type

CLAUDE
GARAMOND
(1480–1561)

ROBERT
GRANJON
(d. 1579)

13

cast in fonts ready for printing. One hundred years after Gutenberg, the period of the one-man craftsman-scholar-printer-publisher-bookseller had come to an end.

The earliest star in the brilliant constellation of printers who appeared in the sixteenth century was a Fleming, Josse Bade, who latinized his name to Jodocus Badius Ascensius. He had been to Italy, then learned his trade in Lyons at the press of Johann Trechsel, whose daughter Thalia he married. Badius, himself a scholar interested in the new learning, moved in 1499 to Paris, where he printed and published ancient classics and contemporary literature including works by Erasmus and the noted scholar Guillaume Budé. Issues by Badius were not limited to his books. His two daughters married highly gifted young men: Michel de Vascosan who was to produce with great distinction in his father-in-law's *métier*, and Robert Estienne who would become the most famous of scholar-printers. Both men became Printers to the King. The families of these artisans of the book lived in the heart of the university quarter in Paris where, affiliated by trade, it is not surprising that there was extensive intermarriage. The most successful wife must surely have been one Guyone Viart who married three printers in turn, and became, with her second husband, matriarch of the most important dynasty in the history of printing. From Elizabeth Armstrong's biography, *Robert Estienne, Royal Printer*, we learn of a turn-of-the-century partnership between two foreign printers at work in Paris, John Higman and Wolfgang Hopyl, with whom a certain Henri Estienne was occasionally associated. According to Mrs. Armstrong, "Nothing is known of Henry Estienne before his sudden appearance as Hopyl's associate. But it is clear that he had married the widow of Hopyl's former partner, John Higman, a Frenchwoman named Guyone Viart. Documents concerning a lawsuit, over two farms which Guyone brought her second husband, speak of the marriage between her and Higman; of their children Damien Higman (later active as a bookseller) and Geneviève (later married to Reginald Chaudière the publisher-printer); and of the status which Higman had been able to claim and which Henry Estienne held in his turn, of *bourgeois de Paris et messager juré de l'Université*." Henri died in 1520. Guyone then married her third partner, Henri's talented associate, Simon de Colines. Whatever other reasons there may have been for this marriage, it preserved the Estienne establishment until Henri's son Robert could take over.

Geoffroy Tory, a versatile genius, born in France in 1480, an artist and a scholar who had traveled widely in Renaissance Italy, returned to France and played a major role in the final transition away from gothic type and the stately books of the fifteenth century. Tory was an accomplished poet; a lecturer in philosophy; a translator of Latin and Greek classics; a philologist who introduced the accent, the cedilla, and the apostrophe to the French language; and a calligrapher and type designer, engraver, printer, and publisher. Tory's beautiful Book of Hours (plate 39) of 1525 (printed by Colines) is a prime example of the new, lighter Renaissance spirit in French printing. The floral borders and decorations are open and charming, free of the crowded pictorial details of earlier woodcuts, and in perfect harmony with the type. Tory also designed several series of imposing initial letters which embellished his own books, those of his contemporaries and of future generations of printers.

In 1529 Tory issued his *Champfleury* (plate 40), a learned, ruminative, and prolix study in three parts, of language and letter forms, including his own drawings of roman capitals constructed by rule and compass on squares divided into a hundred parts, and also references to earlier letter studies by Leonardo da Vinci, Luca de Pacioli, Albrecht Dürer, and others. Here are Tory's own summaries (from the George B. Ives translation): "In the First Book is contained the exhortation to establish and order the French tongue by fixed rules for speaking elegantly in good and sound French diction. In the Second the invention of the Attic [roman] Letters is treated, and their proportions are compared to those of the natural body and face of the perfect man. With many fine conceits & moral lessons concerning the said Attic Letters. In the Third and last Book are drawn in their due proportions all the said Attic Letters in their alphabetical order, of their due height and breadth, each by itself, with instruction as to their right fashioning & correct pronunciation, both in Latin and French, as well in the ancient as in the modern manner." The *Champfleury* was an important factor in the more widespread use of the roman letter and in greater respect for its design.

In 1530 François rewarded Tory with the coveted title *Imprimeur du Roi*. In 1533 Tory died, having taken his place in French typographic history as the chief forebear of a line of Royal Printers.

Simon de Colines continued to manage the Estienne workshop from 1520 when Henri died until 1526 when Robert became the proprietor. Colines then established his own Press and continued as a printer-publisher until his death in 1546. He was one of the key figures in the transformation of the printed book. With his new greek font, and with the several italic and roman faces which he designed and cut (perhaps some in collaboration with Antoine Augereau), Colines introduced a lighter, more open and more mellow quality into the printed page. His books show a refreshing awareness of type and related typographic decoration and an overall artfulness in book design. He worked closely with Geoffroy Tory whose epoch-making *Hours* he printed in 1525. Colines' *De Natura Stirpium* of 1536 (plates 43–44) is typical of his best work, one of the noble volumes of the period, with a fine roman type of his own cutting. In addition to elegant folios, Colines' total output of more than seven hundred editions included

SIMON DE COLINES (d. 1546)

large numbers of pocket-sized volumes printed entirely in italics, to satisfy the popular demand for inexpensive books.

ROBERT ESTIENNE (1503–1559)

Robert Estienne, second in the dynastic line, was a great printer of great books in a period of intellectual growth. He was born into a close-knit society, where, on the Rue Saint Jacques and neighboring streets, printers made and sold their books, and lived in the house above the shop. Households were likely to be conducted in Latin, with apprentices living in, and editors and authors as house guests who came for working visits.

If Robert Estienne was a printer by birthright, he was a scholar by vocation. He was a man of the Renaissance for whom the art of the book would be a logical pursuit. He became a friend of François I and the Court, and fulfilled his duties as *Imprimeur du Roi*, the King's Printer, in Latin, Hebrew, and Greek. He was a classicist and Biblical scholar. According to the British catalogue, *Printing and the Mind of Man, Illustrating the Impact of Print on the Evolution of Western Civilization* (1967), "The series of dictionaries edited and published by the Estienne or Stephanus family is perhaps the most significant, though by no means the sole achievement of the most renowned family of scholar-printers in history. . . . Robert's fame rests on his activities as a typographer of Roman, Greek and Hebrew characters, as an accomplished editor of Latin authors and Latin, Greek and Hebrew Bibles, as a philologist and grammarian in these languages as well as his native French, and, above all, as the first scientific lexicographer of both ancient and modern languages."

Because Estienne turned to early manuscripts in his Biblical research, and did not blindly accept the standard text of the Vulgate, he came into conflict with the Catholic theologians of the Sorbonne and became suspect of heresy. After the death of François I, who had protected "his dear printer," Estienne chose not to risk the fate of other publishers and booksellers who had been burned at the stake with their own books feeding the flames. Late in 1550 he moved to Geneva where he re-established his press and published another sixty titles before his death in 1559. The Geneva printing, in Garamond's roman, italic, and greek types and the Tory initials, was continued by Robert's son

HENRI ESTIENNE II (1528–1598)

Henri II who became an even more highly respected editor and publisher of Greek and Latin texts. Robert's brothers and sons and their descendants carried on the establishment in Paris worthy of the family tradition until late in the seventeenth century.

The Paris workshop during its quarter-century under the direction of Robert Estienne published about four hundred and fifty books, probably used six presses, and employed about fifty men including type casters, compositors, readers, pressmen, paper handlers, and apprentices. Its production of Latin and Greek classics, contemporary works of scholarship and tracts, Bibles, dictionaries, thesauri, grammars, etc.,

16

for students and the educated public, were printed in formats from small vest-pocket editions to the more usual duodecimos and octavos, with a substantial percentage of quartos and massive folios. These books were made to be read. The straightforward, unself-conscious workmanship makes it abundantly clear that these books, including those which achieved typographic distinction, were not made as "collectors' items." Surely, the Estienne folio Bibles in Latin of 1532 and 1540 (plates 50–51) and the Eusebius of 1544 in the first printing of Garamond's *Grecs du Roi* types (plate 52) may be seen as Olympian achievements. The magnificence of these folios lies in their splendid typefaces, the classic proportions of their type pages on fine papers, the harmonious use of occasional decoration, the excellence of the presswork, and the sustained vigilance which is evident in all the minutiae of the Estienne production.

Before taking reluctant leave of Paris during this extraordinary time, it is a privilege to quote from A. F. Johnson, the British Museum's authority on sixteenth-century printed books. "The middle years of the century at Paris were a period of great activity for the printing press, remarkable both for the number of books produced and for the high standard of workmanship. Many famous books appeared, such as the French version of the *Polifilo* [plate 54] published by Jacques Kerver in 1546; Paolo Giovio's *Vitae . . . Mediolani principum*, R. Estienne, 1549 [plate 53]; and Jean Cousin's *Livre de perspective*, J. Le Royer, 1560 [plate 61]. Denys Janot, who became the King's printer for French in 1544, produced many popular books [plate 42] with woodcut illustrations of the Tory school. He and his successors were responsible for the remarkable series of folio volumes of the French *Amadis de Gaula*. Michel de Vascosan, a son-in-law of Badius, favoured a style of simplicity and his imposing volumes are admirable specimens of the use of Garamond romans [plate 60]. There were many printers of Greek texts, like Guillaume Morel and the scholar Adrien Turnèbe. The books of Ronsard and the other members of the Pleiad were excellently produced. It is, in fact, hardly possible to open a Paris book of the period which is not of first-rate quality."

In the commercial city of Lyons, a few leading practitioners among about forty active presses participated in the tradition of the art of the book. The earliest of these men was Sebastien Gryphius who at first imported type and wood engravings from Basle. "His editions of ancient authors," according to S. H. Steinberg, "rivalled those of the Aldus and Stephanus [Estienne] presses. For his critical editions of the classical physicians Hippocrates and Galen, Gryphius obtained no less an editor than François Rabelais. . . . Gryphius was also the first publisher of the free-thinking humanist Etienne Dolet who in 1538 opened a press of his own from which he issued Clément Marot's Calvinist satire *L'Enfer* (1542) and his own heretical tracts which eventually led him and his books to the stake in Paris (1546)."

Jean de Tournes (the Elder), born in 1504, gained his experience in the Trechsel and Gryphius workshops. When his own press was established in 1542 in Lyons, his

JACQUES
KERVER
(fl. 1497–1552)

JEAN COUSIN
(c. 1490–1560)

DENYS JANOT
(fl. 1529–1545)

MICHEL
DE
VASCOSAN
(fl. 1530–1577)

SEBASTIEN
GRYPHIUS
(c. 1491–1556)

work benefited from the persuasive influence of the great Paris practitioners. But de Tournes soon exhibited a felicitous typographic style of his own. He used and popularized decorative fleurons and arabesques designed by his fellow townsman Bernard Saloman. "Le Petit Bernard," as he was called, also made exquisite woodcut illustrations for many of the de Tournes books. To these were added the sparkling italics of another Lyonnais craftsman, the famous type designer Robert Granjon.

JEAN DE TOURNES (1504-1564)

Many of the distinguished books of this fertile epoch in France were large quartos and folios dependent, in part at least, on size to achieve grandeur. De Tournes was most effective in his smaller books. One may enjoy exuberance and charm in the *Marguerites* of 1547 (plate 57), the *Biblia Sacra* of 1558, and Ovid's *Metamorphoses* of 1559, to name but a few, and in the enchanting tiny four volumes, *La Sainte Bible* (plate 58) with Saloman woodcuts.

More than one authority finds de Tournes the "best printer" of his century in Europe. He was, surely, a superb technician and a delightful innovator in book design. But if superlatives are in order, this writer would unhesitatingly choose Robert Estienne as the "greatest" printer of the sixteenth century, and perhaps of all time. The distinction between "best" and "greatest" would seem to lie in the combined capacities of great scholarship and superb craftsmanship within one person.

THE NETHERLANDS: PLANTIN AND ELZEVIR

CHRISTOPHER PLANTIN (1514-1589)

An ambitious young Frenchman, Christopher Plantin, born in Touraine in 1514, spent his apprentice years in Lyons, Caen, and Paris where he learned the various trades of the book during the flourishing years of French printing. When ready to set up on his own, Plantin probably found the oppressive controls of the Catholic theologians of the Sorbonne less than favorable for another printing and publishing venture in Paris. Or he might have been drawn to the Low Countries by reports of their prosperity and the possibilities for raising capital in an atmosphere hospitable to artists and scholars. In any event Plantin went to Antwerp in 1549 and began as a bookseller and bookbinder. An injury to his right arm put an end to this career as a binder. In 1555 he founded his press which, during the next thirty-four years, became the most progressive and the largest printing and publishing establishment in Europe.

Plantin's rise was far from smooth during this period when Spain's army and its Inquisition victimized the Low Countries. He did not escape the prevailing religious persecution and military depredation which saw three Antwerp printers executed for heresy. Although Plantin professed to be a devout Catholic, he was suspected of heretical activities. As a secret member of a sect called "The Family of Love," he was forced to flee to Paris for two years during which his worldly goods were dispersed.

Nevertheless, he was able to clear his name and on his return to Antwerp, and for the rest of his life, he steered an astute course between rival religious and political factions. At the same time he moved ahead to a brilliant career as an industrialist with a sensitive and roving typographic eye. Plantin accumulated a fine collection of well-chosen typefaces, a superb assortment of initial letters and ornamental alphabets, printers' flowers and decoration, and music fonts "of remarkable magnificence."

At the sign of the Golden Compasses, the Plantin workshop eventually consisted of some twenty presses employing about one hundred and sixty men, with a lifetime output of almost two thousand books. Plantin, who had an exalted conception of his craft, and who took as his motto *Labore et Constantia*, made his printing office a meeting place for scholars, scientists, artists, and engravers, and made Antwerp the most important center for book production during the second half of the sixteenth century.

Christopher Plantin must be recognized as one of the great figures in the history of the printed word. He was not a scholar himself but his books were scholarly. He was not an original designer, but his books have considerable style, and many are elegant, if less distinguished than the work of the very eminent French printers of his youth. Plantin's smaller books follow patterns established by Simon de Colines and Jean de Tournes. The tall folios are reminiscent of the Robert Estienne glory. His types too came from French sources where he purchased types and "strikes" at the sales of Colines' and Garamond's material. He commissioned Robert Granjon who came to Antwerp for a time and there designed several series, engaged Guillaume Le Bé for Hebrew, and other type designers by direct employment in the foundry attached to the printing house. Plantin was a chief protagonist for extravagant engraved copperplate title pages which became the vogue all over Europe. In later years Plantin's grandson, Balthazar Moretus, induced his friend and fellow townsman Peter Paul Rubens to decorate several of the books of the Officina Plantiniana with majestic baroque title pages.

In addition to the classics and Bibles, dictionaries, medical books, charming emblem books (plate 62), etc., Plantin made great strides in music printing, and published the work of contemporary Dutch and Flemish geographers, cartographers, and botanists. His most important production and his masterpiece was the massive, eight-volume Polyglot Bible issued in 1572 in Latin, Greek, Hebrew, Syriac, and Aramaic, which Plantin organized, printed, and published (plates 63–64–65). The financial support promised by King Philip II of Spain, for whose greater glory the volumes were produced, was never forthcoming. This almost ruined the printer. However, compensation did later appear with certain exclusive ecclesiastical printing privileges for Plantin and his heirs.

One of Plantin's daughters married a scholar and linguist named Raphelengius who had taught at Cambridge in England. He became Plantin's chief "press corrector" and a source of strength in the conduct of a scholarly printing house. Another daughter married an industrious young assistant, Jan Moretus, who became Plantin's manager. He continued the organization after Plantin's death, and his competent descendants carried on the active Plantin-Moretus typographic dynasty until the nineteenth century when the printing establishment, marvelously intact from the sixteenth century, became a famous Belgian museum. It is a place of pilgrimage for anyone, amateur or professional, concerned with the printed page.

LOUIS
ELZEVIR
(1540–1617)

When the Netherlands had become a maritime world power in the seventeenth century, when its great era of painting included Rembrandt and Vermeer, and when the rich burghers of Amsterdam were a merchant aristocracy, a family of Protestant printers and publishers — the Elzevirs — produced neat, attractive, inexpensive books, and sold them all over Europe. Louis Elzevir issued his first book in 1593; the last was published in 1712. The Elzevirs — father, sons, and nephews — were all good businessmen who built up a large and thriving international publishing house. They employed editors who produced texts in Latin, English, French, German, and Dutch, when printers and publishers elsewhere were harassed by government and ecclesiastical controls. Typographically the Elzevirs found and stayed with a formula of tidy charm, with engraved title pages and compact types which, together with low prices, found wide acceptance among growing classes of readers. Their many series of vest-pocket editions apparently evoked sentimental bookish attachments which must have been widespread among readers of the time, and which have persisted among occasional collectors of "charming little books" ever since.

CENSORSHIP

Within weeks after Martin Luther nailed his ninety-five theses to the door of the Wittenberg church in 1517, printing presses provided copies which were read in every corner of Europe. During Luther's lifetime hundreds of thousands of his tracts and several hundred editions of his Bible in German found readers. "Lutheranism," states A. G. Dickens in *Reformation and Society*, "was from the first the child of the printed book . . . For the first time in history a great reading public judged the validity of revolutionary ideas through a mass medium which used the vernacular languages. . . ."

Church and State found this new threat intolerable. The Papacy issued its Index of proscribed books as did regional bishops and lay leaders, including Henry VIII of England who forbade the printing of any book in the English language unless approved by his delegated authority. A sixteenth-century printer wrote to an impatient author: "I thought you were aware that we are not allowed to send anything to press, from a simple epigram or a small notice to a voluminous work, until the entire manuscript has been read, approved, and countersigned by the theologians appointed for that purpose, and even then we shall have to obtain a license to print from the Council."

Oppressive censorship and supervision continued through the seventeenth century with strict limitations on the number of printers allowed to function, the number of presses they might operate, the number of their employees, etc. Civil wars and religious strife added economic chaos. With these harassments it is little wonder that the quality of book design and production sank to low levels. But if the seventeenth century was not a productive period for the art of the book, it was a period of unparalleled genius in its literature. The work of Shakespeare, Milton, Cervantes, Racine, Molière, and many others appeared in book form. In London, in 1611, the King James Bible was printed by Robert Barker. In the United States, the first press was established by Stephen Daye in 1638–1639 under the auspices of the President of Harvard College, and *The Whole Booke of Psalmes*, commonly known as the Bay Psalm Book, appeared in 1640.

THE IMPRIMERIE ROYALE

From the appointment in 1487 of Pierre le Rouge as first *Imprimeur du Roi*, French kings never lost their interest in types and printing. In the seventeenth century—a typographically bleak period through most of Europe—Louis XIII and Cardinal Richelieu, his prime minister, enjoyed personal presses. The young Dauphin had learned to set type in his private press in the Louvre, while the Cardinal completed a few competent small editions at his château. It is not surprising that Richelieu, having rebuilt the Sorbonne and founded the Académie Française, persuaded Louis to establish the Imprimerie Royale. Its founding was a deliberate effort to raise the standard of printing in France and to add to the glory of the Crown that Richelieu served so well. Cardinal Richelieu's determination to build a thoroughly professional plant is clearly set forth in the letter he wrote to the French ambassador in Holland early in 1640: "I have had for a long time the design of establishing a royal printing-office at the Louvre, and because I wish to execute everything in it with the greatest possible perfection, and I learn that in Dutch printing offices they have a secret method of making ink which renders the impression of the letter much more beautiful and distinct, and that it is something which cannot be made in France, and also that there are a large number of printers in the country, at Amsterdam, Leyden, Blaen, and elsewhere, who would perhaps be very glad to come to earn their living here, I beg you will take the trouble to inform yourself if it is possible to find workmen in said printing offices, at least four pressmen and four compositors, and among them, if possible, one who knows how to make this printing-ink, and to arrange with them at once for the expenses of their journey, and their maintenance, as reasonably as possible and as between private persons; for it is not well to mix up, in any way whatever, the name of the King in this business, nor to disclose our plan to foreigners who may wish in some way to hinder it. You can, if you choose, say that it is Monsieur Cramoisy, the Paris publisher, who has undertaken some big piece of work, who has asked you about the matter."

Within months after Richelieu's letter, the Imprimerie Royale, or Typographia

Regia, with Sébastien Cramoisy as its first director was a functioning institution of government. The first book, a folio *De Imitatione Christi* of Thomas à Kempis (plate 67), was completed by the end of 1640. It is a sumptuous volume, very well printed, with types of the Garamond design in large sizes and with copperplate vignettes by Claude Mellon after the designs of Nicolas Poussin. In 1642, the year of Richelieu's death, came a publication from the Cardinal's pen, *Les Principaux Poincts de la Foy Catholique Défendus*. A whole procession of imposing books – about a hundred titles in the first ten years – came from the seven printing presses operated at the Imprimerie, including a monumental Bible in eight folio volumes. Type for these publications was large, the spacing very ample, with luxurious margins and with copperplate vignettes for decoration. The editing was serious and scholarly. This was subsidized printing and publishing in the grand manner. At this time, it should be noted, the Imprimerie Royale was the only printing office in Europe where the tradition of fine bookmaking was nurtured with typographic enthusiasm, technical skills, and esthetic devotion.

SÉBASTIEN
CRAMOISY
(1585–1669)

The first director of the Imprimerie was succeeded by his grandson, Sébastien Mabre-Cramoisy, who was in turn succeeded in 1691 by Jean Anisson. The next year Louis XIV ordered the design of a new "scientific" typeface which would become the jealously guarded property of the French nation. A distinguished committee of the Académie des Sciences headed by a prominent mathematician was appointed to provide the "perfect" type. Earlier type design had grown out of forms cut by chisel or written with a broad pen in the hands of Renaissance humanist scribes. The warmth of the human touch – the happy accidents – were not lost when transformed into type by great designers such as Griffo and Garamond. Actually these slight irregularities provided vitality and aided legibility, whereas mechanical rigidity creates monotony and tires the eye. However, copperplate engraving had by the end of the seventeenth century superseded calligraphy; the burin replaced the pen, and pure technique became dominant.

The master designs of the Académie committee were finally engraved by the well-known Simonneau based on letters drawn with ruler and compass on a grid of close horizontal and vertical lines. Fortunately, the punches for the final type were cut by Philippe Grandjean, the King's Royal Punch Cutter, who followed his own instinctive genius and avoided excessively mechanical features. Greater contrasts than heretofore between thick and thin lines of the type, with sharp horizontal serifs, gave the type a new brilliance on the smoother papers then being made. The result is brittle and cold but undeniably handsome. Called *Romain du Roi Louis XIV*, the type was an immediate success and paved the way for the even more contrasting types and sharper presswork of Fournier, Baskerville, Bodoni, and Didot, soon to follow.

PHILIPPE
GRANDJEAN
(1666–1714)

The first book to be set in the *Romain du Roi*, printed and published, of course, by the Imprimerie Royale, is a magnificent folio, issued in 1702, *Médailles sur les Principaux Événements du Règne de Louis le Grand* (plates 68–69). In production for eight years, the book's planning and final publication involved the best designers and engravers in France. Its craftsmanship is brilliant—a supreme example of the florid and sophisticated book. Because of the precision of its type and the mechanical excellence of all phases of production, the *Médailles* marks the beginning of the modern, more precisely manufactured artifact, just about halfway in time between the invention of movable type and today's computerized letter composition.

THE EIGHTEENTH CENTURY

The contrasts between Latin and Anglo-Saxon characteristics could not be more clearly mirrored than in the books that appeared during the eighteenth century. The kings of France were not the only proprietors of private presses. Many members of the French aristocracy played with printing as a hobby. Madame de Pompadour, patroness and friend of artists and writers, herself possessed of some artistic competence, installed a press in the north wing of the palace at Versailles which gave her small editions (produced with help from printers of the Imprimerie) the imprint "*Au Nord.*" And let us not forget Benjamin Franklin's private press at Passy where he printed the bagatelles he wrote for his lady friends and colleagues between his more serious duties as minister to the French Court.

During the years of French extravagance in Versailles, the professional printers in Paris, aided by the best French artists and engravers, naturally fostered the spirit of the *livre de luxe*. They turned out charming octavos illustrating themes of love in enchanted gardens and boudoirs, luxurious tomes celebrating royal pageants, and the classics in massive, sumptuous folios richly bound to adorn rococo tables in fashionable drawing rooms. In Italy and Spain, court printers produced spectacular volumes for the wealthy, which were probably never read. In Britain, on the other hand, a few printers appeared who produced excellent literary editions, suitable for the worthiest texts, dependent on sound type design and fine page proportions, free of superfluous ornamentation or ostentation. This was a logical development at a time when, according to G. M. Trevelyan, "British scholars became more than ever separated from their continental brethren, thought and learning became more national, more popular, and more closely allied to literature."

The first influential figure in a century given to new trends in bookmaking is Pierre Simon Fournier—end product of a French family for several generations in the business of typefounding and type design. Born in 1712, Pierre Simon studied art but early turned to type and type ornament. In 1742 he issued his first specimen book, *Modèles des Caractères de l'Imprimerie*. He was an articulate member of his calling who wrote with scholarly and informative grace "about the history and development of the various branches of the Art of Printing." In 1764–1766 he published his beautiful, 16mo, two-volume *Manuel Typographique* (plate 78). Fournier devised our present printers' point system of measurement. His types were designed with an eye to the past but

PIERRE
SIMON
FOURNIER
(1712–1768)

23

drawn to satisfy the new preference for sharpness and contrast. He is best remembered for his great contribution to the decoration of books by means of ornament he made available on type metal. His foundry offered ornamental alphabets and initial letters, garlands, festoons, vignettes, decorated dashes and braces, and printers' flowers on pieces of metal which could be put together to make veritable gardenlike borders, chapter headings, tailpieces, and the like, in endless combinations. These printers' fleurons became standard equipment in every printing office in Europe and America until twentieth-century functionalism drove surface decoration into disrepute.

From the time Caxton returned to his native land late in the fifteenth century, the British relied on the papermakers, printers, and typefounders from across the Channel. During the seventeenth and into the eighteenth century, the dependence was primarily on the Netherlands where type was expertly designed and cast. The Oxford University Press, which began work in 1585, received a handsome gift of Dutch types in the 1660's and 1670's from Dr. John Fell, Dean of Christ Church, later Bishop of Oxford, who was influential in the foundation of the modern University Press. In 1676 Peter Walpergen, brought over from Holland, was engaged as type designer and typefounder. He cut the type and was responsible for a highly creditable three-volume folio publication, Clarendon's *The History of the Rebellion and Civil Wars in England* (plate 70), issued in 1702–1704. Another early eighteenth-century English publication is worthy of notice. In 1733–1737 John Pine, who had studied with a French engraver in Amsterdam, completed a two-volume Horace — a *tour de force* with the entire text and all the illustrations engraved on plates. The edition is curiously un-English, but attractive, with sharp, contrasting letters, and with open spacing ahead of its time; an octavo which foreshadowed much of what lay directly ahead.

WILLIAM
CASLON
(1692–1766) The first Englishman to provide native typographic genius was William Caslon, an engraver of gunlocks and bookbinding tools turned typefounder. He established his foundry in 1720 and issued his first comprehensive type specimen sheet in 1734. The high quality and usefulness of his type immediately reversed English dependence on the Continent. Although the Caslon roman and italic were patterned on contemporary Dutch models, the craftsmanship of Caslon's design and cutting made a better, cleaner font. It is difficult to analyze type except by involvement in technical details which are apt to be more subjective than authoritative. Adjectives must suffice. The Caslon face does lack elegance; but it is eminently clear, forthright, legible, comfortable, "commonsense," and has a good surface for printing. It had immediate success, was then passed over, then has had several periods of active revival, dependent on cycles of fashion and taste. At the present writing it is infrequently seen.

A new concept of book design, which had been several years in the making in England and Scotland, made its dramatic appearance in 1757 with an impressive quarto Virgil, planned and printed by John Baskerville (plate 76). A distinguished and eminently readable volume presented its text honorably and handsomely without ostentation and without the aid of illustration or decoration. This Virgil "went forth and astonished" the librarians and connoisseurs of Europe. Small wonder when Baskerville's forthright handling of type is compared with continental *éditions de luxe* where, usually, typography was the poor relation of elaborate engravings. Baskerville's books surprise us much less today because English and American bookmaking has accepted the Anglo-Saxon precepts of which Baskerville was an illustrious protagonist, i.e., that good design, type, paper, and good presswork are the principal components of the fine book, and that illustration and adornment, if any, may be secondary graces. And, need one add, respect for literary content remains the compelling reason for the book's existence.

Baskerville was born in 1706. At the age of nineteen he went to Birmingham where, during the next ten years, he established himself as a skilled writing master and stonecutter. These admirable gifts were then, as now, their own reward, but they were not lucrative enough for Baskerville. He next became a manufacturer of japanned ware, and as an industrialist, with inventiveness and competence, he acquired an independent fortune. A large and elegant house and a gorgeous equipage established his position in Birmingham society. Whereupon, at age forty-four, he was ready to return to his first love. In his own words: "Having been an early admirer of the beauty of Letters, I became insensibly desirous of contributing to the perfection of them." Baskerville spent the next seven years designing a typeface (cut by a certain John Handy), setting up a foundry and a press, training compositors and pressmen in his methods and, finally, completing his first book. In a letter to a friend Baskerville wrote: "The Ink, Presses, Chases, Moulds for casting and all the apparatus for Printing, were made in my own shops." Because Baskerville did not gain his livelihood from the sale of his books, he has been called an amateur. This has an unfortunate connotation. Baskerville was more professional and more expert in the art and techniques of bookmaking than the hosts of men whose daily bread has been earned by running presses. Baskerville's contributions to the mechanics of book production were threefold: type, paper, and more precise methods of printing. His type, with vertical stresses, is crisp, wide, and very readable, drawn by a master of the pointed pen. If it lacks Gallic charm, it does have masculine grace. The English Monotype version, which you are now reading, is very much in use for all varieties of bookmaking, as is the Linotype version. The Baskerville type has had its periods of greater and less acclaim. Updike found it inferior to Caslon. The present writer would pass the opposite judgment. Benjamin Franklin liked both typefaces. With a copy of the Baskerville Virgil that he presented to the Harvard Library in 1758, Franklin wrote: "... it is thought to be the most curiously printed of any book hitherto done in the world."

Baskerville manufactured his own intense black ink. And, in association with paper mills, he devised a wove mold which produced a smooth sheet (without the ribbed formation of laid papers) receptive to more even presswork. Nevertheless, Baskerville used more laid paper for his books than wove sheets, and occasionally used both in the same volume. After printing, these papers were pressed between polished metal plates. The books must have been brilliant when new, but today the paper is occasionally slightly discolored with brown spots due probably to the hot pressing.

JOHN
BASKERVILLE

Baskerville printed fifty-six titles. In the preface to his Milton in 1758 he wrote: "It is not my desire to print many books; but such only, as are of Consequence, of intrinsic merit, or established Reputation, and which the public may be pleased to see in an elegant dress, and to purchase at such a price, as will repay the extraordinary care and expence that must necessarily be bestowed upon them." His most influential books were the squarish quartos of the Latin classics, especially the Virgil and a Juvenal and Persius of 1761 (plate 77). His most ambitious undertaking was the Bible in royal folio, completed in 1763, during his appointment as Printer to Cambridge University, at great financial loss to himself. With the Bible in production, Baskerville wrote to Horace Walpole requesting a government subsidy. Like other printers buried under the minutiae of bookmaking, Baskerville became restive and writes of "this business of Printing, which I am heartily tired of, and repent I ever attempted. It is surely a particular hardship that I should not get Bread in my own Country (and it is too late to go abroad) after having acquired the reputation of excelling in the most useful Art known to Mankind. . . ." The subsidy was not granted. Baskerville gave up printing for a few years, then returned to it until his death in 1775.

Baskerville's Bible has been widely acclaimed as his masterpiece. It is, certainly, an important labor. But it is not as fully conceived as the noble bibles of Robert Estienne two hundred years earlier, or the Lectern Bible designed by Bruce Rogers and printed at the Oxford University Press less than two hundred years later. Nevertheless, Baskerville's place in typographic history is secure. His open, generous pages brought to a climax the clear, widely spaced treatment, already to be seen in the books of Tonson and Bowyer in London, especially the noble Tonson *Commentaries* of Caesar, 1712 (plate

ROBERT
AND ANDREW
FOULIS
(fl. 1750–1770)

71), and in the superb editions of the Foulis Brothers in Glasgow (plate 79). In crystallizing this trend, Baskerville was the inspiration that set off a fifty-year stretch of native British bookmaking as seen in the work of the printers Bulmer, Bensley, and Bell, and the type designers Martin, Austin, and Wilson. Baskerville's influence in Europe was also profoundly felt, most significantly on the work of Bodoni in Italy and on the Didot books in France. Bodoni and Didot, together with Joaquín Ibarra in Spain, produced works of conspicuous grandeur and had the distinction of being the last entrepreneurs of sumptuous bookmaking before the advent of the machine.

Son of a family of printers, Giambattista Bodoni was born in the north of Italy in 1740. He began his apprentice years in his home town of Saluzzo, then went to the Propaganda Fide in Rome, the missionary press which printed in native languages for all parts of the world. This involved the young Bodoni in exotic fonts for which he cut punches and in which he showed high promise. When his mentor, head of the press, died in 1767, Bodoni made plans to continue his career in England, hoping to work under Baskerville. Meanwhile he was recommended to Ferdinand, Duke of Parma, who wished to establish a press patterned somewhat after the French Imprimerie Royale. Bodoni accepted the call, arrived in Parma in 1768, and remained for life. As printer to the court, he set up a subsidized press and foundry with equipment and personnel. He would soon produce exalted printing for royal occasions, free from the usual mortal concern for costs. It was a rare opportunity. Bodoni rose to it with abundant skills and with a ready aptitude for audacious showmanship. And, of great importance to him, his career spanned the years just before the final curtain fell on unlimited royal privilege.

Bodoni's early work shows French influence, especially the types of Fournier. But he soon developed his own dramatic style, at its best in books of large format which invited extravagant treatment. The first of many volumes in the grand manner was the *Epithalamia* of 1775, a folio celebrating the nuptials of Marie Adelaide Clotilde, sister of Louis XVI, with engravings, and with the short text repeated in a multitude of exotic types. Books of all kinds came from the Stamperia Reale at Parma, and Bodoni's fame spread through Europe. He continued to design and cut type which he showed in a 360-page specimen book in 1788. His romans and italics achieved brilliance by extreme contrast between thick and thin strokes, and, of course, on excellent and original design. For display and exhibition purposes, the Bodoni types, especially in the large sizes, are striking and handsome. In small sizes for average-length books they are too sharp to be easily readable.

Permission to print and publish on his own, as well as for his royal patron, made possible the completion of Bodoni's most renowned titles: the one-volume Horace in 1791 (plate 83), and the Virgil in two volumes in 1793. They are giant folios, page size approximately twelve by eighteen inches. The typography is clear, open, formal, austere, free of decoration. The text type, about equivalent to our present eighteen point and widely spaced between lines, was printed on luxurious paper with intense black ink, with impression scarcely short of perfection. Altogether, these books with their vast margins and bold display are technical and artistic masterpieces. And yet they lack the vital spark of scholarship, which is the heart of the matter, and without which these great undertakings remain dry and cold. Bodoni's books were notoriously replete with textual errors, as pointed out by Horace Walpole whose *Castle of Otranto* Bodoni printed, by Bodoni's rival, Pierre Didot, and by others. But the privileged young men on their "Grand Tour" who bought the books were not troubled by what they did not read. Bodoni became a European personage, honored by the aristocrats and collected by the bibliophiles. He was sought after and complimented by the Pope; the city of Parma struck a medal in his honor; he corresponded with Benjamin Franklin; he received pensions from the King of Spain and the Viceroy of Naples, and from

Napoleon, in whose honor in 1808 he printed a three-volume Homer in Greek, with the Italian dedication emblazoned in capital letters: "Alla Maestà Imperiale e Reale di Napoleone il Grande Imperator de' Francesi Re d'Italia e Protettore della Confederazione del Reno," and signed, "Giambattista Bodoni."

Along with all this acclaim by dignitaries who were unaware of typographic niceties, Bodoni is not without honor among professionals of the book. He was, undeniably, a master of the art and technique of printing and a great and prolific type designer. In the magnificent two-volume *Manuale Tipografico* (plates 84–85) which Bodoni himself planned, but which Bodoni's widow issued in 1818, five years after his death, Bodoni's tremendous lifework is manifest. Giovanni Mardersteig, the eminent designer and printer of the Officina Bodoni in Verona, who has had access to much of the original Bodoni material, told the present writer that Bodoni cut somewhere around three hundred fonts of type, and before he died Bodoni had seen at least one piece of printing in each of one hundred and fifty languages set in his types. And Bodoni himself cut more than twenty thousand punches and struck more than forty thousand matrices. The Bodoni Museum in Parma now contains altogether some eighty thousand punches and matrices.

The Bodoni romans and italics have been extensively copied and have become an essential part of today's typographic equipment, chiefly for newspaper headings, magazines, and promotional printing. With a very few exceptions, most of the socalled "Bodonis" are libelous versions which perpetuate the name but not the designer's skills. In any event, Bodoni should be seen in the originals — in the great folio editions. A good reproduction is at best a simulation of glory.

Benjamin Franklin, always a printer at heart, whose friendship was enjoyed by Europe's foremost practitioners, wrote in a letter from Passy in 1781: "A strong Emulation exists at Present between Paris and Madrid, with regard to beautiful Printing. Here a M. Didot *le jeune* has a Passion for the Art . . . he has executed several charming Editions. But the 'Salust' and the 'Don Quixote' of Madrid are thought to excel them." The printer of these two widely admired books was Joaquín Ibarra, Printer to the Court of Spain. He had been appointed by Carlos III, patron of artists and craftsmen, who had even issued a decree permitting hidalgos to engage in the crafts without loss of caste. The special interest in printing is not surprising since Carlos was an uncle to the Ferdinand who was Bodoni's royal patron.

JOAQUÍN
IBARRA
(1725–1785)

Ibarra performed, with great distinction, the diverse duties which fell to a court printer. His chief fame rests on the Sallust of 1772 (plate 81) and the *Don Quixote* of 1780 in four volumes, the latter commissioned and supervised by the Spanish Royal Academy. Both are elegant editions, with numerous engraved illustrations, type, paper, and all details Spanish, deliberately made to be national treasures, which, indubitably, they are. The translation was by the Infante Don Gabriel Antonio de Bourbon who sent a copy to Franklin.

The eighteenth century which witnessed such an abundant artistic and literary flowering in France naturally brought the publication of many remarkable and beautiful editions in all categories. A few of these should be named before introducing the Didot *Éditions du Louvre*. The century was given a good send-off in 1702 by the Imprimerie Royale's *Médailles* already mentioned. In 1734 a six-volume edition of the Molière *Oeuvres* printed by Pierre Prault included thirty-three designs by François Boucher. From 1755 to 1759, four magnificent folio volumes of La Fontaine's *Fables Choisies Mises en Vers* (plate 74) were issued in a landmark edition combining the paintings of Jean Baptiste Oudry redrawn for engraving by Charles Nicolas Cochin, and floral pieces by J. J. Bachelier cut in wood by J. B. Papillon and Nicolas le Sueur. The books were printed by Charles Antoine Jombert whose composition and press-work rose to the occasion. In 1762 came another title by La Fontaine, *Contes et Nouvelles en Vers* (plate 75), in two charming octavo volumes with designs by Charles Eisen and vignettes by Pierre Philippe Choffard. Joseph Gérard Barbou was the publisher and probably also the printer. The Imprimerie Royale produced one of its most important scientific publications in the superb ten-volume illustrated folio, *Histoire Naturelle des Oiseaux* by the Comte de Buffon in 1771–1786. Among the many lighthearted books published for the entertainment of the less staid members of society are Dorat's *Les Baisers*, 1770 (plate 80), and Montesquieu's *Le Temple de Gnide*, 1772, both illustrated by Charles Eisen.

CHARLES ANTOINE JOMBERT (1712–1784)

The Didot family of typefounders, printers, papermakers, and publishers is the third dynasty (after Estienne and Fournier) to contribute its varied talents and scholarly competence to the sustained leadership of Paris in the art of the book. The ancestor of the family was Denis Didot, printer and bookseller in Paris whose son François (1689–1757), also a printer and publisher, is remembered for having issued a twenty-volume account of the travels of his friend the Abbé Prévost in 1747. Next came sons Pierre François and François Ambroise who in their turn begat sons and grandsons who upheld the family tradition well into the nineteenth century.

FRANÇOIS DIDOT (1689–1757)

The line that most concerns us begins with François Ambroise Didot (1730–1804) known as *l'aîné*. He was the first to give the Didot touch to type and to bookmaking. He was printer by appointment to the Comte d'Artois, the King's brother. By order of Louis XVI he printed and published a famous collection of French authors, *Imprimé par ordre du Roi pour l'éducation de Monsieur le Dauphin*. This same Didot perfected the printers' point system begun by Fournier. In 1780 he arranged for the making of *papier vélin*, a wove sheet similar to the paper introduced by Baskerville. And, finally, it is pleasant to know that in 1785 it was with François Ambroise Didot that Benjamin Franklin placed his grandson, Benjamin Franklin Bache, to learn typefounding and printing. In his diary the lad wrote: "My grandpapa has prevailed upon Mr. Didot,

FRANÇOIS AMBROISE DIDOT (1730–1804)

the best printer of this age and even the best that has ever been seen, to consent to take me into his house for some time in order to teach me his art. I take my meals at his house and sleep at the house of Mrs. LeRoy, a friend of my grandpapa; I went thither today with my cousin and I became acquainted with his family and something more. He combines in his house engraving, the forge, the foundry and the printing-office; it is a very amiable family, as it seems to me; the meals are frugal." Shortly thereafter, he added, "Today I have engraved my first punch with Mr. Didot's younger son. It was an o. They assert that I have not succeeded badly."

PIERRE DIDOT L'AÎNÉ (1761–1853)

FIRMIN DIDOT (1764–1836)

François Ambroise had two famous sons who worked closely together. Pierre *l'aîné* (1761–1853) became the printer; Firmin (1764–1836) took over the foundry where he designed and cut the famous types used by his brother in the printing of the extraordinary *Éditions du Louvre* and other publications. Firmin Didot was also involved in the development of stereotyping with which he was able to produce small books inexpensively. Napoleon appointed him director of the foundry of the Imprimerie Impériale (formerly Royale, later Nationale). In 1830 Firmin was made director of the Institution. Meanwhile he looked to the future, having become involved in new techniques of paper and ink and printing by machine. He was also a Latin scholar and translator. He died in 1836, having lived the full life of craftsmanship and scholarship.

Pierre Didot's reputation rests primarily, but not entirely, on four magnificent publications: La Fontaine, 1795; Virgil, 1798 (plate 91); Horace, 1799; and Racine, 1801 (plates 92–93). They are known as the *Éditions du Louvre* because they were printed at the Louvre in the space vacated by removal of the Imprimerie Royale to other quarters in Paris. Whatever else may have been the *raison d'être* for these noble volumes, there can be little doubt that they were meant to outshine the Horace and Virgil of Bodoni. For this writer, the Didot books are superior. Whereas all these massive tomes are showpieces from a period when extravagant waste was acceptable, the Didot books reap the benefits of scholarship which the Bodoni volumes lack. And although both Bodoni and Didot types are very similar, and both suffer from mechanical rigidity, the Didot type is superior by the considerable margin of the more cultivated Didot sensibilities. Further, the Didot editions gain from magnificent decoration and illustration which add warmth and spirit to these grandiose performances. The Racine, regarded as Didot's masterpiece, is illustrated with full-page engravings after designs by Prud'hon, Girodet, Gérard, and others, in the formal, classical manner of the painter David. These volumes are at the peak of lavish showmanship, breathtaking in the audacity of conception and perfection of execution. The Didots also printed many smaller books—for students and an informed reading public—altogether admirable, and many are beautiful. Nevertheless, the Didot type in small sizes suffers, as did the Bodonis, from an excess of contrast which dazzles the eye—at least our modern eyes addicted to rapid reading.

The large nine-volume "Boydell Shakspeare" (plate 86) was England's answer in folio to Bodoni and Didot. Its publication as a "national" edition was planned by Josiah Boydell with George Nicol, bookseller to George III. In a foreword to Volume I, Nicol states that "splendour and magnificance, united with correctness of text, were the great objects of this edition." Leading British artists were commissioned to make more than a hundred paintings from which full-page illustrations were engraved to accompany the text. "With regard to the typographical part of the work," continued Nicol, "the state of printing in England, when it was first undertaken [1786] was such that it was found necessary to establish a printing-house on purpose to print the work; a foundry to cast the types; and even a manufactory to make the ink."

William Bulmer, who had already spent some time in France and had been work- WILLIAM ing for John Bell, was selected to produce the edition. It was an admirable choice BULMER which brought about the establishment of the press of W. Bulmer and Company in (1757–1830) London. The first of the Shakspeare volumes was issued in 1792, the last of nine in 1802. These tall folios were undeniably opulent, but their straightforward, literate typography and printing spared them from ostentation. Together with a companion three-volume folio Milton, these superb books must have occupied proud places in the stately libraries of eighteenth-century English manor houses. Along with a full schedule of workmanlike production, Bulmer printed two delightful quartos: *Poems by Goldsmith and Parnell*, 1795 (plate 87), and *The Chase* by William Somerville, 1796. Both books, typical of the open British style of these decades, are of special importance because they were the first adequately printed presentations of the wood engravings of Thomas Bewick. Bulmer and Bewick had been apprentices together and remained THOMAS friends and associates from their youth. Bewick's new technique consisted of engraved BEWICK "white lines" on the endgrain of hardwood blocks by a burin as opposed to earlier (1753–1828) cutting on the long side grain with a knife. This method has since, of course, become a choice medium for book illustration.

The excellent, sturdy type used for the above-mentioned Bulmer books was cut by William Martin, brother of the Robert Martin who had been Baskerville's foreman. It is a transitional face derivative of Baskerville and Bodoni. A faithful modern cutting, unfairly baptized "Bulmer," has been made and is available now for hand and machine composition. The Martin and Bell types were modified in English and Scottish foundries during the next decades and evolved into faces known as "Modern" and "Scotch" — both versions widely and continuously used in books and periodicals well into the present century.

Thomas Bensley, who started as a trade printer, later produced some excellent THOMAS work. Among his noteworthy books are *The Seasons* by James Thomson, 1797 (plate BENSLEY 88), with engravings by Bartolozzi and Tomkins from paintings by W. Hamilton; the (d. 1835) Macklin folio Bible, 1800, intended to compare with the Boydell Shakspeare (but not its equal); and Blair's *The Grave*, 1808, with illustrations by William Blake.

THE NINETEENTH CENTURY
AND THE INDUSTRIAL REVOLUTION

Bulmer and Bensley were the last important printers in England whose work was produced on wooden hand presses with ink applied to type by ancient leather ink balls. These men were also factors in the vast changes about to transform society. During the year 1800 the all-iron lever press, invented or at least perfected by Lord Stanhope, was given its first tests in the Bulmer printing office. The greater strength of iron and the more ingenious method of applying pressure enabled printers to more than double sheet size and production. Of far greater importance, during the first decade of the nineteenth century a cylinder press run by steam was built and given trials in the Bensley workshop by its inventor, Friedrich König, a German printer who had settled in London. John Walter, publisher of the London *Times*, ordered two presses to be installed in utter secrecy (fearing conflict with his regular pressmen) in Printing House Square. On the night of November 28, 1814, the first newspaper was printed by power on a cylinder machine, and the lead article next morning included the statement: "Our journal of this day presents to the public the practical result of the greatest improvement connected with printing since the discovery of the art itself."

The enormous increase in the speed of newspaper printing, spurred on by the newly invented stereotype plates and machine-made paper, was followed much more slowly in book production. Satisfactory mechanical type composition was not achieved until the last decades of the nineteenth century because early inventors sought its solution in cumbersome slotted machines which would drop previously cast individual type characters into place. The burdens of standing type and type distribution, time-consuming procedures which harked back to the fifteenth century, were left unresolved. Mark Twain was only one among the many inventors and investors who lost large sums along this fruitless path. Ottmar Mergenthaler, a German-American at work in Baltimore, cut through these difficulties with a machine that simultaneously composed and cast lines of new type for each job. Hence the name, "Linotype." When printed (or reprinted) the metal was thrown back into the melting pot. Tolbert Lanston followed shortly with a composing machine that cast individual letter composition, logically called "Monotype." Each machine claims advantages, but both are facing obsolescence and probably eventual extinction. They are being supplanted by electronic letter composition employing film instead of metal, reproduced at dazzling speeds and at much less cost by offset lithography instead of direct impressional printing.

During the nineteenth century and well into the twentieth, the machine was thought to be an obstacle to fine bookmaking. Actually the machine did bring about a cleavage. Heretofore all printers used the same kinds of equipment and the same methods of production. The great designer-printers, whether Estienne or Bodoni, whether subsidized or not, differed from the lesser members of their craft by the measure of their capacities for scholarship, artistry, and craftsmanship. With the accumulation of complex, expensive machinery, and with accelerating wages, the industrial printer became a merchant who sold machine time at the bidding of publishers, advertisers, and other consumers of printed matter. Craftsmanship sank to low levels. Design and taste, if any, were imposed from without. The ruthless demands of machinery and the vast growth of the capitalistic structure imposed the need for increasing specialization. These conditions gave rise to publishers who set their own typographic standards, led to the establishing of influential private presses, and, in due course, saw the occasional appearance of scholar-printers who would uphold and pass along the traditions of fine workmanship.

The austere neoclassicism of the eighteenth century gave way to greater freedom of treatment after Waterloo. In French books this was reflected in copiously illustrated editions in which wood engravings and lithographs dominated texts set up with less formal and less skillful typographic attention. Notable among editions issued in Paris are, chronologically: Goethe's *Faust*, 1828, with large and flamboyant lithographs by Delacroix; Saint Pierre's *Paul et Virginie*, 1838, overflowing with wood engravings from several hands (plate 96); *Un Autre Monde*, 1844, with wood-engraved illustrations by J. J. Grandville in black-and-white and color; books with multitudes of drawings by Gustave Doré cut in wood by professional engravers (plate 97); and Edgar Allan Poe's *The Raven*, 1875, translated by Mallarmé with lithographs by Édouard Manet. Clearly, these books catered to the French partiality for book illustration, and pointed the way to the extraordinary volumes to be known as *Les Livres de Peintres* illustrated by the most famous of twentieth-century French artists.

In England, as on the Continent, with the passing of the Bodoni-Didot period of austere luxury the inevitable reactions set in. Workmanship drifted to low standards. Instead of sharp, contrasting display type, foundries offered grossly fat faces and other exaggerations and distortions. The new industrialism brought its own confusions. Only one publisher in London, William Pickering, resisted the then current trend and turned back to the fifteenth and sixteenth centuries for inspiration.

William Pickering, a publisher—not a printer—was responsible for the design and execution of a notable program of excellent books. He was, moreover, the first conspicuous figure in the emerging separation of book design from printing and publishing. Born in 1796 the young lad, brought up by a tailor and his wife from whom he took his name, was apprenticed at fourteen years of age to a bookseller and publisher in London. Ten years later he set up on his own as an antiquarian bookseller with capital supplied, so Geoffrey Keynes tells us, by one of his book-loving, aristocratic, if anonymous,

WILLIAM
PICKERING
(1796–1854)

33

parents. Obviously endowed with native acumen and an instinct for sound scholarship, he soon prospered. He made his first venture into publishing in 1820 with the diminutive and enchanting "Diamond Classics" in Latin. The series had a well-deserved success. Full-sized books soon followed in a very comprehensive publishing program during more than thirty years—mainly editions of English authors, including, for example, Francis Bacon's works in seventeen volumes edited by Basil Montague, Dr. Johnson in eleven volumes, and sumptuous liturgical books in black letter (plates 94, 95). In 1830, beginning with Robert Burns, Pickering issued the famous "Aldine Poets," eventually carried to fifty-three volumes.

As an antiquarian bookseller Pickering had seen the work of the early great printers. In homage, in 1828, he adopted as his own publisher's mark the anchor and dolphin of Aldus, to which he added *Aldi Discip. Anglvs*, and as a good disciple, paid his respects to the past with books that were modest in format and costs, distinguished in appearance. Pickering was able to obtain creditable work from several printers.

CHARLES
WHITTINGHAM
(1795–1876) In 1830 he began a lifelong relationship with Charles Whittingham, the younger, proprietor of the Chiswick Press, whose technical competence dovetailed happily with Pickering's activities. Together these men in the 1840's resurrected Caslon Old Face type which marked a return to the warmer and more agreeable types derived from calligraphic sources. Pickering might well be considered an early ancestor of the men and women who design books in today's publishing houses.

BRITISH PRIVATE PRESSES

William Morris, born in 1834, inherited enough financial means to allow himself the luxury of devoting his life to art. He was influenced by the poetry of Chaucer, the painting of Dante Gabriel Rossetti with whom he studied, and the anti-industrialism of John Ruskin. The Middle Ages appealed to the romantic Morris, who collected and studied medi-

WILLIAM
MORRIS
(1834–1896) eval manuscripts and himself became an accomplished calligrapher and illuminator. He believed fervently in the dignity of labor. The heartless industrialism of Victorian England and the debasement of workmanship horrified Morris and impelled him to become an active worker in the Socialist movement which he hoped would provide the working classes with some joy in their work and less injustice in their daily lives.

Morris studied architecture which he never practiced. He did become a professional designer and decorator, and at times a manufacturer in many crafts including furniture, tapestries, wall papers, carpets, hangings, and stained glass. Throughout his life he was also a popular and prolific poet, novelist, and translator of ancient epic romances. Then on an evening in November of 1888 at an Arts and Crafts Exhibition in London, Morris attended a lecture by his friend and neighbor Emery Walker.

34

Walker was a technician and printer, who became an advisor to Morris and a continuing source of strength. The subject was printing, illustrated with lantern slides of early manuscripts and typefaces. As the two friends walked home, Morris, inspired by what he had seen, resolved to carry through a plan he had been harboring—to start a press and print books. Within a few months he was engaged in type design. In January 1891 Morris wrote to William Bowden, a prospective employee, asking him to accept the position of "compositor and press printer in the little typographical adventure I am planning."

Morris clearly did not anticipate that the "typographical adventure" would expand as it did, nor that the Kelmscott Press would become so important and influential. He started with one secondhand Albion hand press, later purchased two more hand presses, and engaged three compositors. Morris was now fifty-seven years of age. In his remaining six years he continued his manifold activities and at the same time turned out fifty-two printed works at the Kelmscott Press in sixty-six volumes for a total of more than eighteen thousand copies. Many of these books were Morris' own writings, and epics in his translation; many were reprints of Caxton's titles; others by Keats (plate 100), Shelley, Ruskin, Rossetti, Tennyson, Swinburne, Thomas More, Herrick, Coleridge, etc., with the crowning typographic achievement in 1896—the majestic Kelmscott Chaucer (plate 101). Morris arranged with "my friend, Mr. Batchelor, of Little Chart, Kent" for a magnificent paper, handmade, entirely from linen rags at a time when cotton was already being widely used. After several failures by English ink manufacturers, Morris turned to Jaenecke in Germany for an intense black that met his standards. Average editions were three hundred copies on paper and a few copies printed on vellum.

In *A Note on His Aims*, in 1895, Morris wrote: "It was only natural that I, a decorator by profession, should attempt to ornament my books suitably; about this matter I will say that I have always tried to keep in mind the necessity for making my decoration a part of the page of type. I may add that in designing the magnificent and inimitable woodcuts which have adorned several of my books, and will above all adorn the Chaucer which is now drawing near to completion, my friend Sir Edward Burne-Jones has never lost sight of this important point, so that his work will not only give us a series of most beautiful and imaginative pictures, but form the most harmonious decoration possible to the printed book." The completed Chaucer contained eighty-seven woodcut illustrations by Burne-Jones engraved by W. H. Hooper, also a woodcut title, fourteen large borders, eighteen different frames around the illustrations, and twenty-six large initial words designed for the book by William Morris.

Morris completed three types. The "Golden" type, so named after *The Golden Legend*, was patterned, in Morris' words, on "the works of the great Venetian printers of the fifteenth century, of whom Nicholas Jenson produced the completest and most Roman characters from 1470 to 1476. This type I studied with much care, getting it photographed to a big scale, and drawing it over many times before I began designing my own letter; so that though I think I mastered the essence of it, I did not copy it servilely; in fact, my Roman type, especially in the lower case, tends rather more to the Gothic than does Jenson's." The "Troy" type (called "Chaucer" in the smaller size) was designed "to redeem the Gothic character from the charge of unreadableness. . . . Keeping my end steadily in view, I designed a black-letter type which I think I may claim to be as readable as a Roman one, and to say the truth, I prefer it to the Roman."

William Morris, whose mentors were the great craftsmen of the Middle Ages, was a romantic idealist who believed that salvation lay in the sanctity of work done by hand. His books, brilliant in conception and resplendent in decoration, may seem intruders in today's hurried world and small living spaces. But Morris meant them to be read for their literary content and enjoyed for their beauty. Paradoxically, Morris, who looked to the past, exerted enormous influence on the future; not only in book production, but also in the larger fields of industrial design where Morris' respect for materials and workmanship were profound stimuli. His passionate craftsmanship (not his typographic design) was the spark which ignited a fifty-year renaissance of book-making in England, on the Continent, and in the United States. His example gave rise to a vital private press tradition and to a generation of amateurs and collectors of fine printing. This man who loathed the machine was an inspiration to professional practitioners who, as men of their time, would make peace with power-driven machinery and learn to direct it adventurously and intelligently.

BRITISH PRIVATE PRESSES

The impact of the Kelmscott Press was quickly seen in a number of British private presses dedicated to grandeur in printing. Best known are the Ashendene Press, 1894–1935, Eragny Press, 1894–1914, Essex House, 1898–1910, Doves Press, 1900–1916, and the Welsh Gregynog Press, 1922–1940. The private press may be described—to avoid confusion with hobby printers—as a sustained enterprise of a person of means, and of taste and ability, who produces books for his own esthetic pleasure, frequently with a newly commissioned proprietary typeface and, usually, with one or more employed journeymen. Books were set by hand and printed on dampened handmade papers and customarily bound in vellum. Most striking among many beautiful press books are the Doves Press five-volume folio Bible, 1903–1905 (plate 104), and the Ashendene folio Dante, 1909 (plate 107). The Doves Press was established by T. J.

T. J. COBDEN-SANDERSON (1840–1922)

Cobden-Sanderson, a friend of William Morris, a barrister turned exquisite hand bookbinder, who induced Emery Walker to become his partner and to design a house type, again based on a Jenson original. The Doves Press books were without illustration or decoration except for handsome initial letters by Edward Johnston and Graily Hewitt. Johnston was the father of the important revival of calligraphy which he raised to professional stature. The Ashendene Press was the solid and very personal venture of C. H. St. John Hornby, managing director of a large British distributor of books and periodicals. These press books are often superlative. They are also inclined to be echoes of the past without the natural strengths of the Renaissance forebears who made books within the economic and social framework of their times. Nevertheless, let it be quickly said that the artistry and craftsmanship of the proprietors of these presses and the regal elegance of many of their books were exemplars to typographically minded practitioners and collectors, and to a few young men for whom fine printing became a rewarding (if not very lucrative) profession.

THE GERMAN REVIVAL

The gospel of fine bookmaking seen in the work of the English private presses found zealous followers on the Continent, except perhaps in France which went its own way. The reception in Germany, the country which gave birth to printing, was especially enthusiastic. From the early years of the century to Hitler's long rise to power, many publishers, printers, typefounders, and designers joined in serious efforts to enhance the state of the physical book. State-supported arts and crafts schools in major cities, notably the State Academy for Graphic Arts in Leipzig, were staffed by prominent artists and designers who were also free to offer their services to industry. Their work was encouraged and used by, among many others, Carl Ernest Poeschel, an excellent printer in Leipzig, by the Insel Verlag, and by publishers Kurt Wolff and S. Fischer. Typefounders produced a host of new typefaces: traditional and modern romans and gothics, decorative scripts, and several excellent sanserifs. These fonts were very successful at home and abroad. Many have survived and are being used today. Among the many book and type designers — Ehmcke, Weiss, Bernhard, Renner, Schneidler, Tiemann — the most unusual figure was Rudolf Koch. Koch revered medieval craftsmanship and regarded the letters of the alphabet as a supreme, mystical achievement of the human spirit. He was leader of the arts and crafts school in Offenbach-am-Main, where he gathered round him in the ancient guild manner a group of brilliant and devoted students. (Several of these young men, later fleeing from Nazi oppression, took their talents to England and to the United States.) Together, Koch and his pupils used lettering to decorate and honor paper and vellum, wood, metal, stone, and textiles. They were artists and craftsmen, calligraphers and printers (plate 109). Several typefaces designed by Koch and cast at the local Klingspor Foundry were welcomed by designers around the world to dress their printed pages.

RUDOLF KOCH (1876–1934)

Numerous German private presses appeared; two became world famous. The Bremer Presse, productive from 1911 to 1939, was established by a group of artists and scholars led by Willy Wiegand, son of a German industrialist, who remained its director to the end. Wiegand designed four typefaces; gothics for his Missal and the five-volume Luther Bible; greek for his Sophocles, Homer (plate 108), and other Greek classics; and roman type in several sizes for "humanistic" literature such as Tacitus, St. Augustine, Dante, Goethe, and Emerson. The only decorations were the spirited initial letters made for each book by Anna Simons, a student of Edward

WILLY WIEGAND (1884–1961)

Johnston. The Bremer Presse books, usually issued in editions of about two hundred and fifty copies for subscribers, were magnificently made in every craftsmanlike detail by a thoroughly professional group of compositors and pressmen. The books were clearly made to glorify the written word and the traditional art of the book, which they do with great distinction.

COUNT HARRY KESSLER (1868–1937)

The Cranach Presse was the private venture of Count Harry Kessler, German diplomat, cosmopolite, and patron of the arts. Established in 1913 in Weimar, the Press was directed by the Belgian designer Henry van de Velde during Kessler's absence in the First World War. The last book was published in 1932, the year that Kessler was forced to flee the Nazis. A Cranach Presse monument is, surely, the Virgil *Eclogues* of 1926 (plate 110) with woodcuts by Aristide Maillol, with a title page and initial letters by Eric Gill, a roman type cut under the direction of Emery Walker, and an italic by Edward Johnston. The magnificent paper was made by hand by Maillol's nephew at Monval near Paris. The book is a fine classical setting with harmonious relations between type, paper, and the exquisite illustrations. The *Tragedie of Hamlet*, 1930, with woodcuts by Gordon Craig on which he is said to have worked for seventeen years, and the 1931 *Song of Songs (Canticum Canticorum)* with wood-engraved illustrations and initials by Eric Gill, are other outstanding publications. Kessler's involvement in contemporary politics and his wide friendships among European artists gave his books elements of daring and originality rarely found in privately subsidized undertakings.

THE TWENTIETH CENTURY

The year 1891 was prophetic on both sides of the Atlantic. In May, William Morris issued his first Kelmscott book, *The Glittering Plain*, in elegant quarto. Then in October, in Portland, Maine, Thomas Bird Mosher, son of a New England sea captain, published *Modern Love* by George Meredith. This small volume of poetry was the first title in a long list of modest and attractive Mosher books, chosen with keen literary judgment. More important, during the 1890's in Boston, a group of brilliant young practitioners appeared who, on their own and in reciprocal ties with the British, would be responsible for a half century of conspicuous bookmaking.

The work of the English private presses exerted a remote and subtle but visible influence. Before and especially after the First World War, several substantial printing houses in England and Scotland, and a number of British trade publishers, were inspired to improve their bookmaking. In 1935 Allen Lane introduced the sixpenny Penguin paperbacks and soon achieved a considerable measure of quality with very large editions. In 1946 Jan Tschichold, "modernist" turned classicist, was called in to set up rules for design and for care in manufacturing details. His Penguin Shakespeare is an excellent example of a very attractive, well-produced book for a mass market. The two university presses — Oxford and Cambridge — have enjoyed printing facilities,

Bible privileges, and erudition since their origins in the sixteenth century. In the present era they have built large modern plants and have produced much distinguished work. Their printing and publishing activities are widespread. It has been said of their directing heads that scholars have become printers and printers have become scholars.

The private press gradually became an anachronism as the twentieth century leveled many economic and social privileges. Luxury was no longer quite acceptable after the First World War. The ample "gentleman's" private library in large houses staffed by servants was fast disappearing. However, the desire for beautiful books remained. The need was met by skilled designers in America and Europe who used the machine to make distinguished books and splendid ephemera. In England, four men were primarily responsible: Stanley Morison, Oliver Simon, Eric Gill, and Francis Meynell.

A first breakthrough in the availability of new typefaces based on historic originals came from the American Type Founders Company with their cutting in 1913 of "Cloister" based on Jenson, and then in 1916–1919 an excellent reproduction of Garamond. The "Garamond" and some early designs by Frederic W. Goudy made considerable impression in Britain where the choice had been restricted to "Caslon" and to the inelegant "old styles" and "moderns." It was the unavailability of good typefaces that had forced the private presses to cut their own designs, based on classical ancestors. In 1922 Stanley Morison, then a young man who had had ten years' involvement in printing and publishing, was appointed typographical adviser to the British Monotype Corporation. With the solid backing of the managing director, W. I. Burch, and the cooperation of the manufacturing plant, Morison during the next decade made available to printers a brilliant galaxy of remarkable types. The faces based on earlier models were "Bembo," "Poliphilus," "Garamond," "Fournier," "Baskerville," "Bell," "Walbaum," and others. New faces by a number of contemporary designers were also cut, most notably, "Perpetua" by Eric Gill, "Centaur" by Bruce Rogers, "Lutetia" by Jan van Krimpen, and "Dante" by Giovanni Mardersteig. In 1932 came Morison's "Times New Roman" made for the London *Times*. After a year's exclusive use by the newspaper, the type was made generally available and became an immediate success. Morison's practical and extensive type program offered designers and printers a range of superb choices for machine composition that had never before existed. Furthermore, as a towering scholar and historian in paleography, calligraphy, typography, and printing, Morison left a body of work that is vital to any study in the manifold areas of the Latin alphabet and the printed book. He gave new typographic stature to his generation, and a brave new impetus to consciously elegant workmanship.

During the prosperous 1920's, Oliver Simon joined The Curwen Press in London, a printing house of substantial reputation. Simon was an ardent spirit who drew into the uses of the machine many of the best contemporary English artists and designers. He commissioned newly drawn decorative type units, ornamental papers, and book

FREDERIC
W. GOUDY
(1865–1947)

STANLEY
MORISON
(1889–1967)

OLIVER
SIMON
(1895–1956)

39

illustration. He was primarily responsible for founding *The Fleuron*, an annual quarto publication, clothbound, which became the international heart of the burgeoning interest and excitement in all matters typographic: design, type, fleurons, calligraphy, book illustration, historical research, contemporary biography, etc. The first four volumes, 1923 through 1926, were edited by Simon and printed at The Curwen Press; the remaining three were edited by Stanley Morison and printed at the Cambridge University Press.

ERIC GILL
(1882–1940)

Eric Gill was an eminent sculptor and stonecutter who became involved in book illustration, type design, and printing. He believed with religious fervor in the sacredness of hand labor. Nevertheless he was induced to design types for mechanical composition. His "Gill Sans" and "Perpetua," on Monotype, both monumental in form as would come logically from a designer of monuments, are still in wide use. For his own press he cut a proprietary font, "Joanna." His most memorable book is *The Four Gospels*, 1931 (plate 118), one of the glories of bookmaking for which he designed the type and himself engraved the beautiful initial letters and illustrations on wood. It is one of many handsome volumes designed, printed, and published by Robert Gibbings at the Golden Cockerel Press in Waltham St. Lawrence.

Two men, Bruce Rogers, American, and Francis Meynell, English, were primarily responsible for crossing the abyss between the grandeur of books produced by inspired amateurs on the hand press and noble books produced by professionals on power-driven machines. Meynell, scion of a distinguished English literary and publishing family, who had spent several years as a printer and in the design of books and advertising matter, established the Nonesuch Press in 1923. The stated purpose in founding the Press was "to choose and make books according to a triple ideal: significance of subject, beauty of format, and moderation of price." These desirable ends were achieved by the editorial courage of Meynell and his literary associate, David Garnett; in books designed by Meynell from specimen pages set in type in his basement; and with books produced in various established plants under the watchful eye of the designer. The first Nonesuch book, *The Love Poems of John Donne*, appeared in 1923 (plate 111), about which the present writer has reported elsewhere: "I recall with nostalgic pleasure how, as a young book salesman, I saw the Nonesuch Donne on a bookstore table. That was in 1924. For about five dollars I carried it away, a handsome tall octavo, set in the Fell types, printed at the Oxford University Press on a wonderful French handmade paper, and bound in quarter-vellum with decorated Italian paper sides. Twelve hundred copies had been printed at ten shillings and sixpence plus postage. It was and still is a dashing piece of bookmaking."

In a dramatic and successful fifteen-year publishing program of great distinction,

Meynell (now Sir Francis) published more than a hundred books which hold their own among the great books of the past. The historical significance of the Nonesuch performance lies in the combination for the first time of beautifully made books in a major publishing program with original editorial scholarship in larger editions at lower prices for less affluent aficionados. By the adventurous use and intelligent control of machine processes, Meynell overcame the limitations and prejudices of the private press. Whereas most private press books followed a fixed house style, Meynell was fortunate to have had much greater freedom in the selection of format, types, papers, illustration, and binding. Each title was separately and differently planned and designed. The novelty of a different design approach for each new publication was first accomplished by Bruce Rogers in Cambridge, U.S.A., from 1900 to 1912. Meynell in his recent autobiography, *My Lives* (1971), writes of his own beginnings that "Bruce Rogers, the great American typographer, was my hero." Typical among the Nonesuch books are a Shakespeare in seven volumes edited by Herbert Farjeon (plate 113), a three-volume Blake with hitherto unpublished material, and a Dante (plate 112). Partway through his program, Meynell wrote: "It remains the ambition of the Press to make a worthy edition, textually and typographically, of every major English writer who has not already been appropriately served. It will make these books for money, and has no shame in that. We are not 'Gentlemen Farmers' but workers at our trade. But we are enthusiasts also, even in our middle years; and still propagandists. Every well-designed book or advertisement or prospectus is the begetter of others; and good printing is one of the graces of life even where life is ungracious."

FRANCIS
MEYNELL
(b. 1891)

THE REVIVAL IN EUROPE

The "Revival" touched several sensitive spots in Europe. The Netherlands sustained its high esteem for the book with concerned publishers and typefounders, and with two type designers of international stature. Early in this century S. H. de Roos, a Dutch painter, established his own private press in the classic tradition, influenced by William Morris but in his own idiom. He designed a private type for his own use and several that were made available to the public by the Typefoundry Amsterdam. Of greater and more lasting significance is the work of type- and book-designer Jan van Krimpen, whose types for hand composition were issued by the ancient and honorable Enschedé Foundry in Haarlem, and some of which were later added to the Monotype repertory for machine composition. Van Krimpen's approach was literary, cultured, aristocratic, restrained, and elegant, as may be seen in his famous typefaces, chiefly the "Lutetia," "Spectrum," and "Romanée."

JAN VAN
KRIMPEN
(1892–1958)

Henry van de Velde, versatile Belgian architect and designer (already mentioned as a temporary associate at the Cranach Presse), became an apostle, in the 1890's, of *art nouveau* which he carried into industrial design and typography (plate 106). His

41

main influence was in Germany where the movement was known as *Jugendstil*. Once *art nouveau* had run its course, the reaction swung to severe "functionalism." Van de Velde was the founder of the Weimar school that gave rise to the Bauhaus established by Walter Gropius. He welcomed sanserif types and made asymmetrical layouts for title and text pages. Van de Velde and other "modernists" have had little influence on traditional book design which is severely tied down by inflexible book-reading habits. However, modern textbooks, books for children, paperback covers, advertising, promotional printing, and related fields, which are outside the province of this discussion, have been profoundly affected by the Bauhaus and other commendable attempts to relate typography more closely to the impact of modern art and contemporary design.

The stark neoclassical Didot type blanketed French typography and bookmaking until the middle of the nineteenth century when a turn toward romanticism paralleled the revival in London of old-style types. In 1846 Louis Perrin cut a series of capitals called Augustaux based on Roman inscriptional forms and, later, a lowercase patterned on earlier French calligraphic models. French printers and publishers revived the conventional types and decorations made popular by the Elzevirs in the seventeenth century. The style which became known as *Elzévirien* stayed within these traditional limits until the turn of the century when Édouard Pelletan struck a fresh personal style in his several series of books, excellently printed, of which a good example is Molière's *Le Misanthrope*, Paris, 1907 (plate 105). Several groups of bibliophiles, such as the *Société des Amis des Livres* commissioned and published meticulously made illustrated books for their members. One of the most interesting of these volumes is *À Rebours* by J. K. Huysmans, Paris, 1903, in characteristic *art nouveau*, with wood engravings by Auguste Lepère printed in several colors, in the then new "Auriol" type (plate 103), issued by *Les Cents Bibliophiles*.

Across the Channel two books issued by general publishers, less lavish than these French books, showed new trends. In 1894 Elkin Mathews and John Lane issued Oscar Wilde's *The Sphinx* designed and with decorations by Charles Ricketts (plate 98), in pages that depart from traditional typography. In 1896 the Chiswick Press printed Pope's *The Rape of the Lock* with photoengraved zinc line plates made from drawings by Aubrey Beardsley (plate 99). This may well have been the first time that a major artist's book illustration was successfully printed from mechanically made plates.

To a non-French typographic practitioner, the twentieth century represents several attempts by French designers, encouraged by typefounder Georges Peignot, to arrive at new forms in type and its arrangement. Many of these experiments have been successful for posters, promotional printing, and advertising, rather than for book design where any arrangement which disturbs the easy and agreeable relation between author and reader has been unwelcome.

The kinship between the artist and the book has been a continuum of paramount

HENRY
VAN DE
VELDE
(1863–1957)

ÉDOUARD
PELLETAN
(1854–1912)

42

interest in France since earliest manuscript times. In the last decade of the nineteenth century Ambroise Vollard, an art dealer in Paris, conceived the idea that France's greatest painters should illustrate books with original work pulled directly from etched plates, lithographic stones, or wood blocks. Among Vollard's first publications were two books illustrated by Pierre Bonnard: *Parallèlement* by Paul Verlaine, Paris, 1900, with lithographs and wood engravings separately printed, with a well-designed text printed at the Imprimerie Nationale; and *Daphnis et Chloé*, Paris, 1902 (plate 102), similarly produced. Out of these volumes grew — or rather exploded — the enormous interest in the books illustrated by the great masters in Paris. Known as *Les Livres de Peintres*, these books reversed the ancient role of the artist who embellished a literary work. In many of these *Livres*, a text was provided which offered skeleton support to a series of illustrations, and the bound book provided a convenient and permanent means of preservation. Illustrated books are outside the scope of this collection. Readers interested in these great volumes are referred to the catalogues of two notable exhibitions: *Painters and Sculptors as Illustrators*, The Museum of Modern Art, New York, 1936, and *The Artist and the Book*, Museum of Fine Arts, Boston, Harvard College Library, 1961.

Significant workmanship in the best spirit of the typographic revival spread through continental Europe. Devoted designers and practitioners appeared in Czechoslovakia, Scandinavia, and Switzerland. The most conspicuous undertaking has been the Officina Bodoni, established in Verona, Italy, by Giovanni Mardersteig, a German by birth. The young Mardersteig's home in Weimar was a meeting place for German writers, artists, and diplomats, where Count Harry Kessler of the Cranach Presse was an intimate. The lad's ancestry included a well-known painter and sculptor on each side of the family. Giovanni's early education was directed toward art and literature. In 1916 he left Germany and went to Switzerland for reasons of health. His business experience after the First World War was with the eminent publisher Kurt Wolff in Munich, where Mardersteig was an editor and involved in book production. Natural predilection led him to direct involvement with fine books, scrupulously edited. Only by having complete control, literally in his own hands, could his aspirations be realized. He first set up a hand press in Switzerland in 1922 and obtained the privilege from the Italian government to cast new type from existing original Bodoni matrices. In 1927 he moved to Verona, having been awarded the commission to design and print the forty-volume edition of D'Annunzio's complete works. In order to accomplish this and other contemporary projects, Mardersteig established another plant, with typesetting machines and automatic presses, also in Verona. Both the hand press and the Stamperia Valdonega, as the machine plant is known, produced fine work, each in its own province. Mardersteig has designed several typefaces: "Griffo," "Zeno," and "Pacioli" for hand composition, and "Dante" which has been cut for Monotype casting, with considerable success. Mardersteig's

GIOVANNI
MARDERSTEIG
(b. 1892)

43

work has been honored in exhibitions in Europe and in the United States. Here shown is his edition of Boccaccio's *The Nymphs of Fiesole*, 1952 (plate 125), with woodcuts by Bartolomeo di Giovanni, recut by Fritz Kredel.

THE PRINTED BOOK IN THE UNITED STATES

A frontier and colonial society concerned with survival does not produce fine printing. The great printed books which appeared in Europe during the first hundred years after the invention of printing were patterned on magnificent manuscript volumes. Thereafter consciously elegant books were made during periods of civilized leisure, when designers and printers were free to plan them and when buyers existed who had the financial resources and personal inclination to acquire them. It is hardly surprising, therefore, that no American practitioner of international stature appeared in the United States until the last decade of the nineteenth century.

BENJAMIN
FRANKLIN
(1706–1790)

The printing done in England and on the Continent during the eighteenth century rubbed off on a few Americans. Benjamin Franklin was an apprenticed journeyman who spent two years in London workshops as a trade compositor. In 1730 at twenty-four years of age he established his own plant in Philadelphia. His financial success during the next twenty years enabled him to retire from active business in his early forties and to devote his wide-ranging mind to a variety of other interests. We know that later he would be enamored of the books of Baskerville, Bodoni, and Didot, but the minutiae of fine bookmaking were not for him. Probably his best volume, said to be his own favorite, is Cicero's *Cato Major*, Philadelphia, 1744 (plate 73), in Caslon type he had imported and with a two-color title page. It is not more than a workmanlike job, here included for historical interest; of special interest, too, because the translation was made by the Chief Justice of the State of Pennsylvania. In his foreword, "Printer to the Reader," Franklin concludes with, ". . . my hearty Wish that this first Translation of a *Classic* in this *Western World*, may be followed with many others, performed with equal Judgment and Success; and be a happy Omen that *Philadelphia* shall become the Seat of the *American* muses."

ISAIAH
THOMAS
(1749–1831)

Isaiah Thomas, another successful colonial printer and publisher, established a workshop in Massachusetts in 1770 which grew into twelve presses, branch offices, a bindery, and a paper mill. His extensive publishing included the first American illustrated folio Bible in 1791, the first Greek grammar, the first American dictionary, a type specimen book, as well as newspapers and miscellaneous printing. Most remarkable, he spent the later years of his life writing a scholarly book in two volumes, *The History of Printing in America* (1810), which also included the European scene from the Gutenberg invention. If he was not an innovative craftsman, he does have the distinction of being the first of several scholar-printers in the United States. He founded the American Antiquarian Society in Worcester, Massachusetts, which still thrives.

In 1807 Fry and Kammerer in Philadelphia printed a deluxe quarto volume, *The*

44

Columbiad, a long epic poem by Joel Barlow. The typographic arrangement and the type cast by Binny and Ronaldson, the first successful typefounders in America, were closely patterned on the work of Bulmer in London. *The Columbiad* is an isolated accomplishment, worthy of some notice in view of the limited resources then available on this continent. As the nineteenth century advanced, the separation of printers and publishers grew quite complete. New York had become the new center of the book trade with Harper, Scribner, Putnam, Appleton, and other publishers.

Theodore Low De Vinne, the cultivated son of a Methodist minister, entered the printing trade as an apprentice compositor in 1843, at fourteen years of age, when books and magazines were still set by hand. In his long career as a highly successful entrepreneur, he welcomed the great changes involved in the new technological improvements. At his death in 1914, his six-story building in New York housed his modern, mechanized plant. De Vinne printed the *Century* magazine with its own type series, the *Century Dictionary*, *Harper's*, and *Scribner's* magazines, to all of which he gave clean, conservative, and workmanlike typographic dress. De Vinne was not a memorable designer, but he maintained high standards in his undertakings and had profound respect for the best traditions of his calling. He accumulated a library of six thousand volumes, including almost a hundred incunabula which he used in the writing of his highly respected *The Invention of Printing*, published in 1876. Stanley Morison wrote of this book as recently as 1963 that "De Vinne's original scholarship has still to be superseded." Among other books, De Vinne completed a four-volume manual, *The Practice of Typography*, which reflects his own thorough research and experience. De Vinne, a man of affairs who paid homage to the civilizing influence of the printed book, received honorary degrees from Columbia and Yale universities. He was a founder in 1884 and an early president of The Grolier Club whose purpose was "the literary study and promotion of the arts entering into the production of books."

Ground swells in the last quarter of the nineteenth century could not be seen for their true worth until much later. In 1870 the great museums of art were founded in New York and Boston. A fresh awareness of the arts and crafts cracked the heavy crust of pervasive industrialism. Soon after a group of prominent New Yorkers formed The Grolier Club in New York, The Club of Odd Volumes was established in Boston. That center of American culture drew together in the 1890's an extraordinary confluence of young men: printers, designers, and publishers with typographic convictions and talents. Out of this group came Daniel Berkeley Updike, a scholar-printer, and Bruce Rogers, a designer, both of whom would for the first time exert an important American influence on the history and development of the printed book.

Thomas Bird Mosher of Portland, Maine, has already had passing mention. Starting in 1891 and continuing until 1923, he published some four hundred titles, modest in format, price, and design, with forthright charm—the first American to sustain a consistent program of fine bookmaking. He designed his books, then supervised pro-

THEODORE
LOW
DE VINNE
(1828–1914)

THOMAS
BIRD
MOSHER
(1852–1923)

duction in local printing shops. Mosher early expressed the wish that someday he would publish books "that would be truly beautiful as well as within the reach of those who appreciate beauty but who cannot possess it at exorbitant rates." He took advantage of the lack of copyright laws to publish without royalties English authors whose work, he claimed, would not otherwise have become available in the United States. He was accused of piracy, but some of his authors did not object. In 1892 George Meredith wrote to Mosher: "Sir, a handsome pirate is always half pardoned, and in this case he has broken only the upper laws. I shall receive with pleasure the copy of 'Modern Love' which you propose to send. I have it much at heart that works of mine should be read by Americans."

DANIEL
BERKELEY
UPDIKE
(1860–1941)

Daniel Berkeley Updike, son of a prominent New England family, started as an errand boy in 1880 at Houghton, Mifflin & Company, publishers of Emerson, Thoreau, and Hawthorne. The publishers were the owners of The Riverside Press, a book printing plant with high standards. After a dozen years at the Press, the young Updike decided rather reluctantly, as he tells in his own *Notes on the Press and Its Work*, to set out for himself. At first he tried to place work he had designed with established printers. Because this lack of direct control over production did not satisfy him, he established his own plant, The Merrymount Press, in 1893. As a printer he succeeded with great style. In his *Notes* he wrote with classic understatement: "Perhaps the reason that I survived, in spite of mistakes, was that a simple idea had got hold of me—to make work better for its purpose than was commonly thought worthwhile, and by having one's own establishment, to be free to do so."

Updike gave stature, dignity, scholarship, and a lofty excellence to the printing shop. He came from an exceptional background. His plant, his large library, his customers, his work, reflected his inheritance. His early work showed some Kelmscott influence, but Updike soon developed his own style, with deference to the clarity of the English eighteenth century. His work had structure and depth. Updike chose his type and ornament with discrimination at a time when sources were few and scattered. He commissioned Bertram Grosvenor Goodhue, an architect (who later designed "Cheltenham") to design the "Merrymount" type, which was not too successful. Updike's customers were universities, publishing houses, collectors, book clubs, cultural institutions, and the church. His most famous book is *The Book of Common Prayer*, 1930 (plate 117), to which he brought mature typographic judgment, an intense personal theology, and a profound knowledge of liturgical printing.

Updike's greatest contribution is to the scholarship of printing. His most lasting monument is his enormously important, two-volume work, *Printing Types, Their History, Forms, and Use*, which grew out of a series of lectures at Harvard University, published by the Harvard University Press in 1922 and since reprinted. It is the keystone to any study in the history of printing.

A regional and cosmopolitan culture on the American Pacific Coast during the

46

first half of the twentieth century produced a group of literate, skillful printers, loyally supported by book clubs in San Francisco and Los Angeles, by the Huntington Library in San Marino, and by collectors. The earliest designer-printer of note was the flamboyant John Henry Nash whose impressive folios had a large following and who printed elaborate catalogues for some of the wealthiest collectors then resident in California. Nash's four-volume Dante, 1929 (plate 116), is his most respected work. The books of Edwin and Robert Grabhorn at their Grabhorn Press in San Francisco were widely collected over a forty-year career of high-spirited, colorful workmanship. Their folio *John Maundevile*, 1928 (plate 114), with woodcuts by Valenti Angelo, was printed in Rudolf Koch's "Jessen" type, and published by Random House, New York. The Grabhorn *Leaves of Grass*, 1930, in Goudy's "Newstyle" type is no doubt their best-known work, but the *Maundevile* is probably more interesting and more "bookish."

JOHN HENRY NASH (1871–1947)

GRABHORN PRESS (fl. 1919–1965)

Elmer Adler as a young man was the advertising manager for a large family clothing business in Rochester, New York. His contact with promotional printing provoked an intellectual curiosity in the important typographic work of the past, and led to the acquisition of a fine collection of old and contemporary books and prints. The collector then put his interests to a hard test by setting up a press in New York City in 1922 — The Pynson Printers — for the production of fine books and ephemera for publishers, collectors, and at least one New York men's furnishing store. During the eighteen years of its existence The Pynson Printers became a meeting place for the makers and collectors of fine books, where, too, Adler became the chief editor, printer, and publisher of *The Colophon*, a lively magazine for book collectors. Adler's favorite book, certainly his most original work, is Voltaire's *Candide*, 1928 (plate 115), profusely illustrated by Rockwell Kent, set in type designed by Lucien Bernhard.

ELMER ADLER (1884–1961)

Dard Hunter, son of a prosperous newspaper publisher in Chillicothe, Ohio, was an American phenomenon. The young Dard was fascinated by paper, pursued its history, and put study into practice by making paper himself, expertly, by hand, on his own equipment. He traveled over the world on visits to surviving handmade paper mills, many in remote corners of the Orient where ancient methods were still practiced, and where he gathered samples which he mounted in his books. Altogether he wrote ten volumes on the history of paper from original research in unexplored areas. His first book, *Old Papermaking*, appeared in 1923. Hunter printed this and subsequent volumes on his own hand press from type he had himself designed and cut, on his own handmade paper. The formats were large, issued in editions of less than two hundred copies. His last personally produced book, and his magnum opus, is *Papermaking by Hand in America*, 1950 (plate 123). Hunter also wrote two books published in trade editions by Alfred A. Knopf, New York: *Papermaking, The History and Technique of an Ancient Craft* in 1947, and a very readable autobiography in 1958, *My Life with Paper*.

DARD HUNTER (1883–1966)

Victor Hammer, a man of many gifts — painter, sculptor, architect, typographer, printer — lived and worked in the spirit of the Italian Renaissance. He was born in

Vienna where he became a prominent portraitist. He established his press (Stamperia del Santuccio) in Florence and there cut two uncial types, and produced books of a pure, personal craftsmanship, "Ad Maiorem Dei Gloriam." He came to the United States in 1939, to Wells College in Aurora, New York, in the art department. A number of distinguished hand-press books in "Emerson" type appeared during his nine years in Aurora. Meanwhile he had begun to cut the punches for his new uncial type. In 1948 he joined the faculty of Transylvania College in Lexington, Kentucky, as Professor in Art. Here Hammer's American career continued and blossomed, sustained by devoted associates, and here in 1949 he completed his masterpiece, the Hölderlin poems (plate 124) on his hand press, beautifully set and impeccably printed in his new American Uncial type in an edition of fifty-one copies.

Limitations imposed on this essay have allowed only brief discussion of major historical trends and their makers. Regretfully we must pass over many designers and printers whose work would deserve discussion in a longer review. Chief among these in the East are Will Bradley, Frederic W. Goudy, Carl Purington Rollins, Walter Gillis, Henry W. Kent, William Edwin Rudge, T. M. Cleland, Rudolph Ruzicka, W. A. Dwiggins, and the publisher Alfred A. Knopf. Time is arbitrary, and selections by anthology are inevitably inadequate. Many younger men and women came along during and since the 1920's, and are still at work here and in Europe, but they must be dealt with by other hands when perspectives have become longer and judgments less personal.

We now approach the end of our historical panorama with Bruce Rogers, born in the American Middle West in 1870, later said by Francis Meynell (and confirmed in a letter to this writer) to have been "the greatest artificer of the book who ever lived." If an artificer employs artful devices, subtle stratagems, and delicate maneuvers, and if these are absorbed into skillful arrangements of type for book design, we will be aware of some of the ingredients that entered into the charm and finish of the Bruce Rogers books.

Soon after graduation from Purdue University, Rogers came to Boston as a free-lance designer for the magazine *Modern Art*. Here he saw Kelmscott books and is quoted by Frederic Warde that "upon seeing Morris's printing, his whole interest in book production became rationalized and intensified. He abandoned the prevalent idea that a book could be made beautiful through the work of an illustrator alone, and determined instead to use that curiosity he had always felt as to type and paper, toward a study of the physical form of printed books." In 1896 Rogers joined The Riverside Press where he designed trade books and book advertisements for the next four years. Then, in the late 'nineties he induced George H. Mifflin, a senior partner at the Press, to establish a special department for the production of limited editions. What a happy combination of personalities and potentialities this was:

the proprietor of a solid, conservative business in Cambridge, Massachusetts, who gave full scope to the young designer out of the American cornbelt at the beginning of a new century.

During the next dozen years (1900–1912) Rogers completed sixty editions which set a wholly new approach to book design. Books were done with rare but somehow lighthearted discrimination. Each new title was an adventure down new paths for the designer, as it was for his collectors. Each book was different in design, format, type, paper, printing, and binding. Some were inventive and experimental, some derivative and allusive. Neither Rogers nor Updike had an American tradition on which to build. With scholarly logic they looked to historical sources for their criteria. Updike, a New Englander, naturally found antecedents in English workmanship. Rogers' blithe spirit was more in sympathy with the eloquence of fifteenth-century Venice and the grace and sophistication of sixteenth-century France. But along with tradition, Rogers had developed a style of his own. Here were the beautiful Riverside Press limited editions made in a commercial printing plant, at least a dozen of which were small masterpieces—the work of an "artist-typographer." In his wide-ranging eclecticism Rogers might well be called the first modern book designer, the progenitor of the typographers who have made books since his time.

After sixteen years at The Riverside Press, Rogers became restive. In a letter he said he had "always looked forward to living, for a term of years at least, either in England or the Continent. . . . My present agreement with the Riverside Press expires next year. . . . They pay very well . . . but they give me no leisure except two weeks' vacation yearly. And now leisure for my own pursuits has come to mean more than money to me." A summer in England in 1912 did not provide working opportunities. He then returned to the United States for five rather lean years, with, however, his newly designed and cut "Centaur" type a conspicuous achievement. It was first used in one of his superb books, Maurice de Guérin's *The Centaur*, printed in 1915 in an edition of one hundred and thirty-five copies at the Montague Press, the idealistic printing shop at the Dyke Mill in Massachusetts owned by Carl Purington Rollins, later the influential printer to Yale University.

In 1916 Emery Walker invited Rogers to come to England to form a partnership for the production of fine printing somewhat in the spirit of the Kelmscott and Doves presses. Rogers accepted with keen anticipation and with a commission in his pocket from The Grolier Club to reprint that part of Dürer's *Geometry* which deals with the design of letters for inscriptions. Entitled *On the Just Shaping of Letters*, the edition was completed late in 1917 under formidably trying working conditions in wartime London which B.R., as he came to be known, described in remarkable letters to his friend Henry W. Kent, then Secretary of the Metropolitan Museum of Art in New York. The partnership with Emery Walker soon foundered. There followed, to quote B.R., "a month of starvation in a miserable boarding house on Trumpington Street." He was about to return to the United States when Sydney Cockerell, Director of the Fitzwilliam Museum, formerly secretary to William Morris at the Kelmscott Press, determined to secure Rogers' services for the Cambridge University Press. Despite the gravity of the war, the Syndics appointed Rogers to be Adviser to the Press and to make recommendations for improvement of their books. Rogers soon delivered a lengthy statement which included the frank comment: "I cannot believe that any

other printing-house of equal standing can have gone on for so many years with such an inferior equipment of types. . . . They are, in my opinion, bad beyond belief." To the credit of the Syndics the report was adopted and implemented as war and postwar conditions allowed. In 1950, in an official publication, Brooke Crutchley, the eminent University Printer, wrote: "It was the example of Bruce Rogers' painstaking quest for perfection as much as the report itself that was to put new life into the University Press, and it is a pleasure, thirty-three years later, to acknowledge once more the debt that Cambridge, as indeed the whole world, owes to a great craftsman and artist."

Many years had slipped by since Rogers had done the kind of work that could nourish his soul. He returned to the United States in 1919 and assumed duties as an active adviser to the Harvard University Press. Then, fortunately, he met William Edwin Rudge whose new building in Mount Vernon, outside New York City, housed a fine and well-equipped printing establishment. This became Rogers' haven during the prosperous and expansive 'twenties. In B.R.'s own words: "All in all, I spent eight productive years working with Rudge, and no collaboration could have been happier for me. He left me an entirely free hand and unhesitatingly backed up nobly even my most unpromising projects, with new types, papers, equipment — everything — whether they were likely to prove profitable or the reverse." Rogers was fifty years of age when he started with Rudge. During the ensuing eight fruitful years he made about a hundred books, many of which have become part of American typographic history. In 1927 B.R. began to stir the ingredients that became one of his masterpieces. He induced T. E. Lawrence to translate the *Odyssey* of Homer, but the scholar who had made a reputation for boldness and courage as Lawrence of Arabia expressed fear that his words would not be worthy of Rogers' bookmaking. With this translation under way, the urge came over Rogers to see his English friends again and to roam the English countryside. Besides, the Monotype people wished to cut his Centaur type under his immediate supervision. In 1928 he sailed for England where, during the next four years, he would produce his finest work.

In the First World War many Canadians lost their lives in the Belgian town of Ypres — pronounced "Wipers" by the soldiers. Ten years later the Canadian government built a memorial chapel where their young had died. The King of England wished to present a lectern Bible worthy of the occasion. But no Bible had been printed in Britain comparable to the Baskerville volume of 1763. The Oxford University Press immediately set out to repair the omission. Bruce Rogers, then resident in London (1928) and recognized as the foremost typographer of his time, was commissioned to design a new folio Bible in the King James Version, in a volume not to exceed twelve hundred and fifty pages. John Johnson, then printer to Oxford University, suggested the Centaur type which was modified to fit. The story of the making of the Bible during its four years in production at the Oxford University Press was told by Rogers in a pamphlet issued by the Monotype Corporation in 1936.

These years in England saw the ultimate flowering of Bruce Rogers' genius. Three books can be chosen from this sojourn as among his best works. They are *The Odyssey of Homer*, 1932 (plate 119), printed with Emery Walker; *Fra Luca de Pacioli*, 1933 (plate 120), printed at the Cambridge University Press for The Grolier Club; and that crowning achievement, the Oxford Lectern Bible (plates 121, 122) published in 1935. This writer has yet to be contradicted in having stated that the Oxford Lectern Bible is the most important printed book of the twentieth century.

After returning to his home in New Fairfield, Connecticut, in 1932, a quarter century of life remained to Bruce Rogers. He clung to his *métier* and was responsible for a few fine volumes, especially for the Limited Editions Club of New York. Bruce Rogers' long life spanned great years in the history of the printed book. He began when printing was still within the province of the hand. It is a mark of his genius that he was able to cross the frontier to the area of the machine and to retain artistry and finesse in the transition. In Rogers' command of this fundamental change he showed himself to be a man of his time.

Having looked back to the impressive monuments of five hundred years of bookmaking, let us glance briefly at our own time and hazard some prophecy for the future. The great and noble folios which graced the libraries of ancestral homes are not relevant to the present way of life. Vast technological changes have already affected the production of books, including those made with esthetic devotion. However, the preservation of human thought has taken many forms since pictures were made on the walls of prehistoric caves and cuneiform strokes were baked into Sumerian clay tablets. A thousand years of the book as we have known it, first written then printed, are links in the long historic chain of the dissemination of accumulated knowledge. Staggering problems of storage and preservation are dictating great changes. The book in its present form may well continue far into the future. But if not, we can be sure that language and the alphabet will remain the fundamental means of communication; that literature, philosophy, and science will never fail man's restless search; neither will the urge for beauty fade. Whatever its name, whatever its form, something will always exist to uphold the civilized word. "In the beginning was the word." So it will be at the end.

PLATES

Page sizes for the following plates are given in inches, width by height. Exact chronological sequence has occasionally been sacrificed for more appropriate grouping.

The ornamental initial letters and decorations in fifteenth-century books were usually added by hand. Initials for plates 12, 13, 18, and 19 were apparently cut in wood and printed simultaneously with the text as were the famous two-color metal-cut initials for the Morgan copy of the 1459 Fust and Schoeffer Psalter, plate 4.

egiptii de manu ysmahelitaꝛ: a quibꝫ
pductus erat. Fuitꝗ dñs cu eo: et erat
vir i cuctis prospe agens. Habitauitꝗ
in domo dñi sui: qui optime nouerat
dñm esse cu eo: et oia que gereret ab eo
dirigi i manu illi⁹. Inuenitꝗ ioseph
graciã coram dño suo: ⁊ ministrabat
ei. A quo ipositus omnibꝫ guberna-
bat creditã sibi domu: ⁊ vniuersa que
ei tradita fuerat. Benedixitꝗ dñs do-
mui egiptii: ppter ioseph: ⁊ multiplicauit tam i edibus ꝗ in agris cunctam
ei⁹ sbstanciã. Nec quicꝗ aliud nouerat: nisi pane quo vescebat. Erat aute
ioseph pulcra facie: et decorus aspectu.
Post multos itaꝗ dies: iniecit dña
oculos suos in ioseph: et ait. Dormi
mecu. Qui nequaꝗ acquiescens operi
nephario: dixit ad eã. Ecce dñs meus
omnibꝫ michi traditis: ignorat qd
habeat in domo sua: nec quicꝗ e qd
non sit in mea potestate: uel no tradidit michi: preter te que vxor eius es.
Quo ergo possu hoc malu facere: et peccare i dñm meu? Huiuscemodi uerbis per
singlos dies loquebat: et mulier mo-
lesta erat adolescenti: et ille recusabat
stuprum. Accidit aute quadã die ut in-
traret ioseph domu: ⁊ opecis quippiã
absꝗ arbitris faceret: ⁊ illa apphensa
lacinia vestimenti eius diceret. Dormi
mecu. Qui relicto i manu eius pallio
fugit: et egressus e foras. Cumꝗ vidisset
mulier vestem in manibꝫ suis: ⁊ se esse
cotemptam: vocauit ad se hoies dom⁹
sue: et ait ad eos. En introduxit virũ
hebreũ: ut illuderet nobis. Ingressus
est ad me: ut coiret mecu. Cumꝗ ego
succlamassem: ⁊ audisset vocem meã:
reliquit pallium qd tenebam: ⁊ fugit foras. In argumentu ergo fidei: retentu
pallium ostendit marito reuertenti domu-

er ait. Ingressus e ad me seru⁹ hebreus
que adduxisti: ut illudet michi. Cumꝗ
audisset me clamare: reliquit palliu
qd tenebam: ⁊ fugit foras. His audi-
tis dñs: ⁊ nimiu credulus verbis con-
iugis: iratus est valde: tradiditꝗ ioseph in carcerem ubi vincti regis custo-
diebant: ⁊ erat ibi clausus. Fuit aute
dñs cu ioseph et misertus est illi⁹: ⁊ dedit ei graciã in cospectu principis car-
ceris. Qui tradidit in manu illi⁹ uni-
uersos vinctos qui i custodia tenebãt:
et quidqd fiebat sub ipso erat: nec nouerat aliquid: cunctis ei creditis. Dñs
eni erat cu illo: ⁊ oia opa ei⁹ dirigebat.

Hijs itaꝗ gestis: accidit ut [peccarent]
peccarent duo eunuchi: pincerna
regis egipti et pistor: dño suo. Iratusꝗ
contra eos pharao: nam alter pin-
cernis perat: alter pistoribꝫ: misit eos
in carcerem principis militu: in quo
erat vinctus ⁊ ioseph. At custos carce-
ris tradidit eos ioseph: ꝗ et ministrabat eis. Aliquantulu tpis fluxerat: et illi
in custodia tenebant. Viderutꝗ ambo
somniu nocte una: iuxta interptatio-
nem congruã sibi. Ad quos cu intro-
isset ioseph mane ⁊ vidisset eos tristes:
scitscitat⁹ e dicens. Cur tristior e hodie
solito facies vestra? Qui responderut.
Somniu vidim⁹: et non est qui inter-
pretetur nobis. Dixitꝗ ad eos ioseph.
Nuquid no dei e interpretacio? Referte
michi quid videritis. Narrauit prior
ipositus pincernar: somniu suu. Vi-
debam coram me vitem in qua erant
tres propagines crescere paulatim i gem-
mas: ⁊ post flores uuas maturescere:
calicemꝗ pharaonis in manu mea.
Tuli ergo uuas ⁊ expressi i calicem que
tenebam: ⁊ tradidi poculu pharaoni.
Respondit ioseph. Hec est interptaco

1 JOHANN GUTENBERG, Mainz, c. 1455

Bible in Latin (42-line) 11¾ x 16

ro pulcriores·Heth.Denigra
ta est sup carbones facies eoz:
et non sunt rogniti in plateis·
Adhesit cutis eoz ossibz:aruit
et facta est quasi lignu·Theth
Melius fuit occisis gladio qz i
terfectis fame:qm isti ertabue
rut cosumpti a sterilitate terre·
Ioth. Manus mulieru mise
ricordiu roxerut filios suos:fa
cti sunt cibz eaz in cotricione fi
lie populi mei·Caph. Lople
uit dns furore suu:effudit ira
indignationis sue·Et succedit
igne in syon:z deuorauit fuda
menta ei⁹·Lameth No credide
runt reges tre et uniusi habita
tores orbis:qm ingredereç hos
tis et inimicus p portas ihrlm·
Mon. Propt pecca phetaz
eius et iniqtas sacerdotu eius:
q effuderut in medio ei⁹ sagui
nem iustoz·Nun. Errauerut
reci in plateis:polluti sunt san
guine·Cunqz no posseut:tenu
erunt lacinias suas·Sameth.
Hecedite polluti clamauerunt
eis:recedite abite:nolite tange
re·Iurgati quippe sunt et com
moti dixerut:inter getes no ad
det ultra ut inhabitet in eis·Phe
Facies dns diuisit eos:no ad
det ut respiciat eos·Facies sac
dotu no erubuert:neqz senu mi
serti sut·Cu adhuc sbsisteremus
defecerut octi nri ad auxiliu nos

tru vanu:cum respiceremus atte
ti ad gente q saluare non pote
rat·Sade Iubricauerut uesti
gia nfa i itinere platearz nfaz:
apropiquauit finis noster:co
pleti sut dies nri:qa uenit finis
noster·Coph. Veliciores fue
rut psecutores nri aquilis celi:
super motes psecuti sunt nos:
in deserto insidiati sunt nobis·
Res. Spiritus oris nri rps dns
captus e in pctis nris:cui diri
mus:in umbra tua uiuemus in
getibz·Sin. Gaude et letare
filia edom q habitas i tra hus
Ad te quoqz pueniet calir:ine
briaberis atqz nudaberis·Thau
Lopleta est iniqtas tua filia sy
on:non addet ultra ut trasmi
gret te·Uisitabit iniqtate tua
filia edo:discooperiet pcta tua.
Erpliciunt lamentaciones
Ieremie.Incipit oro eiusdem.
Recordare dne qd accide
rit nobis:intuere et re
spice obprobriu nrm·
Hereditas nfa uersa est ad alie
nos:domus nfe ad extraneos·
Pupilli facti sumus absqz pre:
mtres nfe qsi uidue·Aqua no
stra pecunia bibim⁹:ligna no
stra pcio coparauim⁹·Ceruici
bz miabamur:lassis no dabaç
requies·Egipto dedim⁹ manu
et assiriis:ut saturemur pane
Pfes nri peccauerut et no sut:

2 JOHANN GUTENBERG (?), Bamberg, c. 1458–1459
Bible in Latin (36-line)   11 5/8 x 16 1/4

poni folet. Ita dic ps in ij ma. In xiiij aut li fic
dic. Et in appone et in cópone inuenif an b o
g l m n r. et ante u et i loco confonantiu pofitas
ut ebeto. educo. egero. eludo. emineo. enarro. euo
eripio euebo. eijcio qd cóponif ab e et iaco. comi
fa a m i. vn debet fcribi per duo i. Reliquif uero
confonantibus feqntibus ex ponitur non e. fcz e
ut excubo. f ut efficio. effundo. effero. in quibus
et fimilibus x in f cómutatur euphonie caufa. H
ut horreo. exhorreo. exhibeo. P ut expello. Q ut
exquiro. T ut extendo. Vocalibus quoqz feqntibz
tam in appone qz in cumpone ex ponitur. ut ex
aro. exegi. exigo. exoletus. exulcero. exequatus.
exaudio. S uero feqnte x abijcitur s. ut exequor
ab ex et fequor. Sed queritur de hoc quod di
cit ps. qz in x nulla fillaba terminatur in media
dicone. nifi in compofitis a ppone ex que integra
mane pt feqnte c ic. Inuenif enim inftantia in dex
tera dextrorfuz fexcenti fexdecim textus fexagin
ta. et fimilibus. Ad hoc dico qz ps obfcure hic lo
cutus e Vnde predicta uba a diuif diuifimoz ex
ponitur. Quida enim dicut qz intelligitur de com
pofitis et non fimplicibus. et fic non e obiecto de
textuf quia fimplex eft. Qz autem definat in x in
media dicone reftat ps dicens in xi li. x anteden
te vniz inuenio in tus. a textuf textus. Sic ergo
intelligitur de compofitis. Sed quidam coartant
hanc regula ad compofita ab aliqua ppone. et fic
non effet queftio de fexcenti. quia non e compofi
tu a prepone fi a nomine. Et tuc eft fenfus. Nulla
fillaba in iunctura compónis definit in x in aliq
buf compofitif a ppone. nifi in compofitis ab ifta
ppone ex. que integra manere pt feqnte c. et cete
ra. Quidam no dicut qz generaliter intelligenduz
eft quod dicit ps. Nam nulla fillaba in iunctura
compónif definit in x nifi in compofitis ab ex. Si
ergo obijciatur de dextrorfum. Dico qz x ibi non
e in iunctura compónis. fiue in media dicone. feu
in fine pmi componentis. vmo e ibi r. Componi
tur enim a dextera et ufum. Et fcias qz tuc dz
x poni in iuctura compónis. qz nichil additur in
ter componentia. Sed tunc opponitur de fexcenti
quia hic x eft in iunctura compónis. Componif
enim a fex et centum. Ad hoc dicut quida qz fef
centi p s debet fcribi. qz x mutatur in s. Alij dnt
qz x abijcif et fic fecenti et fedecim fcributur fine
f et x. et li magis michi placet. Sexaginta eni có
ponitur a fex et genuf quod e decem. vn non e
ibi x in iunctura compónis. quia apponitur et ad
ditur inter componentia. vnde nichil prohibz qn
fcribatur per x. Aliqui funt qui intelligunt pdic
tam regulam in fimplicibus et compofitis. vnde
fic exponitur uba ps. In x nulla fillaba termina
tur in media dicone. nifi feqnte c uf p uf q uel t
et hoc apparet in compofitis a ppone et inte
gra manere pt cu hijs ubis excurro. expello. ex
quiro extendo. Predicta regula fic intellecta eft pla
na. et uerificatur tam in fimplicibus qz in compo
na. et uerificatur tam in fimplicibus qz in compo
uocaf eft. et ideo pt ter fitis generaliter
minare fillam et incipe. quacumqz confo
nante feqnte uf pcedente. ficut omnes uo
In pegrinis dicónibz femp tales faciunt
in pncipio inuenif fillabe. et fi antedat a
lia fillaba neceffe e eam uf in uocalem de
fine. ut gaza. uf in n. ut melanzoros. uf in r. ut a
riobarzanes. Sed opponitur de achaz ubi z nó

in pncipio fi in fine fillie eft. Poteft refponderi qz
nomen hebreum e prifti aute de latinis uel gcis
dicónibus intelligit Et fcias qz pegrinum hic ppe
appellatur gcu. Aliqn autem fub peregrino comp
henditur greca dico et barbara. aliqn omnia dico
que non eft in ppria lingua de quatuor nuiden
Iximus de litteris ter tibg fillabe
minantibus fillam funt de accidentibus
fillabe dicamus Scias ergo qz unicuiqz fil
labe accidit tenor. fpus. tempus. numerus littera
ru. Tenor acutus uel gnis uel circúflexus In dic
ne tenor fiue accentus certus abfqz ea diccone in
certus non pt tamen fine eo effe Similiter fpus
afper uf leuis Tempus unu uel duo. Vel etiaz ut
quibufdam placet. unu et femis. uf duo et femis
uel tria. vnu fi uocal eft breuis p fe. ut eo. vel fi
eam una confonans fimplex confequif. ut caput
Vnu et femis in cómunibus filbis. ut lacme.
Et fciendum qz non folum an l uf r fi edi an m
uf fub docuimus et n pofite mute fadut commu
nes. Preterea m an n pofita fecerunt quida com
munes fillabas. Illud quoqz non e ptermittendu
qz tribuf confonantibuf feqntibuf pt fieri commu
nif fillaba. qn in pncipio fillabe feqntf poft uoca
lem correptam e muta et poft eam liquida feq
tur. quippe cu f in metro fubtrahi more foleat ue
teu. ut oracius fermonu li j. Liquimuf infani riden
tef pmia fcribere. In longis natura uel pone duo
funt tempa. ut dof aro. Duo et femis. qn poft uo
calem natura longam vna fequif confonans. ut
fol. Tria qn poft uocalem natura longam due có
fonantes fequitur uf vna duplex. ut monf rex
tamen in metro neceffe e vnamquamqz fillabam
uf vnius uf duum accipi tempz. Numerus fcilz
lram accidit fillabe. qz ut fup diximus nó minus
qz vnius nec plus qz fex lram apud latinos pt in
uenir. Incipit fecunda pars huius operis
de accentu

xpleta iam p dei gram pri
ma pte huius opis que eft
de orthogphia. nuc de fecu
da pte fcz de accentu uidea
mus. De accentu autez hoc
mó dicemus. Primo often
demus quid fit accentuf et
quot fint. Secudo ponemuf
regulas generales accentus
et queftiones circa eas. Tercio manifeftabimuf q
et quot loca obtineat accentus. et quare. Quarto
aute ponemus quafdam regulas generales ualen
tef ad accentu cuiuflibet fillabe. Quinto fubiuge
muf regulas fpales de accentu pme et medie filbe.
et fumitur li largo mó accentuf edi ad tpus. fex
to dicemuf de accentu ptium indeclinabiliu. Septi
mo de fex impedimentif accentus. et de dubijf cir
ca ea De accentu generali

Ccentuf e regularif modulacó uocis fca in
fignificatiua pronúciacóne pncipaliter ad
iacens vni fillabe. Regularis dz ad drám
metrice modulacónis et mellire. que accentu non
confiderat regularem. Adiacet aute accentuf regu
laris pncipaliter vni fillabe qnis fm ipfum tota
lis dico iudicetur. Et dz accentus ab accinendo .i.
ad confignificandu aliquid canendo. qn accentus
ad hoc inuentus eft ut fignificaó dicónis melius
diftinguaf Tres autem funt accentus fcz acutus.

Eatus

Vir · a̅ · Seruite d̅n̅o · Euouae ·
qui no̅ abijt in co̅silio im-
piox̃ : ⁊ in via peccatox̃ no̅
stetit : et in cathedra pestile̅=
tie no̅ sedit, Sed in lege
d̅n̅i volu̅tas eius : ⁊ in lege ei⁹ meditabit᷑ die
ac nocte, Et eit tanq̃ lignu̅ qd̅ plantatu̅ est
secus decursus aq̅ru̅ : qd̅ fructu̅ suu̅ dabit in
tp̅e suo, Et foliu̅ ei⁹ no̅ defluet : ⁊ oia quecu̅q̃
faciet ṗsperabunt᷑, Non sic impij no̅ sic : sed
tanq̃ puluis que̅ proicit ventus a facie terre,
Ideo no̅ resurgu̅t impij in iudicio : neq̃ pc̅o=
res in co̅silio iustox̃, Q̅m nouit d̅n̅s via̅ iu=
stox̃u̅ : et iter impiox̃ ṗibit, Gl̅a p̅r̅i, Ofdd

Vare fremueru̅t ge̅tes : ⁊ pp̅li meditati
su̅t inania, Astiteru̅t reges t̅re et prin=
cipes ꝯueneu̅t in vnu̅ : aduſus d̅n̅m ⁊ aduſus
xp̅m ei⁹, Dirũpam⁹ vincla eox̃ : ⁊ picam⁹
a nobis iugu̅ iṗox̃, Qui habitat in celis irri=
debit eos : et d̅n̅s subsannabit eos, Tu̅c lo=
quet᷑ ad eos in ira sua : et in furore suo ꝯtur=
babit eos, Ego aut̅ co̅stitutus su̅ rex ab eo

4 JOHANN FUST AND PETER SCHOEFFER, Mainz, 1459
Psalter in Latin   12 x 17

illudentes ad alterutrū cū scribis dicebāt.
Alios saluos fecit: seipm̄ non potest saluuz
facere. Cristus rex israhel descendat nunc
de cruce: ut videamus a credamus. Et q̄ cū
eo crucifixi erant ouinabant ei. Et scā ho
ra sexta: tenebre facte sūt p totam terram
vsq̄ in horā nonā. Et hora nona exclama
uit ihesus voce magna dicēs. Heloy heloy
lamasabactani. Quod est interp̄tatū. Deus
meus. deus meus: ut quid dereliquisti me
Et quidam de circumstantibₐ audiētes di
cebant. Ecce heliam vocat. Currens autez
vnus a implens spongiā aceto. circumpo
nensq̄ calamo: potū dabat ei dicēs. Dimi
te: videamus si veniat helias ad deponen
dū eū. Ihus aūt emissa voce magnī expira
uit. Et velū tēpli scissū: e in duo: a sūmo usq̄
deorsū. Videns aūt centurio q̄ ex aduerso
stabat. q̄ sic clamās expirasset: ait Vere
homo hic filius dei erat. Erant aūt a mulie
res de longe aspicientes: inter quas erat ma
ria magdalene. et maria iacobi minoris. et
ioseph mater. et salome: et cū esset in galilea
sequebantur eum a ministrabant ei: a alie
multe que simul cū eo ascenderāt iherosoli
mā. Et cū iam sero esset factum. q̄ erat pa
rasceue quod e ante sabbatū. venit ioseph
ab arimathia nobilis decurio: qui ipe erat
expectās regnū dei. Et audacter introiuit
ad pilatū: a petijt corpus ihesu. Pilatus au
tez mirabatur si iā obisset. Et accersito cen
turiōe: interrogauit eū si iam mortuus esset.
Et cū cognouisset a centurione: donauit cor
pus ioseph. Joseph autē mercatus sin do
ne. et deponens eū inuoluit sindone: a po
suit eū in monumēto quod erat excisū de pe
tra: a aduoluit lapidē ad ostiū monumenti.
Maria magdalene a maria ioseph aspicie
Et cū trāsisset XVI bant vbi poneret.
sabbatū: maria magdalene a maria
iacobi a salome emerūt aromata: ut venie
tes vngeret ihesuz. Et valde mane vna sab
batorū veniunt ad monumentū: orto iam
sole. Et dicebant ad inuicē. Quis reuoluet
nobis lapidē ab ostio monumēti. Et respi
cientes viderūt ruolutū lapidē. Erat quip
pe magnus valde. Et introeuntes in monu
mentū viderūt iuuenē sedentez in dextris

coopertū stola candida: a obstupuerit. Qui
dicit illis. Nolite expauescere. Ihesū q̄ritis
nazarenū crucifixū: surrexit: nō est hic. Ec
ce locus: vbi posuerūt eum. Sed ite dicite
discipulis eius a petro: q̄ p̄cedet vos in gali
leam. Ibi eū videbitis: sicut dixit vobis. At
ille exeuntes fugerūt de monumēto. Inua
serat eni eas tremor a pauor: a nemini quicq̄
dixerūt. Timebant enim. Surgens autez
ihesus mane prima sabbati apparuit primo
marie magdalene: de qua eiecerat septem
demonia. Illa vadens nūciauit hijs. qui cū eo
fuerāt lugentibₐ a flentibₐ: et illi audientes
q̄ viueret et visus esset ab ea: non crediderit.
Post hec aūt duobₐ ex hijs ambulātibus o
stensus e in alia effigie euntibₐ in villā: a illi
euntes nūciauerūt ceteris: nec illis credide
rūt. Nouissime aūt recumbētibₐ illis vndeā
apparuit: a exprobrauit incredulitatē eorū
et duriciam cordis: q̄ hijs qui viderāt eū
resurrexisse non crediderūt. Et dixit eis. Eu
tes in mundū vniuersū: p̄dicate eū angeliū
oīi creature. Qui crediderit a baptizatus
fuerit saluus erit: qui vero non crediderit: cō
dennabitur. Signa aūt eos. q̄ crediderint
hec sequētur. In nomine meo demonia eiciet:
linguis loquētur nouis: serpētes tollēt. Et
si mortiferum quid biberint: nō eis nocebit.
Super egros manus imponēt: a bñ habe
būt. Et dñs quidē ihesus postq̄ locutus est
eis: assumptus est in celū: a sedet a dextris
dei. Illi aūt p̄fecti p̄dicauerūt vbiq̄: domio
cooperāte a sermonē confirmāte: sequētibₐ signis.
Explicit euangelium secundum Marcum.
Incipit p̄facio beati Ieronimi p̄sbiterum in

Vcas euangelista scōm Lucā.
Syrus nacōe anthiocēs. arte
medicus. discipulus apostolorū
postea paulum secutus usq̄
ad confessionē eius seruies do
mino sine crimine: nam neq̄ vxorē vnq̄ ha
buit: neq̄ filios: septuaginta a quatuor anorū
obijt in bithinia: plenus spū sancto. Qui cū
iam scripta essent euangelia. p matheū qui
dem in iudea. p marcū aūt in italia: scō insti
gante spiritu in achaie partibₐ hoc scripsit
euangeliū: significās etiam ipe in principio
ante suū alia esse descripta. Cui extra ea que

et multa iam diximꝰ: et ubi uisum fuerit
oportunū esse dicemꝰ. Causa ꝗ magnitu-
dínis imperii romani nec fortuita est nec
fatalis: ßm eorū sníam siue opíonem ꝗ ea
dicūt esse fortuita: quę uel nullas cās hñt
uel nõ ex aliquo rõnabli ordíe ueíentes:
et ea fatalia quę pręter dei & hoīum uo-
lūtatē cuiusdã ordis necessitate cõtíngūt.
Prorsus diuía ꝓuidétía ȓgna cõstituunt
hūana. Quę si ꝓpterea qꜱꝗ fato tribuit:
quia ipam dei uoluntatē uel ꝓtátem fati
noíe appellat: sentécíam teneat: linguam
corrigat. Cur. n. nõ hoc ꝓmū dicat quod
postea dictur9est: cū ab illo qꜱꝗ quęsierit
quid dixerit fatū: Nam id hoíes quádo
audiūt usitata loquédi consuetudíne: nõ
íntelligūt n̄ uím posítíois siderū: qualis é
qn̄ qs nascít siue concipít. qd̄ aliꝗ alienác
a dei uolūtate: aliquí ex illa etíã hęc pen-
dere cõfirmãt. Sed illí ꝗ sine dei uolūtate
decernere opínant sidera qd̄ agamꝰ: uel
quid bonoꝛ hêamꝰmaloruue patiamur:
ab auríbꝰoíum repellendi sunt. Non solū
eoꝛ ꝗ ueram religiõē tenêt: ß quí deoꝛ
qualiūcunꝗ licet ßoꝛ uolūt esse cultores.
Hęc ení opío qd̄ agit aliud nisi ut nullus
oíno colãt aut rogetur ds̄: Contra quos
mõ nobis disputatio non est ínstituta: sed

accepta qdeꜩ ꝓtáte a summo deo arbitrio
suo ista decernere: ß ín talibꝰnecessitatibꝰ
ín gerendis illius oío iussa cõplere: ita ne
de ípo senciendum est: qd̄ índigníssimum
uisum est de stellarum uolūtate sentíre:
Quod si dicunt̄ stellę sigmficare potꝰista
ꝗ facere: ut ꝗ locutio quędã sit illa posítío
ꝓdicens futura nõ agés: nõ. n. medíocter
doctoꝛ hoīm fuit ista sentencia. nõ qdem
ita solét loquí mathematicí: ut uerbi gȓa
dicant: Mars ita posítus homícídã sigmí-
ficat ß homícidam nõ facit. Verútamē ut
cõcedamꝰnõ eos ut debét loquí: et a phís
accíper oportere sermoís regulam: ad ea
pręnūcíanda quę í síderū posítíõe repíre
se putant: qd̄ sit de quo nihil unꝗ dicere
potuerūt: cur í uíta gemmoꝛ: ín actíóíbꝰ
et ín euentis: ín professíoníbus: artíbus:
honoríbus: cęterísꝗ rebꝰad hūanã uítaꜩ
ptínétíbus: atꝗ ín ipa morte sit plęrunꝗ
tanta díuersitas: ut símiliores eis sínt ꝗtū
ad hęc actínet multí extraneí: ꝗípí ínter
se gemíní ꝓ exíguo temporis ínteruallo
ín nascédo separatí: ín cõceptu aūt ꝓ unū
concubitū uno etíã momento semínatí.

Cícero dicit Ipocratem ☙Ca. scd̄m.
nobilíssímū medícū sc̄ptū reliꝗsse:
quosdam fr̄es cū simul ęgrotar cępíssent:

Jncipit Quintus liber Augustini
de ciuitate dei

Qvoniam cõstat oĩm rerum optandarum plenitudinẽ esse feli-citatẽ: quẽ non ẽ dea sed donũ dei: et ideo nullũ deũ colendum esse ab hoĩbus: ñ q põt eos facere felices. Vnde si illa dea eẽt: sola colenda merito diceret. Iam conseqter uideam9: qua cã deus qui põt & illa bona dare quẽ habeᵳ possunt etĩa non boni ac per hoc etiam nõ felices: romanũ impiũ tam magnũ tanqz diuturnũ esse uoluerit. Quia.n. hoc deoᵳ flozz illa quã colebãt multitudo non fecit: et multa iam diximq: et ubi uisum fuerit oportunũ esse dicemq. Causa g̃ magnitu-dínis imperii romani nec fortuita est nec fatalis: sm eorũ sníam siue opionem q ea dicũt esse fortuita: quẽ uel nullas cãs hñt uel nõ ex aliquo rõnabli ordie ueientes: et ea fatalia quẽ prẽter dei & hoĩum uo-lũtatẽ cuiusdã ordis necessitate cõtíngũt. Prorsus diuia puidẽta r̃gna cõstituũt hũana. Quẽ si ppterea qfq fato tribuit: quia ipam dei uoluntatẽ uel ptãtem fati noĩe appellat: sentẽciam teneat: linguam corrigat. Cur.n. nõ hoc pmũ dicat quod postea dicturq est: cũ ab illo qfq quẽsierit quid dixerit fatũ? Nam id hoies quãdo audiũt usitata loquẽdi consuetudíne: nõ íntelligũt ñ uim posinois siderũ: qualis ẽ qñ qs nascit siue concipiẽ. qd aliq alienãt a dei uolũtate: aliqui ex illa etĩa hẽc pen-dere cõfirmãt. Sed illi q sine dei uolũtate decernere opmanẽ sidera qd agam9: uel quid bonoᵳ hẽam9maloruue patiamur: ab aurib9oĩum repellendi sunt. Non solũ eoᵳ q ueram religionẽ tenẽt: sz qui deoᵳ qualiũcunqz licet flozz uolũt esse cultores. Hẽc enĩ opio qd agit aliud nisi ut nullus oĩno colaᵳ aut rogetur d̃s? Contra quos mõ nobis disputatio non est ínstituta: sed

contra eos qui pro defensione eoᵳ quos deos putant x̃anẽ religiõi aduersantur. Illi uero q posinoni stellarũ quodãmodo decernentiũ qualis qfqz sit: et qd puemat bõi quidue mali accidat ex dei uolũtate suspendunt: si easdem stellas putant hẽre hãc ptãtem traditam sibi a summa illius ptãte ut uolentes ista decernant: magnã cẽlo faciũt íniuriã: í cui9uelut clarissimo senatu ac splendidissima curia opĩnãtur scelera facienda decerní: qualia si aliqua terrena ciuitas decreuisset: geneᵳ hũano decernẽte fuerat euertẽda. Quale deínde íudiciũ de hoĩm factis deo relinqẽ: qbus cẽlestis necessitas adhibeᵳ: cũ d̃ns ille sit et siderũ & hoĩm? Aut si nõ dicũt stellas accepta qdez ptãte a summo deo arbitrio suo ista decernere: sz ín talib9necessitanb9 ín gerendis illius oĩo iussa cõplere: ita ne de ipo senciendum est: qd índignissimum uisum est de stellarum uolũtate sentiᵳe? Quod si dicũᵳ stellẽ significare pot9ista q̃ facere: ut q̃ı locutio quẽdã sit illa posino pdicens futura nõ agẽs: nõ.n. mediocᵳer doctoᵳ hoĩm fuit ista sentencia.nõ q dem ita solẽt loqui mathematici: ut uerbi gᵳa dicant:Mars ita positus homicidã signi-ficat sz homicidam nõ facit. Verũtamẽ ut cõcedam9nõ eos ut debẽt loqui: et a phis accipeᵳ oportere sermois regulam: ad ea prẽnũcianda quẽ í siderũ posinõe reptir se putant: qd sit de quo nihil unq̃ dicere potuerũt: cur í uita geminoᵳ: ín actioib9 et ín euentis: ín professionibus: arnbus: bonoribus: ceterisqz reb9ad hũanã uitaz ptínẽtibus: atqz ín ipa morte sit plerunqz tanta diuersitas: ut similiores eis sínt q̃tũ ad hẽc actínet multi extranei: q̃ ipi ínter se gemíni p exiguo temporis ínteruallo ín nascẽdo separati: ín cõceptu aũt p unũ concubitũ uno etĩa momento semĩnati.

Cicero dicit Ipocratem Ca.scdm. nobilissimũ medicũ scẽptũ reliqsse: quosdam fres cũ simul egrotaᵳ cẽpissent:

7 CONRAD SWEYNHEYM AND ARNOLD PANNARTZ, Subiaco, 1467

St. Augustine: *De Civitate Dei* 11¼ x 16

ab radice plagam fibrasque aceto acri:& urina uetusta madefacere atq; eo luto obru
ere sepe fodere. Oleax si parum promisere fructus nudatas radices hyberno frigori
opponút eaq; castigatione proficiút.Omnia hęc annua cęli ratione constat & aliquá
do serius pascunt aliquando celerius:necnon ignis aliquibus prodest aut harúdini
Ambusta nanq; densior mitiorq; surgit. Cato & medicaméta quędam cóponit mé
surę quoq; distributione ad maiox arbox radices amphoram:ad minox urná amur
cę & aquę portioé ęqua ablaqueatis prius radicibus paulatim affundi iubés.In olea
hoc amplius stramétis ante circúpositis.Ité fico huius pręcipue ueteré terram aggre
gari radicibus.In futux ut non decidant grossi maiorq; secúditas nec scabra ,pueiat
Simili modo ne conuoluolus fiat in uinea amurcę congios duos decoqui in crassi
tudine mellis rursusq; cubitú in his tertia parte & sulphuris quarta subdi usq; quo
exardescat.Sub tecto hoc uites circa capita ac sub brachiis ungui ita non fore cóuol
uolú. Quidam contenti sunt fimo huius mixturę suffire uineas flatu continuo tri
duo pleriq; non minus auxilii & aliméti arbitrantur in urina quam Cato abdita in
amurca modo pari aquę portione quonia per se noceat.Aliqui uolucre appellát aíal
pręrodés pubescétes uuas quod ne accidat sales cú sint exacutę fibrina pelle detegút
atq; ita putant aut sanguine ursino lini uolút post putatioé eafdé. Sunt arborum
pestes & formicę has abigunt rubrica ac pice liquida perúctis caudicibus:necnó et
pisce suspenso iuxta in unú locum congregant:aut lupino trito cum oleo radices li
niunt Multi & has & talpas amurca necant.Contraq; erucas & mala ne putrescant
lacerti uiridis felle cacumina tági iubét.Priuatim auté contra erucas ambiri arbores
singulas a muliere icitati mensis nudis pedibus recincta.Ité ne quod animal pastu
malefico decerpat frondé fimo boum diluto aspargi folia quotiés imber interueniat
quoniam obluitur ita uirus medicaminis. Mira quędá excogitante solertia humana
quippe cum auerti grandines carmine credát pleriq; cuius uerba inserere nó ęquidé
serio ausim:q̃q̃ a Catone prodita contra luxata mébra & unguéda harúdinum sissu
rę.Idé arbores religiosas lucosq; succidi permisit sacrificio prius facto.Cuius rei ra
tioné notionéq; eodé uolumine tradidit.

C. Plinii Naturalis historiae incipit libe . 18.

Quanti apud maiores studium agriculturę fuerit C. 1.

EQVITVR NATVRA FRVGVM ORTO

rumq; ac flox quęq; alia pręter arbores aut frutices be
nigna tellure pręueniunt uel per se tantum herbarum
imméfa contéplatione si quis existimet uarietaté nume
rum flores odores coloresq; & succos ac uires eax quas
salutis ac uoluptatis hoinum gratia gignit.Qua in pte
primum omniú patrocinari terrę & adesse cunctox pa
renti iuuat:q̃q̃ inter initia operis defensę:quonia tamé
ipsa materia intus accedit ad reputationem eiusdé paré
tis & noxiam nostris eam criminibus urgemus nostrá
que culpam illi íputamus genuit uenena & quis íuenit
illa pręter hominé.Cauere ac refugére alitibus serisq; satis est:atq; cú arbore exequát
liniuntque cornua elephanti & duri saxo rinocerontes & apri détium sicas:sciantq;
ad nocendum preparare se animalia quod tamé eox excepto homine tęla sua ueneis
suis tingit nos & sagittas cingimus & ferro ipsi nocentius aliquid damus. Nos et
flumina inficimus & rex naturę eleméta.Ipsum quoque quo uiuitur acrem in per
nitiem uertimus.Neque est ut putemus ignorari ea ab animalibus quę pręparaue
rint contra serpétium dimicationes quę post pręlium ad medendú excogitarét indi
cauimus. Nec ab ullo pręter hominé ueneno pugnatur alieno. Fateamur ergo cul

oraculis ne pręliū ineat cohibent & exercitus omnis męrore ac ſtupore cōfectus
eſt : Sed eo neceſſitatis uentum eſt ut uel audendo furtuna tentanda ǀuel diucius
ſtando extrema fames expectanda ſit . Hec cū dixiſſet Alexander ariſtidē orabat
ut ipſe conſtius memoria teneret & neminē participē faceret . Cui tunc ariſtides
iniquū eſſe Pauſaniam ǀ cui ſumma retū cōmiſſa erat hęc ignorare . Cum cęteris
aūt nullum ſe ante pręlium uerbum facturū . At ſi uicerint quod dii faxint oībus
Alexandri uirtutem ac promptitudinem notam fore . Iis ultrocitocǫ dictis Rex
macedonū equo reuectus eſt . Tū Ariſtides ad Pauſanię tabernaculū profectus
quo inſtatu res eſſet expoſuit ǀ cęteris poſt aduocatis ducibus imperatū ut quiſcǫ
ſuos in ordinem inſtruerent & paratos quaſi iam pede collato confligendum eſſet
continerent . Per id ferme tempus pauſanias ut ſcribit Herodotus Ariſtide cō⸗
uento dignum putabat mutato loco athenienſes dextro loco conſtitui & aduerſus
perſas obici . melius enim cū ipſis decertaturos : cum & eorum belligerandi arte
experti & recenti uictoria audaciores eſſent . Se aūtē Siuiſtro in cornu futurū quo
ex loco gręcos qui medorum partes cōſectarentur exciperet . Reliqui Athenięſiū
principes ualde ſuperfluis in rebus occupatū & difficilē Pauſaniā dictitabantǀ
ſi cuncti ſuis in locis dimiſſis ſolus Athenienſes uelut ilotes ſupra & infra collo⸗
caret & arbitratu ſuo nūc pugnatiſſimę gēti obiectaret . Ariſtidis aūte eos magno
in errore uerſarii docuit Nam ſi paulo ante cōtēdere cū tegeatis inquit ut ſiniſtrū
cornu haberetis ad ueſtrā amplitudinē pertinere credidiſtisǀ& eis iudicio pręlati
uos honoſtatos cenſuiſtis In preſentia Lacedemoniis ſponte nobis ex dextro cō⸗
cedentibus & quo Dammō ſūmum nobis principatū conferentibus : cur gloriā
nobis propoſitam non amatis : preſertim cum in lucro ponere debeatis ſi uero
aduerſus Tribules & neceſſarios ueſtros ǀſed Barbaros hoſtes nobis a natura da⸗
tos dimicandum ſit . Hęc cum diſſeruiſſēt Athenienſes ſiniſtram Lacedemoniis
aciem ſummo ſtudio dare in dextram ipſi concedere . Plurimę ſe inuicē exortatū
uoces diſperſę hoſtes aduētare : qui nec armis nec aís ſuperiores illi eſſent : quos
apud Marathona profligaſſent . Aſt eoſdem artus maiorem eandem ueſtis uari⸗
etatem eundem aureum circa mollia corpora & iules aíos apparatū . Nobis eadē
arma & corpora & pleriſcǫ ſecundis pręliis maiorem audatiam . Certamen uero
non agrorū aut urbis cauſa ur maiores noſtri ſed pro tropheis quę Marathone
ac Salamine conſtituimus ut non Milciadis aut fortune ſed Athenięſiū potius
eſſe uideantur . Interea mutato loco aciem inſtruere & ſe inuicem cōponere ſoliciti.
Hęc Thebani pertranſſugas explorata Mardonio renuntiant . Qui ex tēplo ſiue
Athenienſes timeret ſiue cum Lacedemoniis maiori cum laude congredi uellet
dextro cornu perſas aduerſus Lacedemonios inſtruxit . ceteros uero gręcos qui
ſecum erāt aduerſus Athenienſes ſtare iuſſit . Palam aūtē mutatione acierū facta
Pauſanias iterū indextrum cornu ſe recepit & Mardonius ſicut initio habuerat
ut manum cum Lacedemoniis cōſereret in ſiniſtrum reuertit . Eo die nihil actū
gręcis in concilium uocatis lōgius caſtra mouere uiſum atcǫ locū indagare unde
oportune aquationes eſſent . propinqua enim omnia fluenta Barbari fedauerāt
& maximo equitatu occupauerant . Sequenti nocte cum duces aꞋd deſtinatum
caſtris locum ſuos agerent multitudo uix conſtare ac difficile ſubſequi . Vt enim
ex prioribus exceſſeruut munimentis magno numero uerſus Plateenſium urbem
paſſim diſcurrere . Vnde cum ſine imperio Palati diſpergerentur & tabernacula

regiis legatis uirtutem scripturæ occultã esse ostendens his uerbis usus est:ut Aristæus alter ex legatis confcripfit. Dignum autem é inquit nõ nulla eorum quæ ab eo audiuimus breuiter poneri:præcipue quoniam temere quædã de puris atqȝ ipuris aïalibus lege fcripta multi arbitrã tur. Interrogatus enim a nobis quãobrem fi a deo uniuerfa creata funt impura nõnulla fcriptura uocitat:a quibus abftinêdum effe iubet:ita differuit. Vides quantã uim habet cõuerfatio atqȝ confuetudo:malos eîm hoies fi cum improbis:laudabiles fi cum probis cõuerfant'facile facit. Primum igitur legum diuinaȝ lator ita cũcta deo patere oftêdit: ut nihil agi nihil excogitari poffit quod eũ lateat:deinde cæteros omnȝ hoies fallo multitudinem deorum introducere docuit:quũ ipfi multo præftatiores fint ȝ dii fui quos ueneratur:quoȝ fimulacra lapidea uel lignea tanȝ magnes eorum qui ad uitam fibi non nihil contulerunt adorant fenfum ipfi habentes ea quæ infenfata penitus funt. Cur aũt oĩo quafi dii a gentibus coluntur illi qui ad ufum humanæ uitæ aliqd inuenerunt:quum non fecerint neqȝ produxerint ipfi quicquam:fed meliorem eorũ quæ funt ufum excogitarĩt'aut cur hodie quoqȝ multi non adorantur:quum antiquioresqȝ funt:Nam de Aegyptus quidê nefcio qd multa fagaciores acutioresqȝ funt:baluas enim & ferpêtes & uiuos & mortuos uenerant'. Hæc igitur fi fpiciês diuinus ille ur mœnibus ferres & fuiolabili uallo a cæteris gêtibus fepare nos uoluit:quo pacto facilius corpore atqȝ aïo imaculatos lõgeqȝ ab huiufcemodi falfis opiniôibus remotos fore unde bat:ut folũ uerũ deum præter cæteras gentes adorantes illi folũmodo inhæreamus. Vnde factum eft ut a nõnullis ægyptiorum facerdotibus qui difciplinam noftram altius cõfiderarunt dei homines gens noftra fit appellata:quod nemini nifi deũ ueru colat accidere poteft. Nec id iniuria:reliquis enim cibo potui ueftituqȝ inhiantibus noftri omnibus iftis contemptis per totam uitam de omnipotêtia dei cogitant. Negitȝ conuerfatione atqȝ confuetudine aliorum corrupti ad ipietaté eorum deferamur:cibi & potus tactus & auditus atque ufionis purificatione legali nos a cæteris feparauit. Cuncta enim ab una potentia ofpotentis dei gubernata naturali ratõe fimilia funt:quis fingula aȝbus abftine mus & quibus utimur profundam habeant rationem:quorum uȝum aut alterum exempli gratia ponam:ne putes temere de rebus tam puis a Moyfe fuiffe cõfcriptum:fed omnia uideas ad probitatem hoium & iuftitiæ pfectionem fancte ptinere. Volucres eĩm omnes qȝbus utimur domefticæ mũdæqȝ funt tritico aut leguminibus cõnutrica:ut colibȝ turtures perdices anferes cæteraeqȝ huiufmodi:quæ uero prohibitæ fũt

eas rapaces carnibusqȝ aliarũ auium nutriri comperies:a quibus agnis hædisqȝ raptis hoibus quoqȝ tam uius ȝ mortuis infertur inuria:quæ omnia merito imunda noĩauit:ut uel hinc rapina & cæde nos deterre ret:& ad iuftitiam hortaretur:moneretqȝ iuftifime atqȝ pacifice uiueri: ficut omnes uolucres mundæ quæ nulli auium nec omnino aliis inu riant'.Ita his quafi fymbolis ad iuftitiã ĩtelligêtes cõuertit. Nã fi aïalia huiufmodi tangenda non funt propter imundiciê fuam:quales erunt homines qui prauitate morũ illis fe fimiles reddũt?Omnia igitur hæc tropologice fanctéqȝ ĩtellecta plurimum conferunt:confiderato eîm ungulæ fiffanæ an contra fit diftinguêdos effe fingulos actus probe fi gnificat:quos qui nõ diftingũt omnes quafi pecora parentes fimul & filiæ forores & fratres:quodqȝ nec in pecudibus inuenintur mares inter fe cõmifcentur:a quibus omnibus nos longe abfumus. Vnde mirifice una & hunc diftinguendi modum docuit:& uitæ conftrutionisqȝ nĩæ habendam effe memoriam monuit. Quum eĩm dixiffet quãcunqȝ un gulam fcindit:adiecit & ruminãt. Nihil enim aliud per ruminationê uere. hoc uita alimento conferuatur. Ita & alibi iubet dicens. Memoria recordaberis domini dei tui qui fecit in te magna & mirabilia. Ingentia enim profecto funt fiquis diligenter confiderat formatio corporis:ali menti difpenfatio:& ad fingula membra mirabilis tranfitus:ac multo magis fenfuum uis mentis agitatio et fumma ueloctias:unde fingulæ quoqȝ artes iuentæ funt.Quare monet memoria tenendũ omnia quæ diximus diuina uirtute et fieri et gubernari:loca deide ac têpora oĩbus accommodauit:ut fem̄p et ubique deĩ memoriã hêamus et incipientes quicqȝ agere et definentes:et quom inter agendum fumus conftitui:iã cibi et potus tã mundiciæ ȝ imundiciæ ȝ primitiis:qȝbus factis poftea utimur ad deum nos conuertit. Præterea per ueftrũ etiam fimile fecit. qd plura?In ipis quoqȝ ianus præcepta dei fcribere iuffit:ut continuã eus hæremus memoriã:et i manibus ipis circũferre ipã uoluit:ut oftê deret omĩa nobis iufte faciunda creatorem timentibus:et nĩæ creatiois memoriam firmam retinentibus. Iubet enim fiue quis dormitum eat: fiue a lectulo recipiat:fiue abulet:fiue fedeat:dei opa fibi effe meditan da:et in fingulis dei potentiam qua fumus et poffumus nõ uerbis tan tummõ: uerũ etiã cogitatione atqȝ aĩo admirandã laudandã amandã. Sed de cibo ac potu dicta fufficiant. De fenfibus aũt ita iuffit ut nihil audiendum nihilqȝ tangendum uelit quod ĩmundum fit:ethoc fimili quadam rõne. Rapaces eĩm prauæqȝ beftiolæ fũtta quaȝ ractu nos pro hibuit ficut catæ ac mures peftifera quædam aïalia et omĩo inutilia

facit. Primum igitur legum diuinaꝝ lator ita cucta deo patere oltedit:
ut nihil agi nihil excogitari poffit quod eū lateat: deinde cæteros omés
hoīes falfo multitudinem deorum introducere docuit: quū ipfi multo
præftātiores fint q̄ dii fui quos ueneratur: quoꝝ fimulacra lapidea uel
lignea tanq̄ imagines eorum qui ad uitam fibi non nihil contulerunt
adorant fenfum ipfi habentes ea quæ infenfata penitus funt. Cur aūt
oīo quafi dii a gentibus coluntur illi qui ad ufum humanæ uitæ aliqd
inuenerunt: quum non fecerint neq; produxerint ipfi quicquam: fed
meliorem eorū quæ funt ufum excogitarīt: aut cur hodie quoq; multi
non adorantur: quum antiquioribus ad inueniédum excogitandumq;
multa fagaciores acutioresq; fint: Nam de Aegyptiis quidé nefcio qd
dicere oporteat: bæluas enim & ferpétes & uiuos & mortuos uenerant.
Hæc igitur ifpiciés diuinus ille uir mœnibus ferreis & īuiolabili uallo
a cæteris gētibus fepare nos uoluit: quo pacto facilius corpore atq; aīo
īmaculatos lōgeq; ab huiufcemodi falfis opinioībus remotos fore uide⁄
bat: ut folū uerū deum præter cæteras gentes adorantes illi folūmodo
inhæreamus. Vnde factum eft ut a nōnullis ægyptiorum facerdotibus
qui difciplinam noftram altius cōfiderarunt dei homines gens noftra
fit appellata: quod nemini nifi deū uerū colat accidere poteft. Nec id
iniuria: reliquis enim cibo potui ueftituiq; inhiantibus noftri omībus
iftis contemptis per totam uitam de omnipotétia dei cogitant. Ne igit'
conuerfatione atq; confuetudine aliorum corrupti ad īpietaté eorum
deferamur: cibi & potus tactus & auditus atque uifionis purificatione
legali nos a cæteris feparauit. Cuncta enim ab una potentia oīpotentis
dei gubernata naturali ratiōe fimilia funt: q̄uis fingula a q̄bus abftine⁄
mus & quibus utimur profundam habeant rationem: quorum uṇum
aut alterum exempli gratia ponam: ne putes temere de rebus tam p̄uis
a Moyfe fuiffe cōfcriptum: fed omnia uideas ad probitatem hoīum &
iuftitiæ pfectionem fancte ptinere. Volucres eī omnes q̄bus utimur
domefticæ mūdæq; funt tritico aut leguminibus cōnutritæ: ut colūbæ
turtures perdices anferes cæteræq; huiufmodi: quæ uero prohibitæ fūt

11   Detail of plate 10. Actual size.

10   NICOLAUS JENSON, Venice, 1470

Eusebius: *De Evangelica Praeparatione*   9⅛ x 13¼

De Marsepia & Lampedone reginis amazonú. C. ri

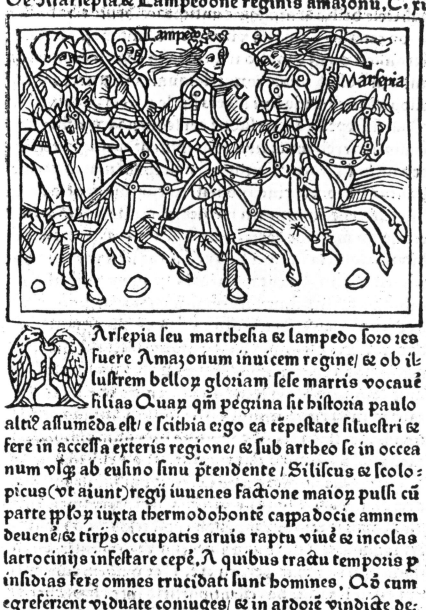

Arsepia seu marthesia & lampedo sorores
fuere Amazonum inuicem regine/ & ob il=
lustrem belloꝝ gloriam sese martis vocauȇ
filias Quaꝝ qm̃ pegrina sit historia paulo
altiꝰ assumȇda est/ e scithia ergo ea tȇpestate siluestri &
fere in acceſſa exteris regione/ & sub artheo se in occea
num vlꝗ ab eusino sinu ꝑtendente ⸓ Siliscus & scolo=
picus(vt aiunt)regij iuuenes Factione maioꝝ pulsi cũ
parte ipsoꝝ iuxta thermodohontȇ cappadocie amnem
deuenȇ/& tirꝑs occupatis aruis raptu viuȇ & incolas
latrocinijs infestare cepȇ⸓ A quibus tractu temporis ꝑ
insidias fere omnes trucidati sunt homines ⸓ Q ȏ cum
egreferzent viduate coniuges/ & in ardoȡ vindicte de=
ueniſſent feruide/ cum paucis qui supuixerint viris in
arma ꝓrupere⸓ Et primo impetu facto hostes a suis
demouere finibus/inde vltro circumstantibus intuleze
bellum/demum arbitrantes hnȋtutȇ potius ꝗ̃ ꝛiugiũ/
si exteris adhererent hoȋnibus ⸓ & feminas solas poſſe

natúrlich kúnſten nit geübet haben·ſunder die natúr
lichen meyſter· võ denen ieronimus damaſo ſchreibet
phiſici·das iſt natúrlich meyſter die ire augen vmb
vrſachen zeerkennen auff in die hymel krbent· vnnd
vnder die erden vntz in die hellen verſencket in leicht
fertigkeit irer ſynn· in vinſteri ires gemütes gand er-
ſüchen tag vnd nacht darumb dz ſy vil wiſſent vnd
wenig nach rechter weyſheit kúndent.

Das ·xxxix· Capitel von der andern kunſt mathe
matice das iſt muſica·von irem lob vñ nutz arbeit
vnd vngemach.

Vſica die ander vnder den ·iiij· wey/
ſenden kúnſten als oben geſaget iſt·
leret die vili der proporcion·in eyni/
keit der ſtymmen zeſamen fügen· di
ſe kunſt iſt auch von den kryechen
allweg in groſſen eren gehaltẽ wor
den. Es ward auch keyner der freyẽ
kúnſt gelert geſchätzet er wäre dañ auch der muſica
gelert worden. Was aber plato lobes õ gúten mithel
lung der ſtymmen gäbe·das wirt auß dem bekant dz
er in thymo ſchreybt·wañ er ſpricht·Muſica iſt die
aller mächtigiſte kunſt der kúnſten·deren ſüſſigkeyt

Segge Jsrahelis kinderē du bpst een volck ee
nes harde nackes · ik schal eens i midde diner
vp staen vñ vordpligē dp · nu vpperstūt legge
vā dp alle dine syrheit · dat ik wete wat ik dō
schal · Darūme leydē Jsrahelis kinder alle ere
syrheit vā en · vā de berge oreb ✳ dat is de kro
nen de en vp ere houet gesat werē an de berge
oreb · Moyses nā dat tabernakel vñ sette dat
werne bute de woninge vñ richtede dat vp · vñ
nomede spnen namē dat tabernackel des vor
bundes · Vñ alle dat volck dat pēnige klaghe
hadde genck vth to de tabernakel des vorbū
des bute de wonynge · Vñ wenne als Moyses
vth wolde gaen tho dem tabernakel der vor
buntnisse · so stunde al dat volck vp · een iewe
lick in der doere spnes paulupns · vnde seghen
Moysi na vp spnē rugge byth he in de tentē
genck · Vñ als he in was gegangē in dat taber
nakel des getuchnisse · so stech nedder een sul
eenes wolckē · vñ stund vor der doer · vnde de
here sprack mit Moysi vñ allermallik sach dat
dat de suple des wolkē stund vor der doer des
tabernackels · vñ se stundē vñ bedē vth de doe
ren erer wonyngen · Vñ de here sprak to Moy
si vā angesichte in angesichte recht als een
mpsche plach to spreke to spnē vrunde · Vñ als
he do wedder quā to den wonynge · spn dener
Josue Nums sone een kint dat en geck nicht
van dem tabernakel · Vñ do sprak Moyses tho
dem herē · gebudestu dat ik dat volck vth lep
de vñ seggest my nicht wen du mit my wpl
lest senden · vñ bysunder na deme du sprekest ·

Jck bekenne dp vth dpnē namē vñ du heuest
gnade vundē by my · Js dat ik nu gnade vun
den hebbe in dpnem angesichte · so wpse my
dpn angesichte vp dat ik dp wytte · vñ dat
ik gnade vynde vor dpnē ogē · see an dpn volk
desse lude · Vñ do sprak god · Mpn angesichte
schal vor dp hen gaen · vñ ik schal dp raste ge
uen · vnde Moyses sprak · vñ efte du vns nicht
sulue vor en geyst so leyde vns nicht vth des
ser stede · war pnne mogen wy denne wete dp
volck vñ ick dat wy gnade hebben vunde in
dpnem angesichte · du en wandeles den mpt
vns dat wy geeret werden van allem volcke ·
de wonet vp der erden · Vñ do sprak de here tho
Moysen · See dat wort dattu gesprakē heuest
schal ik doen · du heuest gnade vunde vor my
vñ ik hebbe dp bekand vth dpnem name · vñ
he sprak · Bewpse my dpn glorie · vñ hee ant
worde · ick schal dp alle gud wpsen vñ vor dp
geesschet werde in den name des here · vñ schal
gnedich sijn in dē dat my behaget vnde sprak
vortmer · Du en machst my angesichte nicht
seen · my en schal neen mpsche seen vñ leuen ·
vnde vortmer sprak he · see dat is een stad by
my · vnde dar schaltu staen vp dem steene · vñ
als mpn glorie en wech geyt · so schal ick dp
setten in den rpt des steenes · vnde schal dp be
schermen mpt myner rechterhant byth ick
gae · vnde ick schal mpn hant aff doen · vnde
du schalt my vp den rugge seen · mpn anghe
sichte en machstu nicht seen ·

14   HEINRICH QUENTELL, Cologne, c. 1478

Bible in Low German   10⅞ x 15⅛

Here endith the Wyff of Bathes prologe.
And here begynnyth her tale.

In olde dayes of kyng Artur
Of Whiche britous spekith gret honour
Al Was this londe ful filled of fayrye
The elf quene With her ioly companye
Daunced ful ofte in mony a greue mede
This Was the olde oppinion as I rede
I speke of many an hundrid peris a goo
But noW can noman se elphis mo
For noW the grete charite and praiers
Of limytours and eke of othir freris
That serchen euery londe and euery streme
As thicke as motis in the sonne beem
Blissinge hallis chambris kechens and boWris
Citees Burghis castellis and eek touris
Shippis bernys Shepens and dayries
This makith that ther be no feyries
For there as Wont Was to Walke an elf
There Walkith noW the limytour hym self
In Vndermelis and in mornyngis
And seith his matyns and his thingis
As he goth forth in his limytacion
A Woman may go sauely vp and doun
Vnder euery bussh or Vnder euery tre
There is none other incubus but he
And he ne Wolde do hem ony dishonour
And so befil that this kyng Artour
Hadde in his hous a lusty bacheler

15 WILLIAM CAXTON, Westminster, c. 1478
Geoffrey Chaucer: *Canterbury Tales*   7½ x 10⅞

quasi ignorantibus ueritatem: sed quasi
scientibus eam:τ qm omne mendacium
ex ueritate nõ est. Quis est mendax nisi
is q negat qm iesus nõ est xpus: Hic est
antixpus q negat prem τ filiũ. Dis q ne
gat filiũ nec bz prem. Qui pfitet filium τ
patrem habet. Uos qd audistis ab iitio
in uobis pmaneat. Si in uobis pmanse
rit qd audistis ab iitio:τ uos i filio τ pre
manebitis. Et hec est repromissio quam
ipse pollicitus est uobis uitã etnaz. Hec
scripsi uobis de his qui seducũt uos.Et
uos unctionẽ quã accepistis ab eo mãe
at in uobis. Et nõ necesse habetis ut ali
quis doceat uos:sed sicut unctio ei' do
cet uos de omnib'. Et uez est τ nõ é mẽ
dacium. Et sicut docuit uos manete i eo.
Et nũc filioli manete in eo:ut cũ apparu
erit habeamus fiduciam:τ nõ confunda
mur ab eo in aduentu eius. Si scitis qm
iustus est:scitote qm τ ois q facit iusticiã
ex ipso natus est. Lectio quarta.

Idete qualem caritatẽ dedit nobis
pater:ut filij dei noiemur τ scim'.
Propter hoc mũdus non nouit uos qz
non nouit eum. Carissimi nũc filij dei su
mus:τ nũdum apparuit nobis quid eri
mus. Scimus qm cũ apparuerit similes
ei erimus:qm uidebimus eũ sicuti é. Et
omnis qui habet hanc spem in eo:sancti
ficat se:sicut τ ille sãctus é. Dis q faé pec
catũ τ iniqtatẽ facit.Et peccatũ est iiqtas.
Et scitis qz ille apparuit ut peccata tolle
ret:τ peccatũ in eo nõ é. Dis q in eo ma
net nõ peccat:τ ois q peccat nõ uidet eũ
nec nouit eũ.Filioli nemo uos seducat.
Qui facit iusticiã iust' é:sicut τ ille iust' é.
Qui facit peccatũ ex diabolo é:qm ab ii
tio diabolus peccat.In hoc apparuit fi
li us dei:ut dissoluat opa diaboli.Dis q
natus est ex deo peccatũ non facit:qm se
men ipius in eo manet:τ nõ põt peccare
qm ex deo natus est. In hoc manifesti sẽ
filij dei:τ filij diaboli. Dis q nõ é iustus:
nõ est ex deo:τ q nõ diligit fratrem suũ.
Quoniã hec est annũciatio quã audistis
ab initio ut diligamus alterutrũ. Non si
cut chain q ex maligno erat q τ occidit

fratrez suũ.Et propter qd occidit eũ:Qm
opera eius maligna erant:fratris autem
ei' iusta. Nolite mirari fratres si odit uoi
mũdus. Nos scimus qm translati sum'
de morte ad uitaz qm diligimus fratres.
Qui nõ diligit manet in morte.Dis qui
odit fratrẽ suũ homicida est. Et scitis qm
omnis homicida nõ habet uitã eternaz
in se met ipo manentem. Lectio quinta.

In hoc cognouimus caritatez dei:
qm ille aiaz suã p nobis posuit:et
nos debemus p fratribus nostris aias
ponere. Qui habuerit substantiam hui'
mundi:τ uiderit fratrem suum necessita
tem habere:τ clauserit uiscera sua ab eo
quomodo caritas dei manet in eo? Fili
oli mei nõ diligamus uerbo neqz ligua
sed opere τ ueritate. In hoc cognoscim'
qm ex ueritate sumus:τ in conspectu ei'
suadebimus corda nostra: quoniaz si re
prehenderit nos cor nostrum maior est
deus corde nostro:τ nouit omnia.Carii
simi si cor nostz non reprehenderit nos
fidutiã habemus ad dnm:ut quicqd pe
tierimus accipiemus ab eo: quoniã mã
data eius custodimus:τ ea que sunt pla
cita corã eo facimus. Et hoc est manda
tum eius ut credamus in nomine christi
iesu filij eius:τ diligamus alterutrum sic
dedit mandatũ nobis. Et qui seruat mã
data eius: in illo manet τ ipe in eo.Et in
hoc scimus quoniam manet in nobis ð
spiritu sancto qué dedit nobis. Lec.vi.
Carissimi nolite õi spũi credere:sed
pbate spũs si ex deo sint:qm mul
ti pseudo prophete exiere in munduz. In
hoc cognoscitur spũs dei.Dis spũs qui
confitetur iesum christum in carne uenis
se.ex deo est:τ omnis spũs qui soluit ie
sum ex deo non est:τ hic est antichristus
de quo audistis quoniã ueniet τ nunc iã
in mundo est.Uos ex deo estis filioli et
uicistis eum qm maior é q in uobis est:
qz qui in mũdo est. Ipi de mũdo sũt:ideo
de mũdo loquũtur:τ mũdus eos audit.
Nos ex deo sumus.Qui nouit deuz au
dit nos. Qui aũt nõ est ex deo nõ audit
nos. In hoc cognoscimus spũm ueritatis

Admirabile cõmerciũ, creator gene=
ris ħumani animatũ corpus sumẽs
de virgine nasci dignatus est,et procedẽs
ħomo sine semine largitus est nobis suaʒ
deitatẽ, Sepe quidẽ diuersis modis mul=
tisʠ mẽsuris, ħumano generi bonitas di
uina cõsuluit, et plurima prouidentie sue
munera, omnibus retro seculis clemen=
ter imptiuit, Sed in nouissimis tempori=
bus omnẽ supħabundantiã solite benig=
nitatis excessit, quãdo in xpo ipsa ad pec=
catores misericordia ad errãtes veritas,

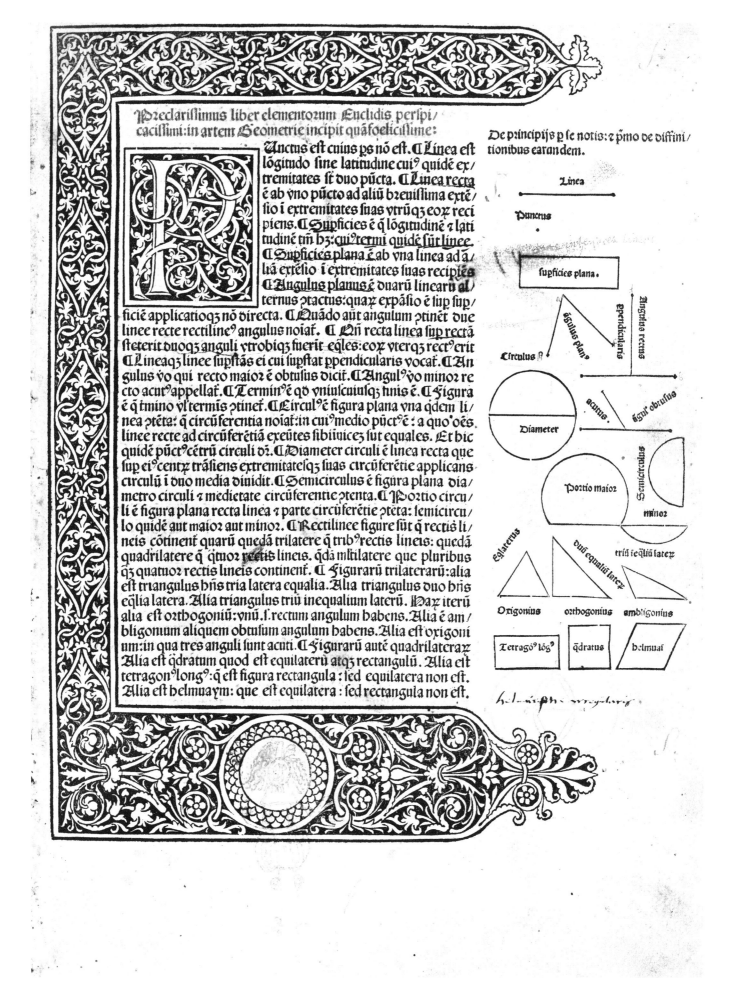

Preclarissimus liber elementorum Euclidis perspi/
cacissimi:in artem Geometrie incipit quāfoelicissime:

Unctus est cuius ps nō est. C Linea est
lōgitudo sine latitudine cui⁹ quidē ex/
tremitates sī duo pūcta. C Linea recta
ē ab vno pūcto ad aliū breuissima extē/
sio i extremitates suas ytrūqz eoꝛ reci
piens.C Supficies ē q̄ lōgitudinē ꝛ lati
tudinē tm̄ bꝫ:cui⁹termi quidē sūt linee.
C Supficies plana ē ab vna linea ad ā/
liā extēsio i extremitates suas recipiēs
C Angulus planus ē duarū linearū al/
ternus ꝓtactus:quaꝛ expāsio ē sup sup/
ficiē applicatioꝗꝫ nō directa. C Quādo aūt angulum ꝓtinēt due
linee recte rectiline⁹ angulus noia�’. C Q̄n̄ recta linea sup rectā
steterit duoqꝫ anguli ytrobiqꝫ fuerit eq̄les:eoꝛ yterqꝫ rect⁹erit
C Lineaqꝫ linee supstās ei cui supstat ꝑpendicularis vocaꝩ.C An
gulus vo qui recto maioꝛ ē obtusus diciꝉ.C Angul⁹ vo minoꝛ re
cto acut⁹appellaꝉ.C Termin⁹ē q̄ vniuscuiusqꝫ finis ē. C Figura
ē q̄ tmino vl termis ꝓtineꝉ.C Circul⁹ē figura plana vna q̄dem li
nea ꝓtēta: q̄ circūferentia noiaꝉ:in cui⁹medio pūct⁹ē : a quo⁹oēs
linee recte ad circūferētiā exeūtes sibiiuiceꝫ sut equales. Et hic
quidē pūct⁹cētrū circuli dꝯ.C Diameter circuli ē linea recta que
sup ei⁹centꝛ trāsiens extremitatesꝗꝫ suas circūferētie applicans
circulū i duo media diuidit.C Semicirculus ē figura plana dia/
metro circuli ꝛ medietate circūferentie ꝓtēta.C Poꝛtio circu/
li ē figura plana recta linea ꝛ parte circūferētie ꝓtēta: semicircu/
lo quidē aut maioꝛ aut minoꝛ. C Rectilinee figure sūt q̄ rectis li/
neis cōtinenꝉ quarū quedā trilatere q̄ trib⁹rectis lineis: quedā
quadrilatere q̄ q̄tuoꝛ rectis lineis. q̄dā mltilatere que pluribus
qꝫ quatuoꝛ rectis lineis continenꝉ. C Figurarū trilaterarū:alia
est triangulus hn̄s tria latera equalia. Alia triangulus duo hn̄s
eq̄lia latera. Alia triangulus triū inequalium laterū. Maꝛ iterū
alia est oꝛthogoniū:vnū.s.rectum angulum habens.Alia ē am/
bligonium aliquem obtusum angulum habens. Alia est oꝛigoni
um:in qua tres anguli sunt acuti.C Figurarū autē quadrilateraꝛ
Alia est q̄dratum quod est equilaterū atqꝫ rectangulū. Alia est
tetragon⁹long⁹:q̄ est figura rectangula : sed equilatera non est.
Alia est helmuaym: que est equilatera : sed rectangula non est.

De principijs ꝑ se notis:ꝛ ꝑmo de diffini/
tionibus earandem.

eodem modo sese habet non omnino satis
explorata sunt & diuturnius tempus eorū
notitiā semp certiorē faciat·circaq̧ cosmog̃
phiā hoc aiaduertendū videtur:cū conces
sum sit:ex traditōibus vario in tpe editis:
nō vnas nostri cōtinentis partes:ob excer
sum sue magnitudinis:nōdū ad nostrā pue
nisse notitia.aliq̧s vero non quéadmodū se
se habet ob paragrantiū negligentiā:nobis
minus diligenter traditas:alias autē esse:q̄
nūc aliter q̄ hacten⁹ se se habet siue ob cor
ruptōes·siue ob mutatōnes.in qbus p par
te corruisse cognite sunt·Necesse nob sit ad
nouas tpis nostri traditōes magis intende
re·liberādo tn̄ in expositōe illoŗ q̄ nūc tra
ctantur.& in se lectione eoŗ q̄ hactenus t̄
dita fuerīt·quid sit:quid ue nō sit credēdū

De editione cosmographie marini·

ARINVS igitur tyri⁹
tēpestatis nostre cosmo
graphorū postremus:
summo videtur studio
huic materie se intulisse
Nā plura explorauisse·
cognoscitur:pterea q̄ hactenus nota fuerāt·
Deīde omnium ferme historicoŗ q̄ eū p̃ue
nerant:notitia diligētissime habita:nō tātū
q̄cunq̧ ab alijs errata fuerāt emēdauit:sed
etiā illa que ipe idē male tractauerat quéad
modum in editionibus pictē sue cosmogra
phie·q̄ q̄ multa elimāt·licet aiadūtere· Sed
si inspiceremus vltimo eius·operi nihil dees
se satis & nobis foret·ex istis eius tātum co
mentarijs:absq̧ alioŗ vestigatōe habitabi
le nostrā describere· Verū cū ipe videatur·
quibusdā aiaduersione haud satis fidei dig
na assentiri.Preterea circa modū designatio
nis noscatur sepius:neq̧ oportune facilita
tis debitā curam agere:nō indigne moti su
mus:vti ad ratione vsumq̧ putauimus fore
comodius operi cōferre & viro· Quod q̄p
pe absq̧ verboŗ insoletia.q̄ maxie id fieri
poterit efficere conabimur·vtrūq̧ erroris ge

nus attingētes breuiter·vti ratio ipa dicta
bit.Primūq̧ id q̄ ad historiā attinet quera
mus·ex q̄ opinatur ipe·ad maiorē longitu
dine versus ortū solis·ac ad maiorē latitu
dine in meridie:quā fas sit:terrā nobis no
tā pro duci. Nō aut iniquius supficiei distā
tiam tendentē ab occasu ad ortuz solis lon
gitudinē appellamus:atq̧ distantiā a septē
trione in meridie latitudinē:cū in motibus
celestibus paralellos similiter nūcupemus·
Preterea q̄ q̄ maxime maiorē distantiā lō
gitudinē dicimus.Plane q̄de cōcessum é ab
ōibus.distantiā nostre habitabilis que ab
ortu solis in occasum extenditur:multo ma
iorē ea esse:q̄ a septetrionē in meridiē ūgit·

Emendatio latitudinis marini·

RIMVM igitur lati
tudinis terminū ponit
& ipe tylem insulā:sub
paralello qui plagam
maxime septetrionalē
terre nobis note diui
dit que paralellū ostendit quā potest dare:
ab eqnoctiali distare sexaginta & tribus g̃
dibus.q̄lium é meridianus circulus trecento
rū & sexaginta.Eam autē latitudinē notat:
triginta & vno millibus ac quingentis sta
dijs:velut g̃dus q̄libet ex qngētis stadijs
proponendum cōstet· Post hec regionem
ethiopū Agisymbam nomie·& prasum pro
montoriū ponit sub paralello : qui plagam
maxime australe nobis cōgitā finit que pa
ralellū sub hyemali tropico sistit.Quare oĩs
latitudo inter eqnoctiale & tropicū hyema
le:ac inter tyle & eqnoctiale in vnū coacta:
gradus fere septe & octuaginta cōplet:sta
dia vero q̄draginta & tria millia ac qngēta·
Conatur aut ratione australis finis ostende
re p obseruatōnes q̄sdā fixaŗ vt ipe putat
& p itinera q̄dam terra mariq̧ facta:quoŗ
q̄dlibet attingemus breuiter·In obseruatōe
quidē fixaŗ:in tertio opis sui volumie sub
his verbis memorat·Zodiacus supra torri

a 4

Ptolemy: *Cosmographia* 12½ x 16⅜

Ce chapitre est par maniere de prolo
gue iusques ou il dist. Ce nest mie chose
conuenable: ou le premier chapitre com/
mence.

Incois que ie dye de
linstitucion de lôme
ou il sera demonstre
la naissance des deux
citez tant côme il tou
che et appartient aux
creatures raisonnables mortelles/si cô
me ou liure precedent il a este demonstre

tes anges/p lesquelles tant côme nous
pourons sera prouue: comment aux hô/
mes et aux anges/ compaignie ne soit
mie dicte estre desconuenable ne mal se
ant/a ce que quatre citez/cest adire qua
tre compaignies ne soiêt mie dictes estre
ordonnees Cestassauoir deux des an/
ges: et deux des hômes Mais qui plus
est deux:cestassauoir Bne aux bons:lau
tre aux mauuais Non mie seulement
aux anges: mais aux hommes.

Declaration de ce liure.

20 PIERRE GÉRARD AND JEAN DUPRÉ, Abbeville, 1486–1487

St. Augustine: *La Cité de Dieu*   10¾ x 15⅛

¶ In die epyphanie. Ad miſſam. Introit⁹

Cce aduenit dñator
dominus ⁊ regnum
in manu eius et po-
teſtas et imperium.
Pſ. Deus iudicium tuũ
regi da:⁊ iuſticiam tuam filio regis. Glo
ria patri. Sicut erat. kyrieleyſõ. Glo
ria in excelſis deo.   ¶   Oratio

Deus qui hodierna die vnigeni
tum tuum gêtibus ſtella du-
ce reuelaſti. concede propicius: vt q̃
iam te ex fide cognouimus : vſqʒ
ad contemplandam ſpeciem tue
celſitudinis pducamur. Per eundẽ
Memoria nulla   Lectio yſaie pphete   lx

Surge illuminare theruſalem
quia venit lumen tuũ.⁊ gloria dñi ſuperte orta eſt. Quia ecce
tenebre operient terrã:⁊ caligo po-
pulos. Super te autẽ orietur dñs:⁊
gloria eius in te videbitur. Et ãbu
labunt gentes in lumine tuo. ⁊ reges in ſplêdore ortus tui. Leua i cir

cuitu oculos tuos ⁊ vide: omês iſti
congregati ſunt: venerũt tibi. Fili
tui delõge venient: ⁊ filie tue de la
tere ſurgent. Tunc videbis ⁊ afflu
es.⁊ mirabitur.⁊ dilatabit cor tuũ:
quãdo conuerſa fuerit ad te multi
tudo maris. fortitudo gentiũ vene
rit tibi. Inundatio camelorʒ operi
et te: dromedarii madian et effa
Omnes de ſabba venient: aurũ ⁊
thus deferentes:⁊ laudẽ dño annũ
ciantes. Ŗ. Omnes de ſabba venient
aurum et thus deferentes et laudem dño
annunciantes. ℣. Surge et illuminare
theruſalem quia gloria domiui ſuper te
orta eſt. Ŗ. Alleluya ℣. Vidimus ſtel
lam eius in oriente et venimus cum mu
neribus adorare dñm   ¶ Proſa

Epyphaniã domino canamus
glorioſã. Qua prolem dei ve
re magi adorant. Immenſã caldei
cuius perſeqʒ venerantur poten
tiam. Quem cuncti prophete ceci
nere venturũ gentes ad ſaluãdas
Cuius maieſtas ita ê inclinata vt
aſſumeret ſerui formã. Ante ſcľa q̃
de⁹⁊ tẽpora homo factus ê i maria
Balaã de quo vaticinãs exibit ex
iacob rutilãs inq̃t ſtella. Et côfrin
get ducũ agmia regiõis moab ma
xima potêtia. Huic magi munera
deferũt preclara aurʒ ſimul thus ⁊
mirrã. Thure deũ predicant auro
regẽ magnũ hominẽ mortalẽ mir
ra. In ſõnis hos monet angelus ne
redeãt ad regẽ cõmotũ ppt regna
Pauebat etenim nimiũ rege naſũ
verês amittere regni iura. Magi

hundert vnd zwelff iar vnd ſtarb. Enos aber le
bet.lrrrr.iar vñ gepar caynan. nach des gepurd
ſebet er achthundert vnd fünffzehen iar vñ ge
par ſün vnd töchter. vnd alſe dye tag enos ſeyn
worden neunhundert vnd fünff iar vnd ſtarb.
Vnd caynan ſebet ſibentzig iar vñd gepar ma
laſehel. vnnd caynan ſebet darnach. So er gepar
malaſehel achthundert vñ viertzig iar vñ gepar
ſün vñ töchter. vnd alſe die tag caynan wurden
neunhundert vñd zehen iar vñ ſtarb. Wañ ma
laſehel ſebet funff vñ ſechtzig iar vñd gepar ia
red. vnnd malaſehel ſebet darnach. So er ge
par iared achthundert vñ dreyſſig iar. vñ gepar
ſün vñ töchter. vnd alſe die tag malaſehel wur
den achthundert vñ funff vñ neuntzig iar vnd
ſtarb. Vñ iared ſebet hundert vñ zwey vñ ſech
tzig iar. vñ gepar enoch. vñ iared ſebet darnach
So er gepar Enoch achthundert iar vnd gepar
ſün vnd töchter vnd alſe die tag iared ſeyn wor
den neunhundert vnd zwey vñ ſechtzig iar vnd
ſtarb. aber enoch ſebet funff vnnd ſechtzig iar

vñ gepar mathuſalé. vñ enoch gieng mit got. vñ
enoch ſebet darnach do er gepar matuſalé drey
hundert iar vñ gepar ſün vnd töchter vñ alle ſy
tag enoch wurdé gemacht dreyhüdert vñ fünf
vñ ſechtzig iar. vñ er gieng mit got vnd erſchyn
nit. wañ got der nä oder erhube in. Vñ matuſa
lem ſebet hundert vnd ſiben vñ achtzig iar. vñd
gebar ſamech vñ mathuſalé ſebt darnach So er
gepar ſamech ſibenhundert vñ zwey vñ achtzig
iar. vnd gepar ſün vnd töchter. vnd alſe dye tag
matuſalé wurden neunhundert vnd newn vnd
ſechtzig iar. vnd ſtarb. Wann ſamech ſebet hü
dert vnd zwey vnd achtzig iar. vnd gepar eynen
ſün. vñ hieß ſei name noe ſagend. Der wirt vnß
tröſté vő dé arbeite vñ vő dé wercké vnſer hend
i der erde. der herr hat geflücht. vnd ſamech
ſebt darnach. So er gebar noe fünff hüdert vñ
fünf vñ neuntzig iar vñ gepar ſün vñ töchter. vñ
alle ſy tag ſamech wurdé ſibéhüdert vñ ſibé vñ
ſibétzig iar vñ ſtarb. Noe aber do er alt ward
funf hüdert iar do gebar ez ſem cham vñ iaphet

Das .VI. Capitel. wie

got der herr vmb Boßheit willen der menſchen
die werlt ließ vergeen in dem waſſer vnd hyeß
noe ein archen machen ſich vnd die ſeynen dar
yn zuenthalten.

Nd do dye menſchen
hetté angefangé manigualtig zewer
dé auf der erdé vñ hetté geboın töch

ter. die ſun gotz ſahé ſy töchter der menſchen
dz ſy waré ſchön ſy name in weyber auß alle dé
die ſy erwelten. Vñ got der ſprach. Mein geiſt
wirt nit Beleybé in den menſché ewigklich. wañ
er iſt fleyſch. Vnnd ſeyn tag werden zwaintzig
vñ hüdert iar. Vñ i dé tagé waré ryſen auf der
erdé. Vñ darnach do ſy ſün gottes waré einge
gangé zu dé töchtern der meſché. vñ ſy gebaré
diß ſein ſy gewaltigé vő der welt der berümté
mañ. Do aber got ſah dz vil vbels der menſché

Jerofolima nomē vrbis in paleſtina metropolis iudeoɽ:pɽ⁹ Jeb⁹.poſtea ſalē. tercio bierofolima. vltio belia dicta. Luius vrbis pɽm⁹ ɒditoɽ fuit (vt Joſeph⁹ teſtaſ) Canaan ǫ iuſt⁹ appellat⁹ erat rex. Et h ǫdē melchiſedech ſacerdos dei altiſſimi dicebatur. Qui cū ibidē phanū edificaſſɜ illud Solimā appellanit. ſolimi fuerūt ppłi iuxta liciā ǫs homeɽ⁹ pugnatiſſimos:ɜ a bellerophōte deuictos dicit. et in mōtib⁹ bitaſſe. Et corneli⁹ tacit⁹ cū de iudeoɽ origine opiōe narrat ait. Alíȷ clara iudeoɽ initia ſolimos carmib⁹ celebɽata homeri gēte ɒditam vɽbe bierofolimā noie ſuo feciſſe. vñ Juuenalis interpɽes legū folimaɽ. ǫ ciuitas cananee gētis vſǫ ad tpa dauid regi bitatio fuit. Nec io ſue iudeoɽū pɽiceps eos cananeos ſeu iebuſeos expellere potuit. Dauid iebuſeis expulſis cū ciuitatem reedificaſſet eā bierofolimā.í.munitiſſimā nūcupauit. Hui⁹ vɽb ſitus ɜ munitio petrofa erat.ɜ triplici muro cingebatur. ǫ vt Strabo ſit inteɽȷ⁹ aǫs abundans exteri⁹ vo oīo ſiccam foſſam bēbat i lapide exciſam.xl.pedū pfundi tate.latitudo vo.cc.l. Elapide aūt exciſo educta erant celeberrimi tēpli menia. Hec bierofolima lōge clariſſima vrbium oɽiētis ſup duos colles erat ɒdita iteruallo diſcretos i quā dom⁹ creberrime deſinebāt. Colliū alter ǫ ſupioɽ citas excelſioɽ ɜ i plixitate directioɽ caſtellū dauid dicebatur. Alter ǫ iſerioɽe ſuſtinet citates vndiǫ declinis ē vallȷ medio ad ſyloā ptins ita fōtē ǫ dulcȷ ē vocabāt. firmiſſime āt dō ſalomōis alioɽūǫ i

terra regū opa oɽnata fuit.agrippa eȷ ptez citatȷ addiderat ɜ cinxerat. Exuberās eñ mľtitudine paulati extra menia ſpebat. Noiata ē ps addita noua citas. Oñe āt citatȷ i giro ſpaciū.xxx.ɜ trib⁹ ſtadíȷs finiebaſ. Et ſi i toto admirabił.ter cius mur⁹ admirabilioɽ ob excellētiaz turriȷ ǫ ad ſeptētrione occidētēǫ ſurgebat i agulo. de ǫ ſole oɽto arabia pſpici poterat ɜ mare vſǫ ad fines hebɽeoɽ. Et iuxta eā turrȷ yppico:ɜ due ǫs herodes i ātiǫ muro edificauerat. Mirabił fuit lapidū magnitudo ex ſecto marmoɽe cādido ita aduati vt ſingle turres ſingła ſaxa videreſ.hȷȷs i ſeptētriōali pte aula ɽgia pſtātiſſima ɽiūgebatur. Muro alto cincta acvarietate ſaxoɽu oɽnata Alte deniǫ poɽtic⁹ p circłm flexe colūneǫ i ſingulis:ǫ iter eas ſb diuo patebāt ſpacia vbi erāt viridaria cū ciſternis eneis.ǫb⁹ aǫ effundebaſ. Pudet dicere h ɽgia ǫł fuerat cū flāma ab iteſtinis iſidiatoɽib⁹ oīa pſumpſit. De excidio tñ h⁹ regie vɽb iſerȷ patebit:vɽbe aūt ſacɽaz reddidit moɽs xpī. Płaɽǫ ſacȷ i eo loco videre poſſumus Amnē.ſ.ǫ lot⁹ē xps. Tēplū ſeu tēpli ruinaz i ǫ docuit.loci vbi cū ſuma būilitate paſſus ē coɽpe vt nos aï paſſionib⁹ libaret.ſepulcɽ vbi ſactiſſimū illo coɽp⁹ ſbſtitit. Et vñ aſcēdit in celū. ǫ ad iudiciū fuerſur⁹ credit. vbi vēȷ ɜ fluctib⁹ ipauit vbi deiǫ elegit idoctos atǫ iopes piſcatoɽes. ǫ rū bamis ɜ rhetib⁹ piſcareſ ipatoɽes ɜ iges gētiuɽ. vbi cecos illuiauit. lepɽoſos mūdauit. paraliticos erexit. moɽtuos ſuſcitauit. Multaǫ ɜ alia ǫ lōge pſeǫ tedioſu cēt.cū ex euāge.nō ſint

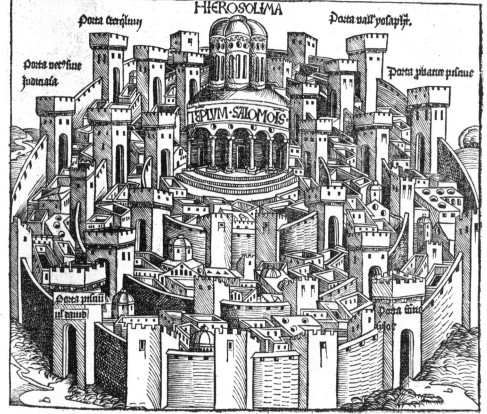

HIEROSOLIMA

TEPLVM·SALOMŌIS

Poɽta Ecɽglim̃   Poɽta vall yoſaphȷ.
Poɽta vet⁹ ſiue Judaica
Poɽta pilani ul dauid
Poɽta phatie piſaue
Poɽta ſtitȷ byfot

23   ANTON KOBERGER, Nuremberg, 1493

     Hartmann Schedel: The Nuremberg Chronicle (Latin)   12⅞ x 18¾

Ca. attn̄. Da. Dauus it̄ercepit ſermonē Carini dicēs: qd ergo petis. ſ. tibi fieri aliud
Ca. ut ducā Philomenā. i. habeā in cōiuḡe. Da. Ridiculū cū exclamatione & irriſio
ne legendū eſt & deeſt hoiem. i. o hoiem. ridiculū. i. plurimū ridendū & illudēdū
Ca. fac ut ad me uenias huc ſiqd poteris. i. uel ſi aliqd poteris inuenire. uel ſi aliquo
modo poteris huc ue／
nire. Da. quid: id ē cur
ueniam ad te. nihil ha／
beo. i. nihil ſum cōmē／
tus quod tibi ex re ſit.
Ca. attamē ſiqd habue
ris ſcilicet uenito. Da.
age hc rtātis aduerbiū
& uix cōcedentis ueniā
ad te ſcilicet Ca. ſiquid

Ca. attn̄. Da. qd ergo. Car. Vt ducā. Da. Ridiculum
Ca. huc face ad me ut uenias／ſi quid poteris. Da.
Quid ueniā: nihil habeo. Ca. Attamē ſi qd. Da age
ueniam. Ca. ſi qd: domi ero. Da. tu miſis (dū exeo)
parūper opire me hic. Mi. quapropter. Da. ita facto
opus eſt. Mi. matura. Da. iam inquā／hic adero.

habueris ſcilicet ero domi: id eſt continebo me domi quo me poſſis facile cōueni
re. Da. tu Miſis operire: id eſt expecta me hic parūper. i. aliquādiu. Mi. quapropter
id eſt quare te opperiar. Da. opuſ eſt facto. i. facere ita. Mi. matura. i. ꝓpera cū mo／
deratione. Da. inquā: i. dico tibi. adero. i. præſens ero. iam. i. ſtatim hic.

24 JOHANNES TRECHSEL, Lyons, 1493

Terence: *Comoediae* 6½ x 9⁵⁄₁₆

Yre hath name for he be
yth the fyre. and is bo
rey of the water as Yſi
dre ſayth / And ſome of
thayre perteyneth to þ
erthi party. and ſome to
heuenly kynde as Beda ſayth / for tho
uer party of thayre is pure & clene. clere
eaſy & ſofte. For meuynge of ſtormes of
wynde & of weder maye not retche ther
to. & ſoo it perteyueth to heuenly kynde /
And the nether party is nyghe to þ ſpe
re of water & of erthe. and is troubli gre
te & thycke corpulent. & full moyſte erthy
vapours as longyth to erthy party / And
this party of ayre bryngith forth of itſel
fe dyuerſe kyndes of thynges / ¶ for as
Yſidre ſayth ayre ſtrongly meuyd ma
kyth wyndes lyghtnynge & thondrynge
drawe togyder it makyth clowdes thyc
ke & reyny / And whan it is congelyd it
makyth ſnowe & hayle. And whan it is
diſparlyd it is clere weder as Yſidre ſa
yth & Beda alſo / And hath more thyk
neſſe & clereneſſe thañe other elementes /
And Conſtantin ſayth þ ayere is a ſym
ple element ſubſtancyalp moyſte & hote
by his owne kynde and ſubſtaůce. he is
moyſte / and by kinde of the roůdneſſe &
ſpere that nygheth therto he is hote. and
therfore by propryte of eyther qualyte þ
ayre ſtretchyth hym kyndly al aboute fro
þ ouer pte of erth & water to the ſpere of
fyre / And by ſubtylte of his ſubſtaůce &
thynneſſe ayre is clere & bryghte / And ſo
by cauſe of his clereneſſe he recepueth in
fluence of the vertue of heuen & Impreſ
ſyon & pryntynge of the lighte of þ ſóne
And ayre peuyth brethe to all men and
beeſtes. & is brethynge of all men & beeſ
tes. and propre dwellinge place of foules
& byrdes / And noo creature wyth ſoule

maye lyue and endure withoute ayre.
¶ And by cauſe of his ſubſtancyall lyg
htneſſe ayre is kyndly meuable and al
ſo chaungable / and maye be tornyd iŋ
to contrary qualytees / Therfore ofte ty
mes he is chaungyd by vapoures of the
erthe and of the ſee / ¶ for yf the vapour
ſtynke and is corrupte and venemouſe /
the ayre is corrupted and Infected to the
whyche ſuche peſtilencyall vapour is me
delyd / ¶ And yf ſmoke is reſolupd and
compth of pure ſubſtaunce and clene. &
is of good ſauour and ſmelle by Incor
poracyon and medelynge wyth ſuche a
ſwete ſmoke the ayre recepupth and ta
kyth a qualitee that is frendly to kynde
¶ Alſo the ayre that biclyppyth vs is to
vs mooſt proufytable and neceſſary for
uedeof breth. and alſo for contynual fou
ſtrynge and nouryſſhynge of the ſpyry
tuell lyfe / ¶ And yf the ayre is clere and
bryghte and clene / thenne the humoures
and ſpyrytes ſhall be clere and bryghte /
And yf he is trowbly aud myſty / humo
urs ſhal be trowblous. and ſpyrytes ſhal
be grete and thycke. and Infecte as Con
ſtantyne ſayth and Philaretus alſo /
¶ And ſoo the ayre is þ element of bodi
es and of ſpyrytes / for ventynge of ayre
compynge to ſpyrytes is cauſe of amende
ment of theym. and of clenſynge and of
purgacyon and of ſwagynge and lettin
ge humours that they be not brennyd /
¶ for ayre recepupd and drawen by the
lounges to the herte. and by the herte to
all the body peupth temperamente ther
to / And ſo the ayre tranſpoſyth and cha
ungyth mooſt the body / for he paſſyth
to the Inuer parties and to the ſpyrytes
And is medelyd wyth the ſubſtaunce of
theym whyche gyuen lyfe to the body /
¶ And ſoo yf that the ayre is pure clere

& iiii

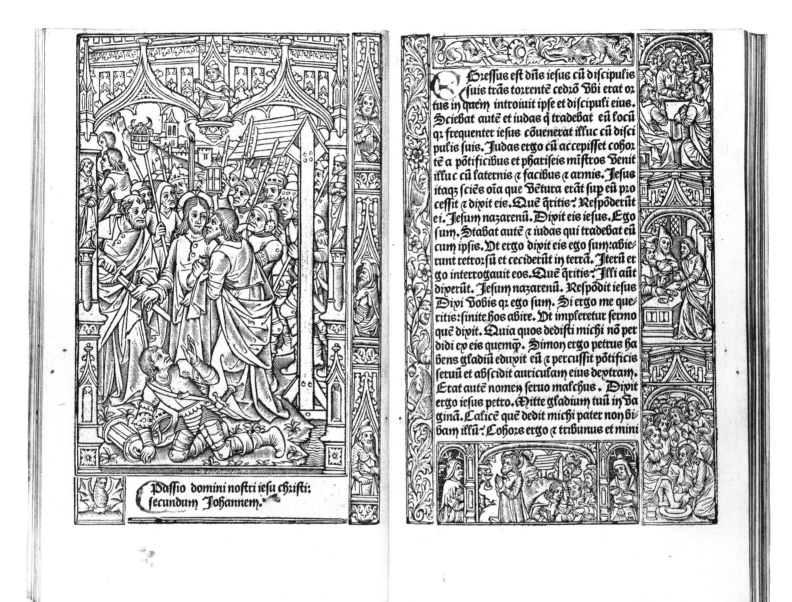

26 PHILIPPE PIGOUCHET, Paris, 1497

Horae in the use of Angers   4¼ x 6½

Ad precedent liure est af/
fez dit du ciel filz de lair
et du iour / mais quant
on explique sa lignee et ge
neracion / on dit titan a/

uoir este son filz de Befte. Et ce dict les
anciens theologiens comme lactence
tesmongne en son liure des diuines in
stitucions. Theodore dit et affeure q̃
la terre fille de demogorgon fut féme

ὅπερ δὲ μὴ διὰ τῶ οἰκείου ἐὰν μὲν ἦ τὸ Δ ὑπὸ τὸ ᾱ, αὕτη
μὲν ἔσται ἀληθής. ἡ ἑτέρα δὲ ψευδής. εἰχωρεῖ γὰρ τὸ ᾱ πλείο
σιν ὑπάρχῃ, ἃ οὐκ ὅσον ὑπά μηλα. ἐὰν δὲ μὴ ἦ τὸ Δ ὑπὸ τὸ
ᾱ, αὕτη μ̄ ἀείδηλον ὅτι ἔστι ψευδής. καταφατικὴ γὰρ λαμ
βάνεται. τὴν δὲ Δ ᾱ οὐδέχεται καὶ ἀληθῆ εἶναι καὶ ψευδῆ.
οὐδὲν γὰρ κωλύει τὸ μὲν ᾱ τῷ Δ μηδενὶ ὑπάρχῃ. τὸ δὲ Δ τῷ β̄
παντὶ. οἷον ζῷον. ἐπιστήμη. ἐπιστήμη δὲ, μουσικῇ. οὐδ' αὖ μήτε
τὸ ᾱ μηδενὶ τῷ Δ. μήτε τὸ Δ μηδενὶ τῷ β̄. φανερὸν οὖν ὅ
τι μὴ ὄντος τῷ μέσου ὑπὸ τὸ ᾱ, ἢ ἀμφοτέρας εἰχωρεῖ ψευ
δεῖς εἶναι καὶ ὁποτέραν ἔτυχε. ποσαχῶς μὲν οὖν καὶ διὰ τί
νων εἰχωρεῖ γίνεσθαι τὰς κατὰ συλλογισμὸν ἀπάτας, ἔν
τε τοῖς ἀμέσοις καὶ ἐν τοῖς δι' ἀποδείξεως, φανερόν. φανερὸν
δὲ καὶ ὅτι εἴ τ' αἴσθησ' ἐκλέλοιπεν, ἀνάγκη καὶ ἐπιστήμη τινὰ ἐκ
λελοιπέναι. ἣν ἀδύνατον λαβεῖν εἴπερ μανθάνομεν, ἢ ἐπα-
γωγῇ ἢ ἀποδείξει. ἔστι δὴ μὲν ἀπόδειξις ἐκ τῶ καθόλου. ἡ δὲ
ἐπαγωγὴ ἐκ τῶν κατὰ μέρος. ἀδύνατον δὲ τὰ καθόλ' θεωρῆ
σαι μὴ δι' ἐπαγωγῆς. ἐπεὶ καὶ τὰ ἐξ ἀφαιρέσεως λεγόμενα, ἔ
σται δι' ἐπαγωγῆς γνώριμα. κἄν τις βούληται γνωρίσαι ποι
εῖν, ὅτι ὑπάρχει ἑκάστῳ γένει ἔνια καὶ εἰ μὴ χωριστά εἰσιν, ᾗ ποι
ὸν δὲ ἕκαστον. ἐπαχθῆναι δὲ μὴ ἔχοντας αἴσθησιν, ἀδύνατον.
τῶ γὰρ καθ' ἕκαστον ἡ αἴσθησις. οὐ γὰρ οὐδέχεται λαβεῖν αὐτῶν
τὴν ἐπιστήμην. οὔτε γὰρ ἐκ τῶν καθόλ' ἄνευ ἐπαγωγῆς. οὔτε
διὰ τῆς ἐπαγωγῆς ἄνευ τῆς αἰσθήσεως. ἔστι δὲ πᾶσ συλλογι
σμὸς διὰ τριῶν ὅρ'. καὶ ὁ μ̄ δεικνῦναι δυνάμενος, ὅτι ὑπάρχει
τὸ ᾱ τῷ γ̄, διὰ τὸ ὑπάρχειν τῷ ᾱ καὶ τοῦτο τῷ γ̄. ὁ δὲ στερη
τικός, τὴν μὲν ἑτέραν πρότασιν ἔχων, ὅτι ὑπάρχει τι ἄλλο
ἄλλῳ. τὴν δὲ ἑτέραν, ὅτι οὐχ ὑπάρχει. φανερὸν οὖν ὅτι αἱ μ̄
ἀρχαὶ καὶ αἱ λεγόμεναι ὑποθέσεις, αὗται εἰσι. λαβόντα γὰρ
ταῦτα, οὕτως ἀνάγκη δεικνῦναι. οἷον ὅτι τὸ ᾱ τῷ γ̄ ὑπάρχει
διὰ τῶ ᾱ. πάλιν δ' ὅτι τὸ ᾱ τῷ β̄. διὰ ἄλλου μέσου. καὶ ὅτι τὸ

28 ALDUS MANUTIUS, Venice, 1495–1498
Aristotle: *Opera* (Greek) 8⅜ x 12¼

falo aliquando fubexefa uentos admi-
ferit aeftuantes , per quos idonea flam-
mae materies incenderetur.   Habes,
unde incendia oriantur Aetnae tuae :
habe nunc quómodo etiam orta per-
durent : in quo quidem nolo ego te illud admirari ,quod uulgus folet:magnũ
effe fcilicet tantas flammas,tam immen
fos ignes poft hominum memoriam fem
per habuiffe, quo alerétur: quid eft enim
magnum ipfi magiftrae rerum omniũ,
et parenti naturae? quid arduum ; quid
illa tandem non poteft ? qui ftellas; qui
folem ; qui coeli conuexa ; qui terras o-
mnes , ac maria ; qui mundum deniq; ip
fum , quo nihil eft admirabilius , uel pò
tius extra quem nihil eft, quod admire-
ris ; faepe fine admiratione intuemur ;
iifdem nobis effe Aetna miraculum poteft ? caue fis tam imprudens filí ; ut tu id
putes:nam fi naturam refpicimus ; nihil
in Aetna eft, quod mirum uoces: fi rem.

POLIPHILO QVIVI NARRA, CHE GLI PARVE AN,
CORA DI DORMIRE, ET ALTRONDE IN SOMNO
RITROVARSE IN VNA CONVALLE, LAQVALE NEL
FINE ERA SERATA DE VNA MIRABILE CLAVSVRA
CVM VNA PORTENTOSA PYRAMIDE, DE ADMI,
RATIONE DIGNA, ET VNO EXCELSO OBELISCO DE
SOPRA. LAQVALE CVM DILIGENTIA ET PIACERE
SVBTILMENTE LA CONSIDEROE.

A SPAVENTEVOLE SILVA, ET CONSTI-
pato Nemore euaso, & gli primi altri lochi per el dolce
somno che se hauea per le fesse & prosternate mébre dif,
fuso relichti, me ritrouai di nouo in uno piu delectabile
sito assai piu che el præcedente. Elquale non era de mon
ti horridi, & crepidinose rupe intorniato, ne falcato di
strumosi iugi. Ma compositamente de grate montagniole di non tro
po altecia. Siluose di giouani quercioli, di roburi, fraxini & Carpi-
ni, & di frondosi Esculi, & Ilice, & di teneri Coryli, & di Alni, & di Ti-
lie, & di Opio, & de infructuosi Oleastri, dispositi secondo laspecto de
gli arboriferi Colli. Et giu al piano erano grate siluule di altri siluatici

arbofcelli, & di floride Genifte, & di multiplice herbe uerdiffime, qului
uidi il Cythifo, La Carice, la commune Cerinthe. La mufcariata Pana-
chia el fiorito ranunculo, & ceruicello, o uero Elaphio, & la feratula, & di
uarie affai nobile, & de molti altri proficui fimplici, & ignote herbe & fio
ri per gli prati difpenfate. Tutta quefta læta regione de uiridura copiofa-
mente adornata fe offeriua. Pofcia poco piu ultra del mediano fuo, io ritrouai uno fabuleto, o uero glareofa plagia, ma in alcuno loco difperfa-
mente, cum alcuni cefpugli de herbatura. Quiui al gliochii mei uno io-
cundiffimo Palmeto fe appræfento, cum le foglie di cultrato mucrone
ad tanta utilitate ad gli ægyptii, del fuo dolciffimo fructo fœcúde & abun
dante. Tra lequale racemofe palme, & picole alcune, & molte mediocre,
& laltre drite erano & excelfe, Electo Signo de uictoria per el refiftere fuo
ad lurgente pondo. Ancora & in quefto loco non trouai incola, ne altro
animale alcuno. Ma peregrinando folitario tra le non denfate, ma inter-
uallate palme fpectatiffime, cogitando delle Rachelaide, Phafelide, & Li
byade, non effere forfa a quefte comparabile. Ecco che uno affermato &
carniuoro lupo alla parte dextra, cum la bucca piena mi apparue.

Francesco Colonna: *Hypnerotomachia Poliphili* 8 x 12¼

E recta, ingenti tedis, atq; ilice secta,
I ntendit'q; locum sertis, et fronde coronat
F unerea, super exuuias, ensem'q; relictum,
E ffigiem'q; toro locat haud ignara futuri.
S tant aræ circum, et crines effusa sacerdos
T er centum tonat ore deos, Herebum'q;, Chaos'q;
T er geminam'q; Hecaten. tria Virginis ora Dianæ.
S parferat et latices simulatos fontis Auerni,
F alcibus et messæ ad lunam quæruntur ahenis
P ubentes herbæ nigri cum lacte ueneni,
Q uæritur et nascentis equi de fronte reuulsus,
E t matri præreptus amor.
I psa mola, manibus'q; piis altaria iuxta
V num exuta pedem uinclis in ueste recincta
T estatur moritura deos, et conscia fati
S ydera, tum si quod non æquo fœdere amantes
C uræ numen habet, iustum'q;, memor'q; precatur.
N ox erat, et placidum carpebant fessa soporem
C orpora per terras, syluæ'q; et sæua quierant
A equora, cum medio uoluuntur sydera lapsu,
C um tacet omnis ager, pecudes, pictæ'q; uolucres,
Q uæ'q; lacus late liquidos, quæq; aspera dumis
R ura tenent, somno positæ sub nocte silenti
L enibant curas, et corda oblita laborum.
A t non infelix animi Phœnissa, nec unquam
S oluitur in somnos, oculis'ue, aut pectore noctem
A ccipit, ingeminant curæ, rursus'q; resurgens
S æuit amor, magno'q; irarum fluctuat æstu.
S ic adeo insistit, secum'q; ita corde uolutat,
E n quid agam? rursus'ne procos irrisa priores

          Experiari

E xperiar? num adum'q; petam connubia supplex,
Q uos ego sum toties iam dedignata maritos?
I liacas igitur classes, atq; ultima Teucrum
I ussa sequar? quia ne auxilio iuuat ante leuatos,
E t bene apud memores ueteris stat gratia facti.
Q uis me autem (fac uelle) sinet? ratibus'q; superbis
I nuisam accipiet? nescis heu perdita, nec dum
L aomedonteæ sentis periuria gentis?
Q uid tum? sola fuga nautas comitabor ouantes?
A n Tyriis, omni'q; manu stipata meorum
I nsequar? et quos Sidonia uix urbe reuelli,
R ursus agam pelago, et uentis dare uela iubebo?
Q uin morere, ut merita es, ferro'q; auerte dolorem.
T u lachrymis euicta meis, tu prima furentem
H is germana malis oneras, atq; obiicis hosti.
N on licuit thalami expertem sine crimine uitam
D egere more feræ, tales nec tangere curas,
N on seruata fides cineri promissa Sichæo.
T antos illa suo rumpebat pectore questus,
A eneas celsa in puppi, iam certus eundi,
C arpebat somnos, rebus iam rite paratis,
H uic se forma dei uultu redeuntis eodem
O btulit in somnis, rursus'q; ita uisa monere est,
O mnia Mercurio similis, uocem'q;, coloremq;,
E t crines flauos, et membra decora iuuentæ.
N ate Dea, potes hoc sub casu ducere somnos?
N ec quæ circumstent te deinde pericula cernis
D emens? nec zephyros audis spirare secundos?
I lla dolos, dirum'q; nefas in pectore uersat,
C erta mori, uario'q; irarum fluctuat æstu.

          G

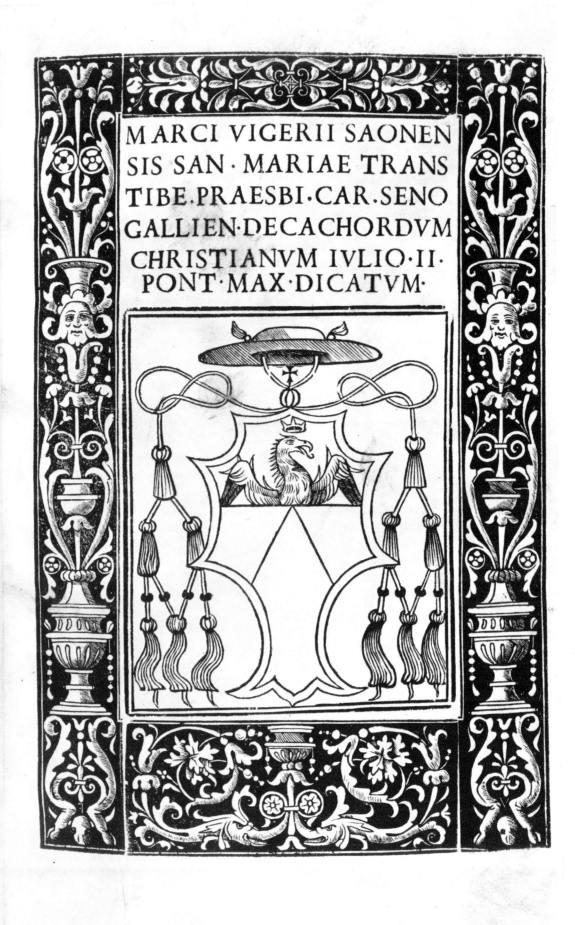

MARCI VIGERII SAONEN
SIS SAN · MARIAE TRANS
TIBE · PRAESBI · CAR · SENO
GALLIEN · DECACHORDVM
CHRISTIANVM IVLIO · II ·
PONT · MAX · DICATVM ·

33   GERSHOM SONCINO, Fano, 1507

Marcus Vigerius: *Decachordum Christianum*   7½ x 12

36

Nfalo dem was nicht züuil
Khein schalkheit als Jch sagen wil
Es was in rechter winterzeit
Darinn gewonnklich vil schnie leit
Ging Onfalo zum Helden dar
Sprach herr Jch sage Euch furwar
Dort steet in der aw vil wildpret
So ferr Jr darzü ein lust het

35 JOHANN SCHÖNSPERGER, Nuremberg, 1517
Melchior Pfinzing: *Theuerdank*   8⅞ x 13⅝

intrare. Quatinus radiis vere lucis

perfusi:ibi in die examinis. leti cum

hymnidicis angelozum chozus valea

mus videre faciem indefessi solis.

Hic mutet vocē suā quasi legendo. Qui
tecū viuit ⁊ regnat in vnitate spirit⁹ san
cti deus. Per oīa scl'a scl'oz. Respōdetur
Amen. *Hic aspergantur cādele aqua be
nedicta ⁊ thurificetur. Deinde sequatur*
Dūs vobiscum. Ozemus.   Oratio.

Omine sancte pater ops lumē in
deficiēs.q̄ es cōditoz oīm luminū
bene ✠ dic hoc lumen tuis fidelibus. in
honoze nois tui poztādum.quatin⁹ a te
sanctificati.atq̄ bñdicti lumine tue clari
tatis accendamur et illuminemur.et p
picius cōcedere digneris: vt veluti eodē
igne.quondā illuminasti moysen famu
lū tuū:ita illumines cozda nr̄a et sensus
nr̄os.quatmus ad visionē eterne clarita
tis puenire mereamur. Per xp̄m dn̄m
nostrum. ℟. Amen. Ozemus.   Oratio.

Ops sempiterne deus q̄ vnigeni
tū tuū āte tēpoza de te genitū. sed
tēpozaliter de maria virgine incarnatū.
lumē verū et indeficiēs. ad repellendas
humani generis tenebzas.et ad incedē
dū lumē fidei et veritatis misisti in mū
dū.cōcede ppicius:vt sicut exterius coz
pozali.ita etiā interius luce spūali.irra
diari mereamur. Per eunð. *Peracta cā
delarū bñdictiōe distribuātur:⁊ interim
cātetur ān. Lumen ad reuelationē.* p̄s. Nūc
dimittis.totus p̄s.dicitur cum Glozia pa
tri.et post vnūquemq̄ ℣. repetatur ān.
❡ Ad missam.   Officium.

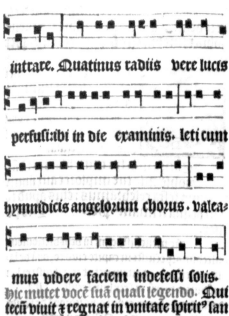

Ulcepim⁹
deus mise
ricozdiā tu
am:in me
dio templi
tui:secūdū
nomē tuū de⁹:ita et laus
tua in fines terre:iustitia
plena est dextera tua. p̄s.
Magnus dn̄s et laudabilis nimis: in ciuitate
dei nostri in monte sancto eius.   Oratio.

Ops sempiterne deus. maiestatē
tuā supplices exozam⁹ vt sicut vni
genitus filius tuus hodierna die. cū no
stre carnis substātia in tēplo est psentat⁹
ita nos facias purificatis tibi mentibus
psētari. Per eūð. *Lcō malachie ppb̄ē. iii*

Ec dicit dn̄s deus Ecce ego mitto
angelū meū.q̄ pzeparabit viā an
te faciē meā. Et statim veniet ad tēpluz
sanctū suum dn̄atoz quē vos queritis: ⁊
angelus testamenti quē vos vultis. Ec
ce eñ venit dicit dn̄s exercituū. Et quis
poterit cogitare diē aduētus eius Et q̄s
stabit ad vidēdū eū: Ipe eñ quasi ignis
cōflans:et quasi herba fullonū. Et sede
bit cōflans et emundās argentū:et pur
gabit filios leui. Et conflabit eos quasi
aurū. et quasi argentū. ⁊ erūt dn̄o offerē
tes sacrificia in iustitia. Et placebit dn̄o
sacrificiū iuda ⁊ hierusalem:sicut dies se
culi. et sicut anni antiqui. Dicit dn̄s:ops
Gz̄. S uscepimus deus miam tuā :in medio
tēpli tui.scd̄m nomē tuū dn̄e:ita et laus tua in fi
nes terre. ℣. Sicut audiuimus.ita et vidimus
in ciuitate dei nostri in mōte sctō eius. A lfa·v
Adozabo ad tēplū sctm̄ tuū:et cōfiteboz noi tuo.
*Hac die dicitur sequentia:licet infra. lxx.
hoc festum contigerit.*   Sequentia.

Ac clara die turma:festiua dat p̄
conia. Mariam cōcrepando:synt
phonia nectarea. Mundi dn̄a:q̄ es sola
castissima:vginū regina. S alutis cau
sa:vite pozta:atq̄ celi referta grā Nam
ad illam sunt nūcia:olim facta angelica.
Aue maria:gratia dei plena per secula
℣. precedens ter dz̄ hac die tin. Mulierū
pia agmina:intra semp benedicta. Vir
go et grauida:mater intacta:ple glozio
la. Qui cōtra maria:hec reddit famina
b.iii.

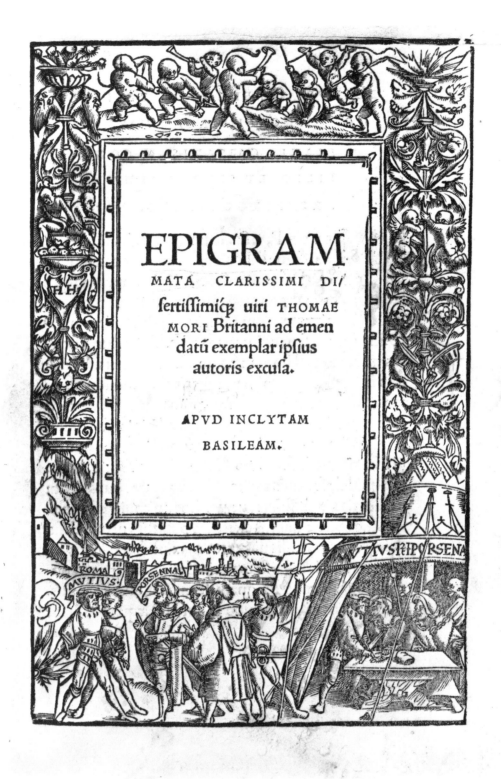

EPIGRAM

MATA CLARISSIMI DI
sertissimíq; uiri THOMAE
MORI Britanni ad emen
datũ exemplar ipsius
autoris excusa.

APVD INCLYTAM
BASILEAM.

37 JOHANN FROBEN, Basle, 1520

Thomas More: *Epigrammata*   5⅞ x 8

CANZONE
DEL TRISSINO
AL SANTISSIMO
CLEMENTE
SETTIMO
P.M.

Prendi dunque Signor la bella impresa,
  Che t'ha serbato il ciel mill'anni, e mille,
  Per la piu gloriosa, che mai fosse;
E certo, al suon de l'honorate squille
  Si moverà l'Europa in tua difesa,
  E farà l'armi insanguinate, e rosse
Del Turco sangue; e pria vorrà, che l'osse
  Restin di là, che la vittoria resti.
  Non è da dubitar, che Dio non presti
  Ogni favor a quel, che ti destina.
  Parmi, che la ruina
  D'e' Turchi posta sia ne' le tue mani,
  E 'l tor la Grecia da le man d'e' cani:
Veggio ne' la mia mente il grave scempio
  Di quelle genti; e con vittoria grande
  Tornarsi lieto il mio Signore in Roma.
Veggio che fiori ogniun d'intorno spande;
  Veggio le spoglie opime andare al tempio;
  Veggio a molti di lauro ornar la chioma;
Veggio legarsi in verso ogn'Idioma,
  Per celebrar si gloriosi fatti;
  Veggio narrar sin le parole, e gliatti,

LUDOVICO ARRIGHI, Rome, c. 1523
G. G. Trissino: *Canzone* 5 x 7¼

℣.Diffusa est gratia in labijs tuis. ℞.Propterea
benedixit te deus in æternũ. Kyrie eleison. Chri
ste eleison. Kyrie eleison. ℣.Domine exaudi ora
tionẽ meã. ℞.Et clamor meus ad te veniat. oͬo
Eus qui salutis æternę beatæ Mariæ vir
ginitate fœcunda humano generi præ
mia preſtitiſti, tribue quæſimus, vt ipſa
pro nobis intercedere ſentiamus, per quã me
ruimus autorem vitæ ſuſcipere dominum no
ſtrum Ieſum Chriſtum filium tuum. ℞. Amẽ.
℀Pro ſanctis añ. Sancti dei omnes intercedere
dignemini pro noſtra omniumͥͥ ſalute. ℣.Læ
tamini in domino, & exultate iuſti. ℞. Et glo
riamini omnes recti corde.   Oratio.
Rotege domine populum tuum, & apo
ſtolorum tuorum Petri, & Pauli, & alio
rum apoſtoloꝛũ patrocinio confidentem
perpetua defenſione conſerua.   Oratio.
Mnes ſancti tui queſimus domine nos
vbiꝗ adiuuẽt, vt dum eoꝛũ merita reco
limus, patrocinia ſentiamus, & pacem
tuã noſtris concede tẽporibus, & ab eccleſia tua
cunctã repelle nequitiã: iter, actus, & volũtates
noſtras, & omniũ famuloꝛũ tuoꝛũ in ſalutis tuę
proſperitãte diſpone. benefactoribͥ noſtris ſem
piterna bona retribue, & omnibus fidelibus de
functis requiẽ æterna concede, Per dominũ no
ſtrũ Ieſum Chriſtũ filiũ tuũ, qui tecũ viuit, & re
gnat in vnitate ſpiritus ſancti deͥ, Per oĩa ſecu
la ſeculoꝛũ. Amẽ. ℣.Dñe exaudi oratio̅ẽ meã.
℞.Et clamor meͥ ad te veniat.℣.Benedicamus
dño.℞.Deo gͬas.℣.Fideliũ animæ defunctoꝛũ
per miſericordiã dei requieſcãt in pace. Amen.

Ad ſextam Verſus.

Eus in adiutorium meũ intende.
℞.Domine ad adiuuandũ me fe
ſtina. Gloria patri, & filio, & ſpi
ritui ſancto. Sicut erat in princi
pio, & nunc, & ſemper, & in ſecu
la ſeculorum. Amen. Alleluia.   Hymnus.

39 GEOFFROY TORY (SIMON DE COLINES), Paris, 1525
   Horae in the use of Rome   5⅜ x 8¼

L Afpiration a doncques fon tra=
uerfant traict fus la ligne centri=
que & diametralle, iuftement au def=
fus du penyl du corps humain, pour
nous monftrer que nofdictes lettres
Attiques veulent eftre fi raifonable=
ment faictes, quelles defirent fentir
en elles auec naturelle raifon, toute
conuenable proportion, & lart dar=
chitecture, qui requiert que le corps
dune maifon ou dũg Palaix foit plus
efleue depuis fon fondement iufques
a fa couuerture, que neft la dicte cou
uerture, qui reprefente le chef de tou
te la maifon. Si la couuerture dune
maifon eft exceffiuemét plufgrande

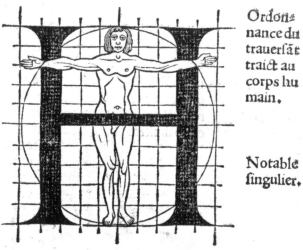

Ordõ=
nance du
trauerfát
traict au
corps hu
main.

Notable
fingulier.

que le corps, la chofe eft difforme, fi non en Halles & Granches, defqlles la cou
uerture commance pour la plus part bien pres de terre, pour euiter limpetuofi
te des grans ventz, & tremblemens de la terre. Doncques noz letttes ne volát
craindre le vent des enuyeux maldifans, veullent eftre erigees folidemét en qua
drature, & brifees, comme iay dict, au deffus de leur ligne centrique & diame=
tralle. Excepte le dict A, qui a fon traict trauerfant iuftement affiz foubz la di=
cte ligne diametralle.

O N peult veoir a la figure cy pres
defignee commát la brifeure de
la lettre K, eft affize fus le point de la li
gne trauerfant par le centre & penyl
du corps humain, ayát les piedz ioints
lequel centre cóme iay toufiours dict,
eft fus le penyl. La brifeure des aultres
lettres que ie laiffe pour cefte heure a
faire, les renuoyant en leur renc abece
daire, fera toufiours auffi affize fus la
dicte ligne centrique & diametralle.

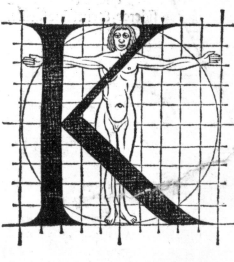

Ordon=
nance
pour la
brifeure
des let=
tres au
corps hu
main.

I Ay dict nagueres ou ie traictois de
lafpiration, que noz lettres Atti=
ques veulent fentir larchitecture : & il
eft vray, confidere que A, reprefente vng pignon de maifon, veu quil eft figu=
re en pignon. Lafpiration H. reprefente le corps dune maifon, entendu que la
partie de deffoubz la ligne trauerfante que iay dicte centrique & diametralle,
eft pour foubz elle conftituer Sales & Chambres baffes. Ft la partie de deffus
eft pour faire pareillement Sales haultes, ou Chambres grandes, & Chambres
moyennes . Le K. a caufe de fa brifeure, nous fignifie degrez a monter en
droicte ligne iufques a vng eftage, & dicelluy pour móter auffi en droicte li=

Lettres
Attiques
veulent
fentir lar=
chitectu=
re.

E.f.

Princeps induetur mœrore. Et
quiescere faciam superbiã po
tentium.

EZECHIE. VII

Vien, prince, auec moy, & delaisse
Honneurs mondains tost finissantz.
Seule suis qui, certes, abaisse
L'orgueil & pompe des puissantz.

Ipse morietur. Quia nõ habuit disci-
plinam, & in multitudine stultitiæ
suæ decipietur.

PROVER. V

Il mourra, Car il n'a receu
En soy aulcune discipline,
Et au nombre sera deceu
De folie qui le domine.

D iij

XLIII.

Vertu de bras fait uoguer la gallée,
  Malgré des uentz ses forces & renfors.
Ce que nous fait demonstrance assez claire,
De ceulx qui ont les couraiges peu fors,
Si d'auenture on n'est par ses effors,
Du premier coup paruenu ou l'on tend,
Sans desespoir oste ce que l'on pretend,
Par aultre endroit il fault qu'on y pouruoye:
Car qui ne peult uenir ou il s'attend,
Par ung costé, si cherche une aultre uoye.

G

De Natura ſtir-
PIVM LIBRI TRES,
Ioanne Ruellio authore.

Cum priuilegio
REGIS.

PARISIIS
Ex officina Simonis Colinæi.
1 5 3 6

43   SIMON DE COLINES, Paris, 1536
     Jean Ruel: *De Natura Stirpium*   9⅞ x 14⅜

aperiat,& humores exugat. Ad eofdem vfus lignum valet, minore tamen effe
ctu. Ex aqua coctum potu torminibus, côuulfis, cruditatibus, venenatorum icti=
bus, item quibus vrina ægrè it, auxilio eft. Capitis vulneribus cum iride ficca
conuenit: offium fquamas extrahit. Spiffamentis vnguentorum ad domandum
5 oleum adijcitur. Calfacit & reficcat in fecundo ordine. Opobalfamum tenuio=
ribus conftat particulis. hoc nihil efficacius effe ad glutinanda vel citra cicatri=
cem vulnera, fibi vulgus perfuafit. Quod fi recipimus, mirû eft Theophraftum,
Diofcoridem, Galenum aut ignoraffe, aut nihil prodidiffe: nam Strabo ad capi=
tis tantum dolores commendauit.

10 ⁌ *Agalochum.* Cap. X X X V I.

Galochum noftro orbi tantum nomine cognitum, quum (vt
Diofcoridi placet) ex Arabia & India lignum aduehatur, thyi=
no fimile, varium punctis maculofúmque, guftu fpiffante, cum
quadam amaritudine. cute corióque verius quàm cortice ve=
15 ftitur, qui penè verficolor eft. Commanducatum aut collutum
decocto, fuauitatem commendat animæ. Aëtius è Græcis pri=
mus quantum equidem inuenerim, à nonnulla fimilitudine coloris aloës, vt ar=
bitror, xylaloën appellauit: quem pofteriorum medicorum vulgus nomine te=
nus infequitur. Officinæ *lignum aloës* vocant. Galenus hoc in fimplicium cenfu
20 filentio prætermifit. Paulus Aegineta Indicum effe lignum teftatur, thuiæ pro=
ximum, odoratum, quod fua iucunditate ijs os commendat, quibus anima fœ=
tet: fingularem in fuffitionibus gratiam habet. Radix denarij pondere pota me=
detur, quibus lentore putri ftomachus languet. Solutum eundem firmat ven=
triculum. iocinerofis, dyfentericis, laterum doloribus præfidio eft. Aëtius arbo=
25 ris effe lignum tradit in varijs orientalium oris, fimul & eorum qui plus ad Au=
ftrum fpectant, natum, nullóque ab alijs lignis difcrimine notatur. Quantum
ad odoris rationem pertinet, non aliàs odoratius futurum, quàm vbi teredini=
bus diu patens computruit: fiquidem marcore fibi fuauiorem adfcifcit odo=
rem. Quare locorum incolæ in frufta diffectum fub terra condunt, & aggere
30 multo obruunt. deinde quum fufficienti tempore emarcuerit, negotiatoribus
vendunt. Aegyptij & alij delibrant ipfum, corticémq; ligni abijciunt. Huius fa=
ftigia fumma quatuor celebrantur, quorum notius eft Indicum, deinde Sapphi=
cû ex vrbe Sappho, Speon & Hygron, quod ipfum deinde in quaternas fpecies
côciditur, de quibus nunc dicere fuerit operofum. Arabicæ familiæ authores vo=
35 lunt agalochum baccas ferre purpureas piperis minuti fimilitudine, quapropter
piperallam cœperût nominare. Sed lignû duntaxat in vfu eft, quod nulli volunt
cariei effe obnoxiû, verum odorem fpirare non anguftû. Quod ex meridie deue=
nit, fragrantius quidé effe, fed tineofum. Agalochum in myrepfico thymiama=
te idem effe putat Aëtius quod taron, quod authore Plinio ex cafiæ & cinnami
40 confinio inuehitur per Nabathæos Troglodytáfq; ijs vicinos. Verùm mágones
officinarû perfæpe pro agalocho afpalathum fubftituunt manifefto errore: quû
agalochum maculis interftinctû, ac punctis quibufdam variatû fpectetur: afpala=
thus verò fubrubefcit, fubtérq; corticê atra quadam rutilat purpura, vnico cô=
tentus colore. is fpinarum vallo cingitur, illud glabrû potius, nec vllis armatum
k.ij.

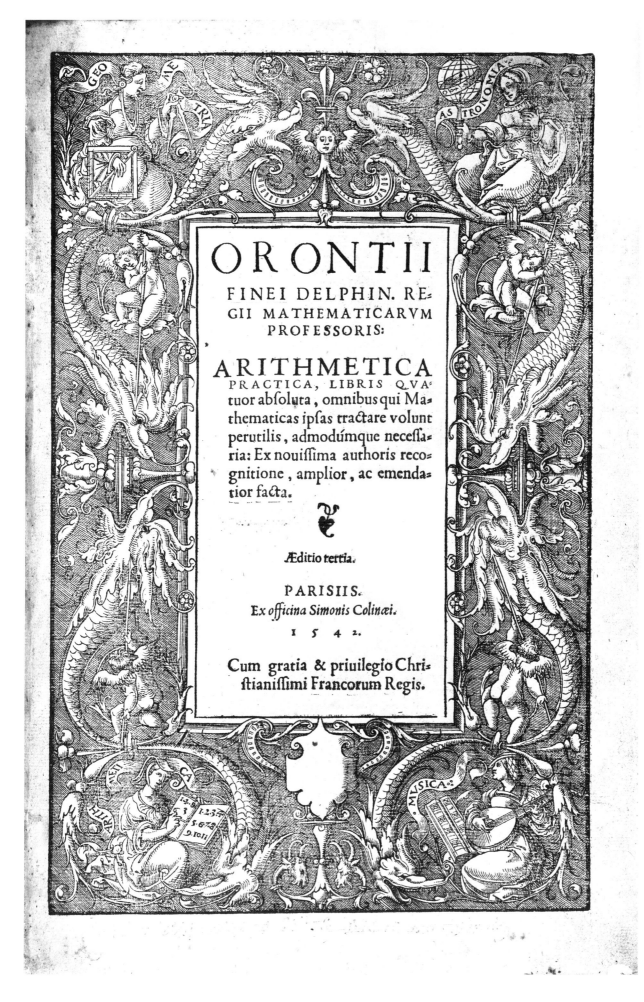

ORONTII

FINEI DELPHIN. RE=
GII MATHEMATICARVM
PROFESSORIS:

ARITHMETICA

PRACTICA, LIBRIS QVA=
tuor abſoluta, omnibus qui Ma=
thematicas ipſas tractare volunt
perutilis, admodúmque neceſſa=
ria: Ex nouiſſima authoris reco=
gnitione, amplior, ac emenda=
tior facta.

Æditio tertia.

PARISIIS.
Ex officina Simonis Colinæi.
1 5 4 2.

Cum gratia & priuilegio Chri=
ſtianiſſimi Francorum Regis.

c Creticum,cuius etiam herbæ notę omnes huic noſtrę cõueniunt,necɣ etiam facul-
tates quas ſimiles Dauco cretico habet,diſcrepãt. Alterum Apio ſylueſtri,uel,ut
antea diximus,Laſerpitio ſimile eſt:aromatũ modo odoratum,acre,guſtanti odoratum & feruens. Tertiũ folijs Coriandro aſsimilatur,flore candido,capite & ſemine Anethi,in quo umbella erraticæ Paſtinacæ ſimilis eſt,ſemine oblongo ple-
num,ſapore ut Cuminum acri.

LOCVS.

Primum in petroſis & apricis locis naſcitur,nuſquam uerò in Germania copio-
ſius quàm in Martianæ ſyluæ quibuſdam pratis prouenit. Reliqua duo genera in
altis montibus gignuntur.

TEMPVS.

Iunio &Iulio menſibus florent.

TEMPERAMENTVM.

Semen Dauci admodum calefacit & exiccat.Idem etiam,ſed minori efficacia,fa-
cit herba.

VIRES. EX DIOSCORIDE.

Omnium Daucorum ſemen calefaciendi uim obtinet.Potum menſes,fœtus,&
urinas mouet.Torminibus liberat.Tuſſes diutinas lenit. Succurrit phalangiorum
morſibus cum uino potum.Oedemata illitum diſcutit. Ex alijs ſeminis tantũ uſus
eſt,ex Cretico radicis etiam,quæ cum uino præſertim ad uenenata bibitur.

EX GALENO.

Dauci ſemen efficax admodum tum mouendæ urinæ medicamentũ, tum pro-
uocandis menſibus.Multum etiam diſcutere foris impoſitum ualet.Ipſa etiam her
ba eandem uim obtinet, ſemine tamen inferiorem, nimirum ob aqueæ humidita-
D tis miſturam.

EX PLINIO.

Vehementer urinam impellit.Creticum magis contra ſerpentes pollet.Bibitur
è uino drachma una,datur & quadrupedibus percuſsis,aduerſatur phalangio,ca-
pitis dolori medetur,tuſsi ſubuenit,ſtranguriæ medetur drachma ſeminis. Eius ra
dix in uino pota,dyſenteriam ſiſtit.Contuſis & euerſis potũ duobus obolis in mul
ſi cyathis tribus ſubuenit, aut ſi febris adſit in aqua mulſa. Menſes & ſecundas po-
tum facillimè pellit.Calculos eijcit.Folia omnia tela infixa corpori extrahunt.

DE DRACONTIO MAGNO CAP. LXXXVI.

NOMINA.

Serpentaria maior.
Dracunculus un de dicta.

Colubrina.

PAKONTIA μεγάλη,ἢ δρακόντιον μέγα Græcis, Dracunculus maior Latinis,nonnullis Serpentaria maior dicitur. Officinis ignota herba. Ger-
mani Schlangenkraut uocant.Nomen autem à figura ſumpſit: caulis
enim glaber, purpureiſɣ reſperſus lituris, uerſicolori facie, corpus an-
guinum repreſentat & æquat longitudine. Vertex quoque ſinuoſo oris hiatu linguam exerens cruentam,caput exprimit.Atque hinc eſt quod ueteribus etiam Ro-
manis Colubrina ac Serpentaria nuncupata ſit: uel ſic dicta, Plinio autore, quod è
terra ad primas ſerpentiũ uernationes exeat,rurſuſɣ cum ijſdem ſe in terram recon
dat,nec omnino occultata ea appareat ſerpens.

FORMA.

Caulē habet glabrũ læuumɣ,rectũ,bicubitalē,baculi craſsitudine,uerſicolorē, ut
angui ſimilis uideat̃,purpureis etiã maculis abundat. Folia fert Rumicis inflexa, &
plicata. Fructũ in ſummo caule racemoſum,coloris inter initia cineracei, poſtea ɵ
maturuit crocei &punicei.Radicē grandē, rotundã, candidã, tenui cortice ueſtitã.
Ex qua deliniatione omnib. perſpicuũ ſit,plantã eam cuius picturã exhibemus,eſſe
Dracunculũ maiorē.Simplici enim caule attolliť, binũ cubitûm alto,lęui glabróue,
recto, baculi craſsitudine, uerſicolorib. anguiũ maculis uariegato, purpureis etiã
intercur-

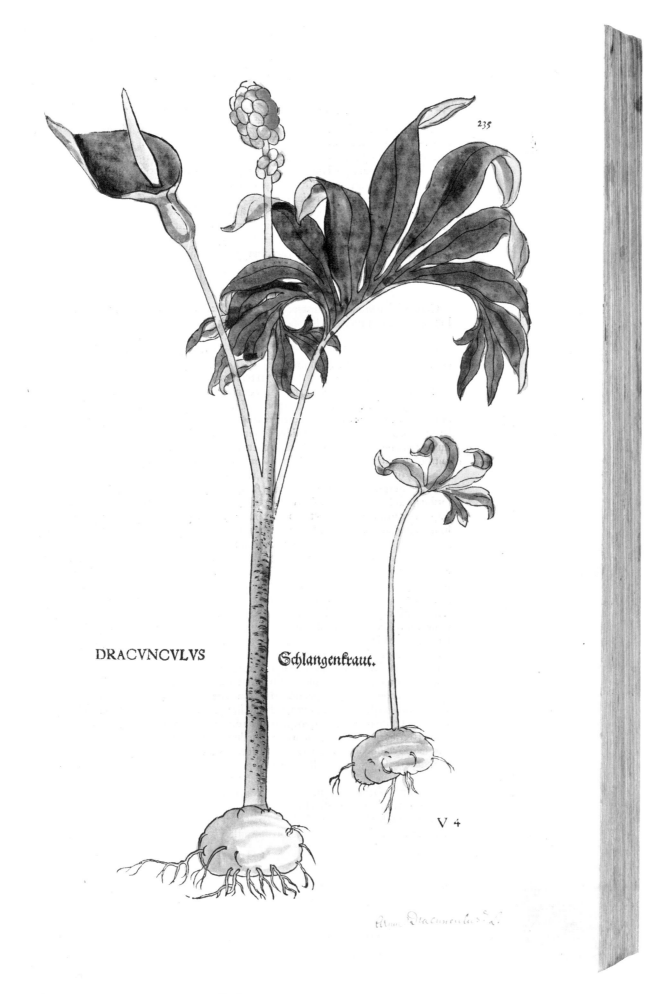

DRACVNCVLVS   Schlangenkraut.

235

V 4

47   MICHAEL ISENGRIN, Basle, 1542

Leonhard Fuchs: *De Historia Stirpium*   9⅝ x 14⅞

femur à coxendicis offe diuulfi. trahentiḗ mihi, unà cum brachijs ac manibus, fcapulæ quoḗ
fubfecutę funt. deerāt tamen alterius manus digiti, & patella utraḗ, unà cum pede altero. Quu
itaḗ crura & brachia (relicto cū totius corporis trunco, capite) clam repetitis uicibus domum
detuliffem, ut thoracē qui catena alte firmabatur nancifcerer, extra ciuitatē me uefperi excludi
paffus fum : tantoḗ obtinendorum offium defiderio & ftudio ardebam, ut media nocte in illa
corporum multitudine quod expetebā diuellere nō horruerim, haud mediocri labore ac indu
ftria, fine arbitris, palum cōfcendens. Verū detracta offa procul illinc deferēs, in fecretiori loco
condidi, fruftatimḗ altera die per aliā ciuitatis portā domū detuli. Porrò quū ligamenta refcin
dere cœpiffem, nihil ob egregiā eorum duriciē promoui, ac illa feruēte aqua emollire coactus
fum : utḗ uoti compos redderer, omnia offa tandē tacite ita coxi, illisḗ emūdatis illud fceleton
extruxi, quod Louanij apud longe amicifsimum mihi GISBERTVM CARBONEM,
infignē ac uario difciplinarū genere inftructū medicū, meumḗ à puero ftudiorū commilitonē
afferuatur. Atḗ id fceleton adeò præpoperē paraui, & manū ac pedem, duasḗ patellas nō mi
nori labore & induftria aliunde conquifiui, ut omnibus perfuaferim id me Lutetia aduexiffe,
quo omnē fubreptorū offium fufpicionē delerem. quamuis eius urbis Prætor poftmodū adeò
medicinæ candidatorū ftudijs fauit, ut quoduis corpus à fe impetrari gauderet: ac ipfe nō uul
gariter Anatomes cognitione afficeretur, mihiḗ illic Anatomen adminiftranti fedulò aftaret.
Quum igitur primum tentantibus nobis adeò promptè negociū fuccefferit, quid nunc futurū
exiftimandum, poftquam cōponendi quoḗ rationem alijs defcripfimus? & præter fubiungen
das nunc tabulas, in plurimis Academijs, uel noftra opera, fceleta uifuntur? Verùm non ho
minis folum offa, fed, uel Galeni nomine, fimiæ & canum, ac Ariftotelis etiam gratia auium pi
fciumḗ & reptilium inuicem connexa, aut faltem difiuncta apud medicinæ & naturalis philo
fophiæ ftudiofum effe oporteret. Nifi forte hanc philofophiæ partē ad nos nihil pertinere ar
bitremur, fatisḗ effe nobis perfuadeamus, fi noftris fyrupis, citra Anatomen imponere morta
libus, & loculos opplere pofsimus.

DE OSSIVM NVMERO.   CAP. LX.

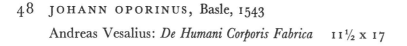

PARVM dubito plerofḗ alicubi à me offium quoḗ numerū defideratu
ros: quibus nullum aliud confiliū dari uelim, quàm, ut ex fingulis huius li
bri Capitibus illū petant. prolixius enim effet, hic omnia recēfere. Quāuis
ne tantillum laboris fubterfugiffe uidear, non enumeratis appendicibus,
& offibus ita ut in prouectioris ætatis hominibus fe habent, cōftitutis, ad
hunc modum ea recenfere nihil impediet. Caluariæ offa uiginti funt, octo
quidem capitis, & maxillæ fuperioris duodecim : ita tamen, ut iugalia pri
uatim nō enumerentur, quum quorundam illorum uiginti offium partes feu fedes tantū fint,
propriaḗ circūfcriptione deftituantur. auditus organi offa quatuor funt, duo fcilicet ad fingu
las aures. dentes funt triginta duo. maxillæ inferioris os unicum. offis v referentis officula funt
ferè undecim. Vertebræ uiginti quatuor. facri offis offa fex. coccygis autem quatuor. coftæ ui
ginti quatuor. Pectoris offis tria numerauimus offa, alijs autē feptena recenfentur. fed age hac
enumeratione tria tantum fint: & aliàs ex tuo arbitratu, quot uifum tibi fuerit. fcapulæ duæ: to
tidem clauiculæ. & humeri duo. ulnæ duæ. radij duo. brachialis offa fedecim, utriufḗ fcilicet
manus octo. octo item poftbrachialis offa, in utraque manu quatuor. digitorum offa triginta:
utriufḗ manus nimirū quindecim. fefamina officula in fingulis manibus ut minimū funt duo
decim, ac proinde iam uiginti quatuor illa in manibus recenfeamus. Offa facri offis lateribus
commiffa, duo. femora duo. duo tibiarū offa. fibulæ duæ. duæ patellæ. duæ calces. tali duo. na
uicularia offa duo. tarfi offa octo, in utroḗ pede quatuor. decem pedij offa, in utroḗ pede quin
que. uiginti octo digitorum pedis offa, cuiufḗ nimirum pedis quatuordecim. pedis fefamina
ofsicula fimiliter atḗ in manibus uiginti quatuor, quāuis nonnulla fint prorfus cartilaginea. Ac
proinde fi hæc offa in unum numerū reijcies, uniuerfa erunt (fi rectè addo) trecēta & quatuor.
quibus fi pectoris offa quatuor adhuc adijci uelles, & maxillæ inferioris duo offa ftatueres, ef
fent trecenta & feptem. Verum fi priuatim omnes appendices (quū offa fint propria circūfcri
ptione in pueris terminata) enumerare lubeat, facile dictum nuper numerū femel, ac rurfus di
midio duplicares. quod uel hinc colliges, fi uertebras, femora, tibiæ offa, atque alia quæ multis
appendicibus donantur, in memoriā reuocaueris. Rurfus fi offa ut in pueris uifuntur fubduxe
ris, Dij boni quantū ofsium aceruum cumulabis? quum omnes uertebræ, aut tribus aut duo
bus conftent offibus: & offa quæ facro coarctantur, tribus, idḗ generis reliqua : adeò ut cuiḗ
fuo arbitratu ofsium numerum confingere fit integrum.

HVMA

HVMANI COR-
SIMVL COMPACTO-
EX FACIE EXPRES-

PORIS OSSIVM
RVM ANTERIORI
SIO.

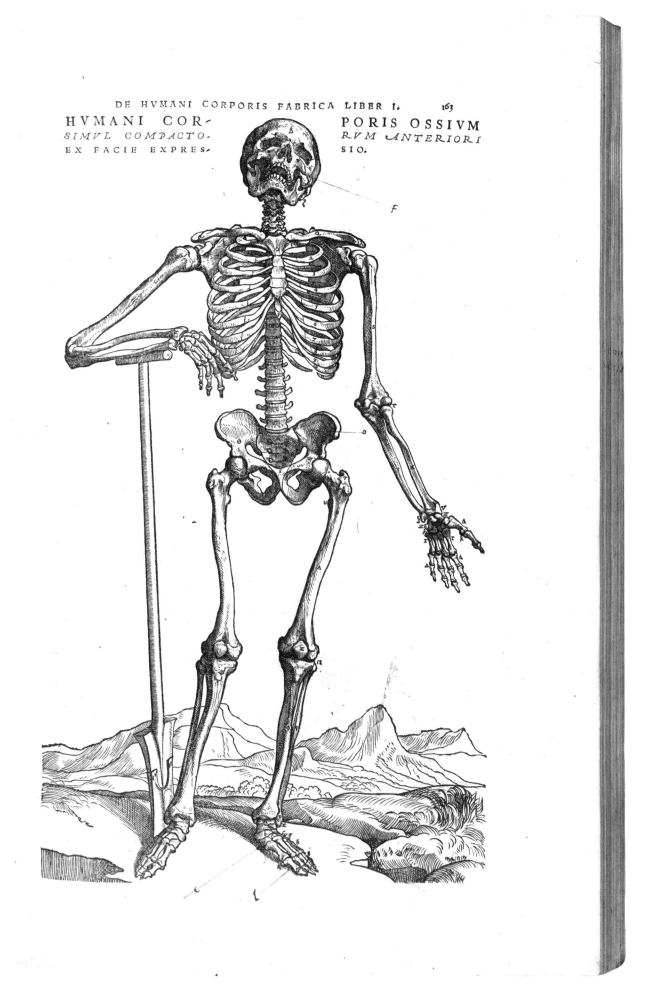

49   JOHANN OPORINUS, Basle, 1543

Andreas Vesalius: *De Humani Corporis Fabrica*   11½ x 17

BIBLIA

HEBRAEA, Chaldæa, Græca & Latina nomina virorum, mulierum, populorum, idolo-
rum, vrbium, fluuiorum, montium, cæterorúmque locorum quæ in Bibliis leguntur, re-
stituta, cum Latina interpretatione.
Locorum descriptio è Cosmographis.

INDEX præterea rerum & sententiarum quæ in iisdem Bibliis continentur.

HIS accesserunt schemata Tabernaculi Mosaici, & Templi Salomonis, quæ præeunte Francisco Vatablo Hebraicarum literarum Regio professore doctissimo, summa arte & fide
expressa sunt.

PARISIIS

EX OFFICINA   TYPOGRAPHI REGII.

M.   D.   XL.

CVM PRIVILEGIO REGIS.

Liber Deuteronomii, hebraice
Elle haddebarim.

CAP. I.

HAEC SVNT VERBA quæ locutus eſt Moyſes ad omnem Iſ- A
rael trãs Iordanem in ſolitudine campeſtri, contra Mare-rubrum,
inter Pharan & Thophel & Laban & Haſeroth, vbi auri eſt pluri-
mum.vndecim diebus de Horeb per viam mõtis Seir vſque ad Ca-
def-barne. Quadrageſimo anno, vndecimo mēſe,prima die mē-
ſis locutus eſt Moyſes ad filios Iſrael omnia quæ præceperat illi
Dominus vt diceret eis:‖poſtquã percuſſit Sehon regē Amorrhæorũ,qui habitauit in Heſebon: & Og regē Baſan,qui manſit in Aſta-
roth,& in Edrái trãs Iordanē in Terra-Moab.Cœpítq; Moyſes ex- B
planare legē & dicere,Dominus Deus noſter locutus eſt ad nos in Horeb,dicens, Sufficit vobis quod in hoc mõte mãſiſtis:reuertimini,& venite ad montē Amorrhæorũ,& ad cætera quæ
ei proxima ſunt campeſtria atque montana & humiliora loca contra meridiem,& iuxta litus
maris,Terram-Chananæorũ,& Libani vſque ad flumē magnũ Euphraten.En,inquit, tradidi
vobis: ingredimini & poſſidete eam, ſuper qua iurauit Dominus patribus veſtris Abraham,
Iſaac,& Iacob,vt daret illã eis,& ſemini eorũ poſt eos. Dixíque vobis illo in tempore, Non
poſſum ſolus ſuſtinere vos: quia Dominus Deus veſter multiplicauit vos, & eſtis hodie ſicut
ſtellæ cæli,plurimi.Dominus Deus patrũ veſtrorũ addat ad hunc numerũ multa milia,& be- C
nedicat vobis ſicut locutus eſt. Non valeo ſolus negotia veſtra ſuſtinere,& põdus ac iurgia.
Date ex vobis viros ſapientes & gnaros, quorũ conuerſatio ſit probata in tribubus veſtris, vt
ponã eos vobis principes.Tunc reſpõdiſtis mihi,Bona res eſt quã vis facere.Tulíque de tribubus veſtris viros ſapientes & nobiles,& conſtitui eos principes,tribunos,& cēturiones,& quin-
quagenarios ac decanos,qui docerent vos ſingula. Præcepíq; eis,dicēs,Audite illos,&‖quod
iuſtum eſt iudicate: ſiue ciuis ſit ille,ſiue peregrinus.‖Nulla erit diſtantia perſonarum,ita par-
uum audietis vt magnum:nec accipietis cuiuſquam perſonã,quia Dei iudicium eſt. Quòd ſi
difficile vobis viſum aliquid fuerit, referte ad me, & ego audiam. Præcepíque omnia quæ fa- D
cere deberetis. Profecti autem de Horeb, tranſiuimus per eremum terribilē & maximã ſo-
litudinem'quam vidiſtis,per viam mõtis Amorrhæi, ſicut præceperat Dominus Deus noſter
nobis. Cúmq; veniſſemus in Cadeſ-barne,dixi vobis,Veniſtis ad montē Amorrhæi,quē Dominus Deus'veſter daturus eſt vobis.'Vide Terrã quã Dominus Deus tuus'dabit'tibi:aſcende
& poſſide eam,ſicut locutus eſt Dominus Deus noſter patribus tuis:noli timere, nec quicquã
paueas. Et acceſſiſtis ad me omnes,atque dixiſtis, Mittamus viros qui conſyderēt Terrã: &
renuntient per quod iter debeamus aſcendere,& ad quas pergere ciuitates. Cúmque mihi ſer
mo placuiſſet,miſi ex vobis duodecim viros,ſingulos de tribubus ſuis.Qui cum perrexiſſent,
& aſcendiſſent in montana, venerunt vſque ad Vallem-botri:& conſyderata terra ſumētes de
fructibus eius,vt oſtenderēt hubertatē,attulerũt ad nos,atque dixerũt,Bona eſt Terra quã Do E
minus Deus noſter daturus eſt nobis. Et noluiſtis aſcendere,ſed increduli ad ſermonem Domini Dei'noſtri' murmuraſtis in tabernaculis veſtris,atque dixiſtis, Odit nos Dominus,& id-
circo eduxit nos de Terra-AEgypti, vt traderet nos in manu Amorrhæi, atque deleret. Quò
aſcēdemus?nũtii terruerũt cor noſtrũ,dicētes, Maxima multitudo eſt, & nobis ſtatura proce-
rior:vrbes magnæ,& ad cælum vſque munitæ, filios enacim vidimus ibi.Et dixi vobis,Nolite
metuere,nec timeatis eos:Dominus Deus qui ductor eſt veſter,pro vobis ipſe pugnabit, ſicut
fecit in AEgypto cunctis videntibus,& in ſolitudine ipſi vidiſtis. Portauit te Dominus Deus
tuus, vt ſolet homo geſtare paruulũ filiũ ſuũ,in omni via per quã ambulaſtis, donec veniretis
ad locũ iſtũ.Et nec ſic quidē credidiſtis Domino Deo veſtro,qui præceſſit vos in via,& meta- F
tus eſt locũ in quo tētoria figere deberetis,‖nocte oſtendēs vobis iter per ignē,& die per colũ-
nam nubis. Cúmq; audiſſet Dominus voce ſermonũ veſtrorũ, iratus iurauit & ait,Non videbit quiſpiam de hominibus generationis huius peſſimæ Terrã bonã,quã ſub iuramēto pollicitus ſum patribus veſtris:præter Caleb filiũ Iephone. ipſe enim videbit eã,& ipſi dabo Terrã quã calcauit,& filiis eius,quia ſecutus eſt Dominũ. Nec mirãda indignatio in populũ,cum

Breuis repeti-
tio geſtorũ,à
manſione in
mõte Horeb,
vſque ad man
ſionem in Ca-
deſ-barne.

Nume.11.e.

Moyſes legem
explanat.

Moyſes nõ va
lens ſolus ad-
miniſtrare po
pulũ,cõſtituit
ſecũ & alios.
exod.18.c.

Pricipes qua-
les eſſe debeãt

Iudiciũ iuſtũ.
iohan.7.d.
Infra 16.d.le-
uit.19.c. pro-
uer.24.c. eccſi
42.a,iac.2.a.

Mittuntur ex-
ploratores. nu
me.13.a.

Popul⁹ incre-
dulus nõ vult
aſcendere.

Exod.13.d.

Incredulus po
pulus non vi-
debit Terram
promiſſam.
num.14 d.
Caleb.

*&(Vet.Di.o.
Ge.p.

▸Vet.Di.l.Ge.l.
p.S.

'noſter datur⁹ eſt
nobis.(Vet.Di.o.
l.Ge.o.l.p.
'dat(Vet.Ge.p.
S.Di.o.

'veſtri(Vet.Cõpl.

51 ROBERT ESTIENNE, Paris, 1540

Bible in Latin 11⅛ x 17

Ζωγράφοι μὲν σανίσι καὶ τοίχοις τὰς παλαιὰς ἐγγράφοντες ἱστορίας, τέρπουσι μὲν τοὺς ὁρῶντας προσφέρουσι. τῶν δὲ γεγενημένων τὴν μνήμην, ἐπὶ πλεῖστον αἰθοῦσαν φυλάττουσι. λογογράφοι δὲ αὐτὶ μὲν σανίδων, ἢ βίβλοις, αὐτῇ δὲ χρωμάτων, τοῖς τῶν λόγων ἄνθεσι κεχρημένοι, διαρκεστέραν τε μονιμωτέραν τῶν πεπραγμένων ποιοῦσι τὴν μνήμην. ὁ γὰρ χρόνος λωβᾶται τὴν ζωγράφων τὴν τέχνην. τούτου δὴ χάριν κἀγὼ τῆς ἐκκλησιαστικῆς ἱστορίας τὰ λείποντα συγγράψαι πειράσομαι. οὐ γὰρ ὅσιον ὡρᾶν λαμπροτάτων ἔργων καὶ ὀνησιφόρων διηγημάτων τὸ κλέος παριδεῖν, ὑπὸ τῆς λήθης συλώμενον. διὰ γὰρ δὴ τοῦτο καὶ τῶν σιωπήσαι τινὲς, ἐπὶ τόνδε με τὸν πόνον πολλάκις προύτρεψαν. ἐγὼ δὲ τῇ μὲν ἐμαυτοῦ δυνάμει τόδε τὸ ἔργον σταθμώμενος, τὴν ἐγχείρησιν ὀρρωδῶ. θαρρῶν δὲ τῷ φιλοτίμῳ δοτῆρι τῶν ἀγαθῶν, μείζοσιν ἢ κατ' ἐμαυτὸν ἐγχειρῶ. Εὐσέβιος μὲν οὖν ὁ παλαιστῖνος, ἀπὸ τῶν ἱερῶν ἀποστόλων τῆς ἱστορίας ἀρξάμενος, μέχρι τῆς κωνσταντίνου θεοφιλοῦς βασιλείας, τὰ τῇ ἐκκλησίας συμβεβηκότα συνέγραψεν. ἐγὼ δὲ τῆς συγγραφῆς ἐκείνης τὸ τέλος, ἀρχὴν τῆς ἱστορίας ποιήσομαι.

α'. Τῶν δυσσεβῶν ἐκείνων καὶ δυσσεβεῖν καταλυθέντων τυράννων, μαξεντίου φημὶ καὶ μαξιμίνου καὶ λικιννίου, κατηυνάσθη τῆς ἐκκλησίας ἡ ζάλη, καὶ οἱ δυσώδεις ἐκεῖνοι καθάπερ τινὲς καθηγίδες ἐκινήθησαν, καὶ γαλήνης λοιπὸν ἀπήλαυε σαφοῦς, τῶν στροβίλων παυσαμένων ἀνέμων. καὶ κωνσταντῖνος δὲ ὁ πολυθρύλλητος βασιλεύς, ὃς οὐκ ἀπ' ἀνθρώπων, οὐδὲ δι' ἀνθρώπου, ἀλλ' οὐρανόθεν κατὰ τὸν θεῖον ἀπόστολον τῆς κλήσεως ταύτης ἔτυχε, τὴν αὐτῆς ἐφυτεύσατο. νόμους γὰρ ἔγραψε, τῶν μὲν εἰδώλοις ἀπείργων, δομᾶσθαι δὲ τὰς ἐκκλησίας προσευρίσαι. καὶ ἐξ ἀρχόντας μὲν πιστῇ κοσμουμένοις ἐφίστη τοῖς ἔθνεσι, γραφὴν κελεύων τοῖς ἱερέας, καὶ τοῖς παριοῦσιν εἰς τούτοις ὑπεχθροῦσιν, ὀλέθρου ἀπειλῶν. ὥστε δὴ, οἱ μὲν τὰς καταλυθείσας ἐκκλησίας ἀνήγειραν· οἱ δὲ ἑτέρας εὐρυτέρας ᾠκοδόμουν καὶ λαμπροτέρας. τούτων οὕτω δρωμένων, τὰ μὲν ἡμέτερα, χαρᾶς ἦν ἔμπλεα καὶ θυμηδίας· τὰ δὲ τῶν ἐναντίων, κατηφείας καὶ ἀθυμίας μεστά. τὰ μὲν γὰρ τῶν εἰδώλων ἀπεκέκλειστο τεμένη· ἐν δὲ ταῖς ἐκκλησίαις ἑορταὶ καὶ πανηγύρεις ἐπετελοῦντο συχναί. ἀλλ' ὁ παμπόνηρος καὶ βάσκανος δαίμων, ὁ τῶν ἀνθρώπων ἀλάστωρ, οὐκ ἤνεγκεν εὖ οὐρείων φερομένην τὴν ἐκκλησίαν ὁρᾶν, ἀλλὰ ταῖς κακομηχάνοις ἐκίνει βουλὰς καταλῦσαι φιλονεικῶν τὴν ὑπὸ τοῦ ποιητοῦ καὶ δεσπότου τῶν ὅλων κυβερνωμένην.

✣ACTIVS ❧

Actius egregii artificis manu depictus in templo Diui Gothardi ad læuam introeuntibus conspicitur.
Videmus etiam parem eius effigiem in templo Diui Marci, extra Beatricem portam . Sed statua exi-
miæ cælaturæ ex Lunensi marmore sepulchro im-
posita,depictæ similitudinem exactè reddit.

Paolo Giovio: *Vitae . . . Mediolani Principum*   6½ x 9⅜

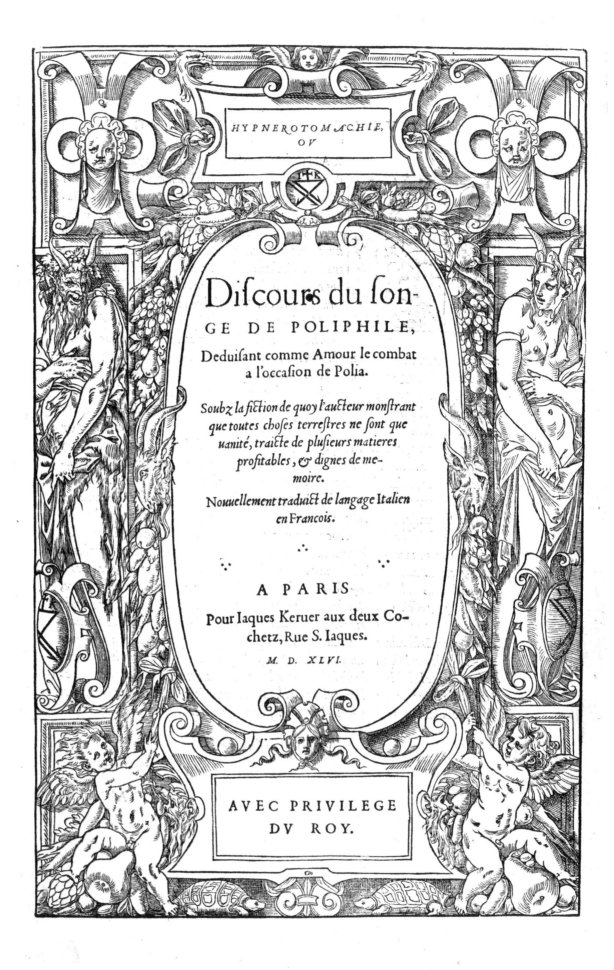

HYPNEROTOMACHIE,
OV

Discours du son-
GE DE POLIPHILE,
Deduisant comme Amour le combat
a l'occasion de Polia.

Soubz la fiction de quoy l'aucteur monstrant
que toutes choses terrestres ne sont que
uanité, traicte de plusieurs matieres
profitables, & dignes de memoire.

Nouuellement traduict de langage Italien
en Francois.

A PARIS
Pour Iaques Keruer aux deux Co-
chetz, Rue S. Iaques.
M. D. XLVI.

AVEC PRIVILEGE
DV ROY.

54 JACQUES KERVER (LOUIS CYANEUS), Paris, 1546
Francesco Colonna: *Discours du Songe de Poliphile* 8¼ x 12¼

L'ARCHITETTVRA
DI LEONBATISTA
ALBERTI

Tradotta in lingua Fiorentina da Cosimo
Bartoli Gentil'huomo & Accade-
mico Fiorentino.

Con la aggiunta de
Disegni.

IN FIRENZE.　　　M. D. L.

Appresso Lorenzo Torrentino Impressor Ducale.

TRIOMPHO QVARTO DI

MESSER FRANCESCO PETRARCA,
NEL QVALE SI VEDE LA FAMA DELLE
NOSTRE OPERATIONI, MAL GRADO
DELLA MORTE, RESTAR NELLA
MEMORIA DE GLI HVOMINI.

DEL TRIOMPHO DI FAMA.
CAPITOLO PRIMO.

D A P O I, *che morte
triomphò nel uol=
to,
Che di me spesso triom
phar solea;
Et fu del nostro mon
do il suo sol tolito;
Partißi quella dispie=
tata & rea*

*Pallida in uista, horribile & superba,
Che'l lume di beltate spento hauea;
Quando mirando intorno su per l'herba
Vidi da l'altra parte giunger quella,
Che trahe l'huom del sepolcro, e'n uita il serba.*

H AVENDO
noi ueduto il sen-
sitiuo appetito del
mondo, La ragio
ne de l'appetito,
Et la morte de la
ragione triomphare, Hora nel pre
sente quarto triopho, in tre cap.
distinto, uedremo, com'a principio dicemmo, la fama da infinita
moltitudine d'huomini famosi ac
compagnata, a la morte predomi
nare. Onde'l Poeta dice, Che da-
poi che morte triomphò del bel
uolto di Madonna Laura per essa
ragione intesa, quale spesse uolte
di lui soleua triomphare, e del no

MARGVERITES

DE LA MARGVERITE

DES PRINCESSES,

TRESILLVSTRE

ROYNE

DE

NAVARRE.

A LYON,

PAR IEAN DE TOVRNES.

M. D. XLVII.

Auec Priuilege pour six ans.

LA COCHE. 319

Ainsi pourrez, par ce tresseur refuge
Auoir le Roy que desirez, pour iuge.
Qui sans refus d'vn cœur doux & humain
Regardera venant de telle main
Tout ce discours ; qui est digne de luy,
Et l'Escriture aura pour son appuy
Celle qui peult la defendre de blasme,
Et l'excuser comme vne œuure de femme.
Ainsi pourra couurir sa charité
Deuant les yeux de la seuerité
Du Roy qui fait à tous iugement droit,
Ce que i'ay trop failly en chasque endroit.

Lors d'vn accord, sur le poinct, nous trouuasmes
Dedens la Coche au logis arriuasmes.
La nuict me feit aux trois donner l'Adieu
Non pour dormir ; mais pour trouuer vn lieu,

Ou

57 JEAN DE TOURNES, Lyons, 1547

Marguerite de Navarre: *Marguerites de la Marguerite*   4¼ x 6½

seens, qui n'estoiét point des enfans d'Israël:
c'estasauoir, les enfans de ceux là, qui estoiét
demourez apres eux en la terre, lesquelz les p
enfans d'Israël n'auoient peu abolir. Mais
Salomon ne permit point seruir aucun des
enfans d'Israël: mais ilz estoient gens de
guerre, & ses ministres, & ses Princes, & ses
Capitaines, Ducs de ses chariots, & de ses
cheuaucheurs. Ceux ci estoient les Princes
a.chr.8 b.c des officiers constituez sus les ouurages de
Salomon ‖ cinq cens cinquante, qui auoient
la domination sus le peuple qui faisoit les
ouurages. Or la fille de Pharao monta de
la cité de Dauid, en sa maison que Salomon
lui auoit edifice, lors il edifia aussi Mello.
Chacun an, par trois fois Salomon offroit
holocaustes, & oblations pacifiques sus l'au-
tel qu'il auoit edifié au Seigneur, & faisoit
encensemens sus icelui, deuant le Seigneur.
Ainsi ayant paracheué la maison, le Roy
Salomon fit des nauires en Aziongaber, qui
estoit pres d'Eloth, au riuage de la mer rouge en la terre d'Edom. Et Hiram enuoya ses
seruiteurs en ceste multitude de nauires, qui
estoient mariniers, & sauoient que c'estoit
de la mer, auec les seruiteurs de Salomon:
lesquelz vindrent en Ophir, & de là prin-
drent de l'or, quatre cens & vingt talens: &
les apporterent au Roy Salomon.

La

---

*La Royne de Saba vient à Salomon pour voir la
magnificence & ouir la sapience d'icelui, &
lui fait grans presens.* CHAP. X.

LA Royne de Saba oyant la renommee
de Salomon, au nom du Seigneur, ‖s'en 2.chr. 9.a
vint pour le tenter par questions obscures. matt.11.d
Laquelle entra en Ierusalem, auec moult Luc 11.d
grosse puissance de gens, & chameaux portans espiceries, & grande abondance d'or, &
pierres precieuses: & s'en vint à Salomon,
& parla à lui, tout ce qu'elle auoit en son
cœur. Et Salomon lui declaira toutes ses
paroles, & rien n'estoit caché au Roy qu'il rdemádes,
ne lui enseignast. Lors la Royne de Saba
voyant toute la sagesse de Salomon, & la
maison qu'il auoit edifice, & les viandes de
r dessus

---

la plora par sept iours. Aussi en toute l'es-
pace de sa vie nul ne troubla Israël, ne aussi
par plusieurs ans apres sa mort. Et le iour de
la feste de ceste victoire, est receu des
Ebrieux au nombre des saints
iours, & est honnoré des
Iuifs, depuis ce temps
là iusques au
iour pre-
sent.

Fin du liure de Iudith.

LE LIVRE DE
ESTHER.

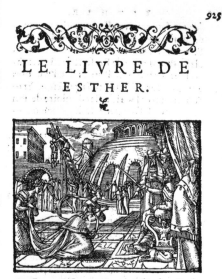

*Assuerus faisant vn grand festin ha reietté
Vasthi sa femme; par ce qu'elle n'auoit obeï
à son commandement.* CHAP. I.

APRES qu'Assuerus, qui re- Assuerus,
gnoit depuis Inde iusques en qui est aus-
Ethiopie, sus cent vingt & sept si appellé
Prouinces, se fut assis sus le thro- Artaxerses
ne de son Royaume en Susan, ville capitale
de

Cy commence le Prologue de meſsire Iehan Froiſſart, ſur les Croniques de France & d'Angleterre, & autres lieux voiſins.

✱

A F I N que les honnorables empriſes & nobles auétures & faicts-d'armes, par les guerres de France & d'Angleterre, ſoyent notablement enregiſtrés & mis en memoire perpetuel, parquoy les preux ayent exemple d'eux encourager en bien faiſant, ie vueil traicter & recorder Hiſtoire de grand' louenge. Mais, auant que ie la commence, ie requier au Sauueur de tout le monde, qui de neant crea toutes choſes, qu'il vueille creer & mettre en moy ſens & entendement ſi vertueux, que ie puiſſe continuer & perſeuerer en telle maniere que tous ceux & celles, qui le lirõt, verront, & orront, y puiſſent prendre ebatement & exemple, & moy encheoir en leur grâce.

On dit, & il eſt vray, que tous edifices ſont maſſonnés & ouurés de pluſieurs ſortes de pierres, & toutes groſſes riuieres ſont faictes & raſſemblees de pluſieurs ſurgeons. Auſſi les ſciences ſont extraictes & compilees de pluſieurs Clercs : & ce, que l'un ſcet, l'autre l'ignore. Non-pourtant rien n'eſt, qui ne ſoit ſceu, ou loing ou pres.

Donc, pour attaindre à la matiere que i'ay empriſe, ie vueil commencer premierement par la grâce de Dieu & de la benoiſte vierge Marie (dont tout confort & auancement viennent) & me vueil fonder & ordonner ſur les vrayes Croniques, iadis faictes par reuerend homme, diſcret & ſage, monſeigneur maiſtre Iehan le Bel, *De qui Froiſſart a pris la preſente Hiſtoire.* Chanoine de Sainct-Lambert du Liege : qui grand' cure & toute bonne diligéce meit en ceſte matiere, & la continua tout ſon viuant au plus iuſtement qu'il peut, & moult luy couſta à la querre & à l'auoir : mais, quelques fraiz qu'il y fiſt, riens ne les plaingnit. car il eſtoit riche & puiſſant (ſi les pouuoit bien porter) & eſtoit de ſoy-meſme large, honnorable, & courtois : & voulontiers voyoit le ſien deſpendre. Auſſi il fut en ſon viuant moult aimé & ſecret à monſeigneur meſſire Iehan de Haynaut : qui bien eſt ramenteu, & de raiſon, en ce liure. car de moult belles & nobles aduenues fut il chef & cauſe, & des Roys moult prochain. parquoy le deſſuſdit meſſire Iehan le Bel peut delez luy veoir pluſieurs nobles beſongnes : leſquelles ſont contenues cy-apres. Vray *† De quel temps eſtoit Froiſſart. ſur quoy faut noter qu'il ne porta que partie de ce premier Volume à la Royne Philippe. car vous verrez qu'il racomptera la mort d'icelle, ſelon l'ordre des temps, en cedit premier & preſent Volume.* eſt que ie, qui ay empris ce liure à ordonner, ay par plaiſance, qui à ce m'a touſiours encliné, frequenté pluſieurs nobles & grans Seigneurs, tant en Fráce qu'en Angleterre, en Eſcoce, & en pluſieurs autres païs : & en ay eu la congnoiſſance d'eux : & ay touſiours, à mon pouuoir, iuſtement enquis & demandé du faict des guerres & des auentures, & par eſpecial depuis la groſſe bataille de Poitiers, où le noble Roy Iehan de France fut pris.† car deuãt i'eſtoye encores moult ieune de ſens & d'aage. Nonobſtant ſi empris ie aſſez hardiment, moy iſſu de l'eſcole, à dicter & à ordonner les guerres deſſuſdites, & porter en Angleterre le liure tout compilé : ſi-comme ie fei, & le preſentay adonc à Ma-dame Philippe de Haynaut, Royne d'Angleterre : qui liement & doucement le receut de moy, & m'en fit grand profit. Et peut eſtre que ce liure n'eſt

a   mie

Neptune. Et lon facrifie auffi à Neptune tous les huictiemes iours de chafque F
mois,à caufe que le nóbre de huict eft le premier cubique,procedant de nombre per, & le double du premier nombre quarré, qui reprefente une fermeté
immobile,proprement attribuee à la puiffance de Neptune, lequel pour cefte
raifon nous furnommons Afphalius & Gæiochus, qui ualent autant à dire
comme,affeurant & affermiffant la terre.

Romulus.

G

ES Hiftoriens ne f'accordent pas à efcrire, par qui ne
pour quelle caufe le grand nom de la uille de Rome,
la gloire duquel feft eftendue par tout le monde, luy
ait efté premierement impofé:pource que les uns tié-
nent que les Pelafgiés, apres auoir couru la plus grá-
de partie de la terre habitable, & auoir dompté plu-
fieurs nations,finablement farrefterent au lieu ou elle eft à prefent fondee: & que pour leur grande puiffance en armes, ilz impoferent le nom de Rome à la
uille qu'ilz baftirent,qui fignifie en langage Grec,puiffance. Les autres difent H
que apres la prife & deftructió de Troie, il y eut quelques Troiens qui feftans
fauluez de l'efpee, fembarquerent fur des uaiffeaux qu'ilz trouuerent d'auenture au port, & furent iettez par les uens en la cofte de la Thofcane, ou ilz po-
ferent les ancres pres la riuiere du Tybre: & là leurs femmes fe trouuans defia
fi mal, qu'elles ne pouuoient plus nullement endurer le trauail de la mer, il y
en eut une,la plus noble & la plus fage de toutes,nommee Rome,qui cófeilla
à fes compaignes de mettre le feu en leurs uaiffeaux. ce qu'elles feirent: dont
leurs marys du commencement furent bien mal contens : mais depuis eftans
contrains par la neceffité de farrefter au pres de la uille de Pallantium,quand
ilz ueirent que leurs affaires y profperoient mieux qu'ilz n'euffent ofé efperer, I
y trouuans la terre fertile, & les peuples uoifins doulx & gratieux qui les re-
ceurent amiablement, entre autres honneurs qu'ilz feirent en recompence à
cefte dame Rome, ilz appellerét leur uille de fó nom,cóme de celle qui auoit
efté caufe de la baftir. Et dit on que de la cómencea la couftume qui dure encores auiourdhuy à Rome, que les femmes faluent leurs parés & leurs marys
en les baifant en la bouche, pource que lors ces dames Troienes faluerent &
carefferét ainfi leurs marys,apres leur auoir bruflé leurs nauires,en les priant
de uouloir appaifer leur courroux & maltalent contre elles.Les autres difent
que Rome fut fille d'Italus & de Lucaria, ou bien de Telephus filz de Her-
cules,& femme d'Æneas,autres difent,d'Afcanius filz d'Æneas,laquelle dó- K
na fon nom à la uille.Autres y en a qui tiennét, que ce fut Romanus filz d'V-
lyffes & de Circe,qui fonda Rome : autres ueulent dire que ce fut Romus filz
d'Emathion, que Diomedes y enuoia de Troie. Les autres efcriuét que ce fut
un Romis tyran des Latins,qui chaffa de ce quartier la, les Thofcás, lefquelz
partans de la Theffalie eftoient premierement paffez en la Lydie, & puis de
la Lydie en Italie. Qui plus eft,ceulx mefmes qui tiennent que Romulus (cóme il y a plus d'apparence) fut celuy qui donna le nom à la uille, ne font pas
d'accord

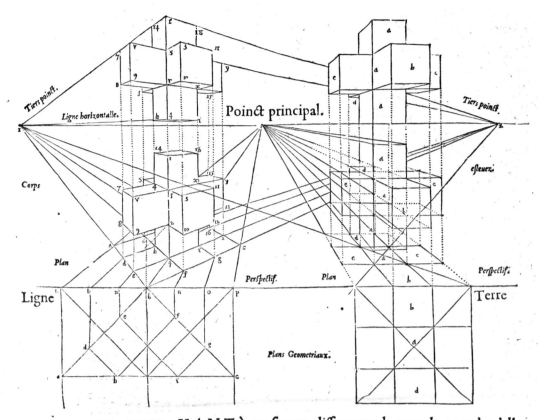

Q V A N T à ces figures differentes de regards, encor' qu'elles foient femblables, fi y a il difference quant à l'execution. Touchãt les interieures parties de ces figures ne vous en diray rien: pource que cefte precedente vous en donne fuffifante intelligence d'icelles. En cefte figure les regards font differents, & les corps veuz fus la ligne Horizontalle, & fouz icelle: & veuz auffi par l'angle, comme voyez en cefte cy fouz la ligne Horizontalle, laquelle cómenceray par fon plan Geometrial, lequel eft icy fouz la ligne Terre, n'eftant que demy, & veu angulairement, comme en voyez icy trois pointes, a.b.c.diftinct de trois portions egalles, d.e.f.g: lefquelles portions font tirees de lignes droittes felon la fituation d'iceluy quarré, comme eft icy, d.h:e.i:f.h:g.i. Icelles lignes & coings, a.d:e.f:g.c:font renuoiez par lignes droittes iufques à la ligne Terre, comme eft icy, a.k:d.l:e.m: (le.b.n'a point de renuoy, pource qu'il touche à la ligne Terre), f.n:g.o:c.p: depuis la ligne Terre, font renuoyez au poinct Principal: puis de.b.tireres lignes aux deux Tiers poincts, merquez, 1.2. Icelles deux lignes k & p.tireres au poinct Principal, faifants leurs fections fus les lignes Vifualles, comme voyez fus ce plan Perfpectif, merqué de mefmes caractheres que le Geometrial: & toutes icelles lignes, f.g.c.tirees au Tiers poinct, 1. & auffi, a.d.e, tirees au Tiers poinct. 2: vous donnent voftre plan Perfpectif femblable au Geo-

G j

HADRIANI
IVNII MEDICI
EMBLEMATA,
AD
D. ARNOLDVM COBELIVM.

EIVSDEM
AENIGMATVM LIBELLVS,
AD
D. ARNOLDVM ROSENBERGVM.

ANTVERPIÆ,
Ex officina Christophori Plantini.
M. D. LXV.
CVM PRIVILEGIO.

EMBLEMA XXVII.   33

Sermo de Deo apertus, mens ſit occulta.
Ad Iohannem Becanum Medicum clariſſimũ.

Perſea fert linguæ ſimiles, ſacra Iſidi, frondes:
Typum'que cordis poma turgida exprimunt.
Sermo, index animi, de numine ſentit apertè;
Cor cæco operculo intus arcanum tegit.

C   Prin-

62   CHRISTOPHER PLANTIN, Antwerp, 1565
Hadrianus Junius: *Emblemata*   3⅝ x 5⅞

BIBLIA SACRA

HEBRAICE,
CHALDAICE,
GRÆCE, &
Latine

PIETATIS CONCORDIÆ. Iſaiæ, 11

PHILIPPI II. REG. CATHOL. PIETATE,
ET STVDIO AD SACROSANCTÆ
ECCLESIÆ VSVM

CHRISTOPH. PLANTINVS EXCVD. ANTVERPIÆ.

63 CHRISTOPHER PLANTIN, Antwerp, 1569–1572
Bible, Polyglot 11 x 16⅝

Hebrew column

וַיִּ֣מַח אֶת־כָּל־הַיְק֣וּם אֲשֶׁ֣ר עַל־פְּנֵ֣י הָֽאֲדָמָ֗ה מֵאָדָ֤ם

עַד־בְּהֵמָה֙ עַד־רֶ֙מֶשׂ֙ וְעַד־ע֣וֹף הַשָּׁמַ֔יִם וַיִּמָּח֖וּ מִן־הָאָ֑רֶץ

וַיִּשָּׁ֧אֶר אַךְ־נֹ֛חַ וַֽאֲשֶׁ֥ר אִתּ֖וֹ בַּתֵּבָֽה׃   וַיִּגְבְּר֥וּ הַמַּ֛יִם

עַל־הָאָ֖רֶץ חֲמִשִּׁ֥ים וּמְאַ֖ת יֽוֹם׃

ח   וַיִּזְכֹּ֤ר אֱלֹהִים֙ אֶת־נֹ֔חַ וְאֵ֤ת כָּל־הַֽחַיָּה֙ וְאֶת־

כָּל־הַבְּהֵמָ֔ה אֲשֶׁ֥ר אִתּ֖וֹ בַּתֵּבָ֑ה וַיַּֽעֲבֵ֨ר אֱלֹהִ֥ים ר֨וּחַ֙ עַל־

הָאָ֔רֶץ וַיָּשֹׁ֖כּוּ הַמָּֽיִם׃   וַיִּסָּֽכְרוּ֙ מַעְיְנֹ֣ת תְּה֔וֹם וַֽאֲרֻבֹּ֖ת

הַשָּׁמָ֑יִם וַיִּכָּלֵ֕א הַגֶּ֖שֶׁם מִן־הַשָּׁמָֽיִם׃   וַיָּשֻׁ֣בוּ הַמַּ֗יִם

מֵעַ֤ל הָאָ֙רֶץ֙ הָל֣וֹךְ וָשׁ֔וֹב וַיַּחְסְר֣וּ הַמַּ֔יִם מִקְצֵ֕ה חֲמִשִּׁ֥ים

וּמְאַ֖ת יֽוֹם׃   וַתָּ֤נַח הַתֵּבָה֙ בַּחֹ֣דֶשׁ הַשְּׁבִיעִ֔י בְּשִׁבְעָֽה־

עָשָׂ֥ר י֖וֹם לַחֹ֑דֶשׁ עַ֖ל הָרֵ֥י אֲרָרָֽט׃   וְהַמַּ֗יִם הָיוּ֙ הָל֣וֹךְ

וְחָס֔וֹר עַ֖ד הַחֹ֣דֶשׁ הָֽעֲשִׂירִ֑י בָּֽעֲשִׂירִ֗י בְּאֶחָד֙ לַחֹ֔דֶשׁ נִרְא֖וּ

רָאשֵׁ֥י הֶֽהָרִֽים׃   וַֽיְהִ֕י מִקֵּ֖ץ אַרְבָּעִ֣ים י֑וֹם וַיִּפְתַּ֣ח נֹ֔חַ

אֶת־חַלּ֥וֹן הַתֵּבָ֖ה אֲשֶׁ֥ר עָשָֽׂה׃   וַיְשַׁלַּ֖ח אֶת־הָֽעֹרֵ֑ב

וַיֵּצֵ֤א יָצוֹא֙ וָשׁ֔וֹב עַד־יְבֹ֥שֶׁת הַמַּ֖יִם מֵעַ֥ל הָאָֽרֶץ׃

וַיְשַׁלַּ֥ח אֶת־הַיּוֹנָ֖ה מֵֽאִתּ֑וֹ לִרְאוֹת֙ הֲקַ֣לּוּ הַמַּ֔יִם מֵעַ֖ל

פְּנֵ֥י הָֽאֲדָמָֽה׃   וְלֹֽא־מָֽצְאָה֩ הַיּוֹנָ֨ה מָנ֜וֹחַ לְכַף־רַגְלָ֗הּ

וַתָּ֤שָׁב אֵלָיו֙ אֶל־הַתֵּבָ֔ה כִּי־מַ֖יִם עַל־פְּנֵ֣י כָל־הָאָ֑רֶץ

וַיִּשְׁלַ֤ח יָדוֹ֙ וַיִּקָּחֶ֔הָ וַיָּבֵ֥א אֹתָ֛הּ אֵלָ֖יו אֶל־הַתֵּבָֽה׃

וַיָּ֣חֶל ע֔וֹד שִׁבְעַ֥ת יָמִ֖ים אֲחֵרִ֑ים וַיֹּ֛סֶף שַׁלַּ֥ח אֶת־הַיּוֹנָ֖ה

מִן־הַתֵּבָֽה׃   וַתָּבֹ֨א אֵלָ֤יו הַיּוֹנָה֙ לְעֵ֣ת עֶ֔רֶב וְהִנֵּ֥ה

עֲלֵה־זַ֖יִת טָרָ֣ף בְּפִ֑יהָ וַיֵּ֣דַע נֹ֔חַ כִּי־קַ֥לּוּ הַמַּ֖יִם מֵעַ֥ל

הָאָֽרֶץ׃   וַיִּיָּ֣חֶל ע֔וֹד שִׁבְעַ֥ת יָמִ֖ים אֲחֵרִ֑ים וַיְשַׁלַּח֙

אֶת־הַיּוֹנָ֔ה וְלֹֽא־יָֽסְפָ֥ה שׁוּב־אֵלָ֖יו עֽוֹד׃   וַֽיְהִ֠י בְּאַחַ֨ת

וְשֵׁשׁ־מֵא֜וֹת שָׁנָ֗ה בָּֽרִאשׁוֹן֙ בְּאֶחָ֣ד לַחֹ֔דֶשׁ חָֽרְב֥וּ

הַמַּ֖יִם מֵעַ֣ל הָאָ֑רֶץ וַיָּ֤סַר נֹ֙חַ֙ אֶת־מִכְסֵ֣ה הַתֵּבָ֔ה וַיַּ֕רְא

וְהִנֵּ֥ה חָֽרְב֖וּ פְּנֵ֥י הָֽאֲדָמָֽה׃   וּבַחֹ֙דֶשׁ֙ הַשֵּׁנִ֔י בְּשִׁבְעָ֧ה

וְעֶשְׂרִ֛ים י֖וֹם לַחֹ֑דֶשׁ יָבְשָׁ֖ה הָאָֽרֶץ׃

וַיְדַבֵּ֥ר אֱלֹהִ֖ים אֶל־נֹ֥חַ לֵאמֹֽר׃

צֵ֖א מִן־הַתֵּבָ֑ה אַתָּ֕ה וְאִשְׁתְּךָ֛ וּבָנֶ֥יךָ וּֽנְשֵֽׁי־בָנֶ֖יךָ אִתָּֽךְ׃

Latin column

23   ‡ Et deleuit omnem substantiam quæ erat super terram, ab hominevsque ad pecus, tam reptile, quàm volucres cæli : & deletæ sunt de terra. Remansit autem solus Noe, & qui cum eo erant in arca . ‡ Obtinueruntq; aquæ terrã 24 centum quinquaginta diebus. CAP. VIII.

1   **R**Ecordatus autem Deus Noe, cunctorumque animantium , & omnium iumentorum quæ erant cum eo in arca: adduxit spiritum super terram, & imminutæ sunt aquæ:

2   ‡ Et clausi sunt fontes abyssi, & cataractæ cæli : & prohibitæ sunt pluuiæ de cælo. ‡ Reuersæque sunt aquæ de terra, euntes & redeuntes: & cœperunt minui post centum quinquagin 4 ta dies . ‡ Requieuitque arca mense septimo, vicesimoseptimo die mensis super montes Armeniæ . ‡ At verò aquæ ibant & decrescebat vsque ad decimum mensem . Decimo enim mense, prima die mensis, apparuerunt cacu 6 mina montium ‡ Cúmque transissent quadraginta dies , aperiens Noe fenestram arcæ 7 quam fecerat, ‡ Dimisit coruum; qui egrediebatur & reuertebatur, donec siccarétur a 8 quæ super terram. ‡ Emisit quoque columBbam post eũ , vt videret si iam cessassent aquæ 9 super faciem terræ . ‡ Quæ cùm non inuenisset vbi requiesceret pes eius , reuersa est ad eum in arcam. Aquæ enim erant super vniuersam terram. Extendítque manum suam, & ap 10 prehensam intulit in arcã. ‡ Expectatis autẽ vltra septẽ diebus aliis, rursum dimisit columbã 11 ex arca. ‡ At illa venit ad eũ ad vesperã, portans ramũ oliuæ virentibus foliis in ore suo. Intellexit ergo Noe q̃ cessassent aquæ super terrã. 12 ‡ Expectauítq; nihilominus septẽ alios dies, & emisit colũbã, quæ nõ est reuersa vltra ad eũ. 13 ‡ Igitur sexcentesimo primo anno, primo men C se, prima die mensis, imminutæ sunt aquæ super terram . Et aperiens Noe tectum arcæ, aspexit, viditque quòd exiccata esset superfi 14 cies terræ. ‡ Mense secundo, septimo & vicesi 15 mo die mésis, arefacta est terra. ‡ Locutus est au 16 té De⁹ ad Noe, dicens: ‡ Egredere de arca tu, & vxor tua, filij tui, & vxores filiorũ tuorũ tecũ.

תרגום אונקלוס

Targum column (Aramaic)

23 וּמְחָא יָת כָּל יְקוּמָא דְעַל אַפֵּי אַרְעָא מֵאֱנָשָׁא עַד בְּעִירָא עַד רִחְשָׁא וְעַד עוֹפָא דִשְׁמַיָא וְאִתְמְחִיאוּ מִן אַרְעָא וְאִשְׁתְּאַר בְּרַם נֹחַ וְדַעֲמֵיהּ בְּתֵבוֹתָא׃ 24 וּתְקִיפוּ מַיָא עַל אַרְעָא מְאָה וְחַמְשִׁין יוֹמִין׃

ח

1 וּדְכִיר יְיָ יָת נֹחַ וְיָת כָּל חַיְתָא וְיָת כָּל בְּעִירָא דְעִמֵיהּ בְּתֵבוֹתָא וְאַעֲבַר יְיָ רוּחָא עַל אַרְעָא וְנָחוּ מַיָא׃ 2 וְאִסְתְּכַרוּ מַבּוּעֵי תְהוֹמָא וְכַוֵי שְׁמַיָא וְאִתְכְּלִי מִטְרָא מִן שְׁמַיָא׃ 3 וְתָבוּ מַיָא מֵעַל אַרְעָא אָזְלִין וְתָיְבִין וַחֲסַרוּ מַיָא מִסוֹף מְאָה וְחַמְשִׁין יוֹמִין׃ 4 וְנָחַת תֵּבוֹתָא בְּיַרְחָא שְׁבִיעָאָה בְּשִׁבְעַת עֶשְׂרָא יוֹמָא לְיַרְחָא עַל טוּרֵי קַרְדּוּ׃ 5 וּמַיָא הֲווֹ אָזְלִין וְחָסְרִין עַד יַרְחָא עֲשִׂירָאָה בַּעֲשִׂירָאָה בְּחַד לְיַרְחָא אִתְחֲזִיאוּ רֵישֵׁי טוּרַיָא׃ 6 וַהֲוָה מִסוֹף אַרְבְּעִין יוֹמִין וּפְתַח נֹחַ יָת כַּוַת תֵּבוֹתָא דַעֲבַד׃ 7 וּשְׁלַח יָת עוֹרְבָא וּנְפַק מִיפַּק וְתָאִיב עַד דְיִבִישׁוּ מַיָא מֵעַל אַרְעָא׃ 8 וּשְׁלַח יָת יוֹנָה מִלְוָתֵיהּ לְמֶחֱזֵי אִם קַלוּ מַיָא מֵעַל אַפֵּי אַרְעָא׃ 9 וְלָא אַשְׁכַּחַת יוֹנָה מְנָח לְפַרְסַת רַגְלַהּ וְתָבַת לְוָתֵיהּ לְתֵבוֹתָא אֲרֵי מַיָא עַל אַפֵּי כָל אַרְעָא וְאוֹשֵׁיט יְדֵיהּ וְנַסְבַהּ וְאָעֵיל יַתַהּ לְוָתֵיהּ לְתֵבוֹתָא׃ 10 וְאוֹרִיךְ עוֹד שִׁבְעָא יוֹמִין אָחֲרָנִין וְאוֹסֵיף שְׁלַח יָת יוֹנָה מִן תֵּבוֹתָא׃ 11 וַאֲתַת לְוָתֵיהּ יוֹנָה לְעִדָּן רַמְשָׁא וְהָא טְרַף זֵיתָא חֲבִיר מָחַת בְּפוּמַהּ וִידַע נֹחַ אֲרֵי קַלוּ מַיָא מֵעַל אַרְעָא׃ 12 וְאוֹרִיךְ עוֹד שִׁבְעָא יוֹמִין אָחֳרָנִין וּשְׁלַח יָת יוֹנָה וְלָא אוֹסִיפַת לְמֵתַב לְוָתֵיהּ עוֹד׃ 13 וַהֲוָה בְּשִׁית מְאָה וַחֲדָא שְׁנִין בְּקַדְמָאָה בְּחַד לְיַרְחָא נְגוּבוּ מַיָא מֵעַל אַרְעָא וְאַעֲדֵי נֹחַ יָת חוֹפָאָה דְתֵבוֹתָא וַחֲזָא וְהָא נְגוּבוּ אַפֵּי אַרְעָא׃ 14 וּבְיַרְחָא תִנְיָנָא בְּעַסְרִין וְשִׁבְעָא יוֹמָא לְיַרְחָא יְבֵישַׁת אַרְעָא׃ 15 וּמַלֵיל יְיָ עִם נֹחַ לְמֵימַר׃ 16 פּוּק מִן תֵּבוֹתָא אַתְּ וְאִתְּתָךְ וּבְנָךְ וּנְשֵׁי בְנָךְ עִמָּךְ׃

* Et deleuit omne surgens quod erat super faciem terræ, ab homine vsque ad pecus, & reptilia, & volucres cæli: & deleta sunt de terra. & remansit Noe solus, & qui cum eo in arca. 23	23 * καὶ ἐξήλειψε πᾶν τὸ ἀνάσημα, ὃ ἰω ἐπὶ πϱσώπου τῆς γῆς, ἀπὸ ἀνθρώπȣ ἕως κτήνος, ὅ ἑϱπετῶν, ὅ πετεινῶν τȣ ȣϱανȣ· καὶ ἐξηλείφθησαν ἀπὸ τῆς γῆς. ὅ κατελείφθη νῶε
* Et exaltata est aqua super terram diebus cen tum quinquaginta. 24	24 μόνος, ὅ οἱ μετ᾽ αὐτȣ ἐν τῇ κιβωτῷ. καὶ ὑψώθη τὸ ὕ δωϱ ἐπὶ τῆς γῆς ἡμέϱας ἑκατὸν πεντήκοντα. η'.

CAP. VIII.

ET recordatus est Deus Noe, & omnium bestia- rum, & omnium iumentorum, & omnium vo- latilium, & omnium reptilium reptantium, quæcun que erant cum eo in arca. & induxit Deus Spiri- tum super terram, & cessauit aqua: * Et cooperti sunt fontes abyßi, & cataractæ cæli. * Et remis- sa est aqua vadens à terra: & imminuebatur aqua post centum quinquaginta dies. * Et sedit ar- ca in septimo mense, septima & vigesima mensis, su per montes Ararat. * Aqua diminuebatur vs- que ad decimum mensem. apparuerunt autem capi- ta montium in decimo mense, prima mensis. 1 2 3 4 5	1 Καὶ ἀνεμνήθη ὁ θεὸς ἑ νῶε, ἑ πάντων τῶνθηϱίων, ἑ πάν- των τῶν κτηνῶν, ἑ πάντων τῶ πετεινῶν, ἡ πάντων τῶν ἑϱπε- τῶν τῶ ἑϱπόντων, ὅσα ἰω μετ᾽ αὐτȣ εἰς τὴν κιβωτόν. ὅ ἐπή- γαγεν ὁ θεὸς πνεῦμα ἐπὶ τῆς γῆς, ὅ ἐκόπασεν τὸ ὕδωϱ. 2 καὶ ἐπεκαλύφθησαν αἱ πηγαὶ τῆς ἀβύσσε, ἡ καὶ κατα- ϱάκ) ȣ ȣϱανȣ. 3 καὶ ἐνεδίδȣ τὸ ὕδωϱ ποϱδυόμψον ἀπὸ τῆς γῆς. ἡ ἠλαπονοῦτο τὸ ὕδωϱ, μῆ ἑκατὸν πεντήκονα ἡμέ- 4 ϱας. ὅ ἐκάθισεν ἡ κιβωτὸς ἐν τῷ ἑβδόμω μηνὶ, ἑβδόμη 5 ὅ εἰκάδι ἑ μηνός, ἐπὶ τὰ ὄϱη τὰ ἀϱαϱάτ. * Τὸ ὕδωϱ ἠ- λατονοῦ τὸ ἕως ἑ δεκάτȣ μηνός. ὤφθησαν ῇ αἱ κεφαλαὶ τῶ 6 ὀϱέων ἐν τῷ δεκάτω μηνὶ, τῇ πϱώτῃ ἑ μηνός. ὅ ἐγένε-
Et factum est post quadraginta dies, & aperuit Noe fenestram arcæ, quam fecit: * Et misit cor- uum ad videndum, si cessauit aqua. & exiens, non est reuersus, donec siccaretur aqua à facie terræ. 6 7	7 το μετὰ τεσσαϱάκονα ἡμέϱας· ὅ ἀνέωξε νῶε τὴν θυϱίδα τῆς κιβωτȣ ῇ, ἣν ἐποίησε. ὅ ἀπέςειλε τὸν κόϱακα ἰδεῖν, εἰ κε- κόπακε τὸ ὕδωϱ. ὅ ἐξελθὼν, ȣκ ἀνέςϱεψεν, ἕως ἑ ξηϱανθῆ- 8 ναι τὸ ὕδωϱ ἀπὸ πϱσώπȣ τῆς γῆς. * ὅ ἐξαπέςειλε τὴν
* Et emisit columbam post eum, vt videret, si cessauit aqua à facie terræ. * Et non inue- niens columba requiem pedibus suis, reuersa est ad eum in arcam; quia aqua erat super omnem faciem terræ: & extendens manum suam, accepit eam; & induxit eam ad se in arcam. 8 9	πεϱιςεϱὰν ὀπίσω αὐτȣ, ἰδεῖν, εἰ κεκόπακε τὸ ὕδωϱ ἀπὸ πϱ- 9 σώπου τῆς γῆς. * ὅ μὴ εὑϱοῦσα ἡ πεϱιςεϱὰ ἀνάπαυσιν τοῖς ποσὶν αὐτῆς, ὑπέςϱεψεν πϱὸς αὐτὸν εἰς τὴν κιβωτόν, ὅτι ὕδωϱ ἰω ἐπὶ πᾶν τὸ πϱόσωπον τῆς γῆς ὅ ἐκλείνας τὴν χεῖ- ϱα αὐτȣ, ἔλαβεν αὐτὴν, ὅ εἰσήγαγεν αὐτὴν πϱὸς αὐτὸν εἰς τὴν 10 κιβωτόν. ὅ ἐπισχὼν ἔπ ἑπ ἡμέϱας, ὅ ἐξαπέςειλε τὴν
* Et exspectans vltra septem dies, emisit colum- bam ex arca: * Et reuersa est ad eum columba, & habebat folium oliuæ festucam in ore suo. & co- gnouit Noe, quòd cessauit aqua à facie terræ. 10 11	11 πεϱιςεϱὰν ἐκ τῆς κιβωτȣ. ὅ ἀπέςϱεψε πϱὸς αὐτὸν ἡ πεϱιςεϱά ὅ εἶχεν φύλλον ἐλαίας κάϱφΘ ἐν τῷ σόμαλι αὐ- τῆς. ὅ ἔγνω νῶε, ὅτι κεκόπακε τὸ ὕδωϱ ἀπὸ πϱσώπȣ τῆς 12 γῆς. * ὅ ἐπισχὼν ἔπ ἑπ ἡμέϱας, ὅ ἐξαπέςειλε τὴν πε-
* Et expectans adhuc septem dies, emisit colum- bam: & non addidit reuerti ad eum vltra.	ϱιςεϱὰν, ὅ ȣ πϱσέθετο τȣ ἐπιςϱέψαι πϱὸς αὐτὸν ἔπ.
* Et factum est in vno & sexcentesimo anno, in vita Noe, primo mense, defecit aqua à facie terræ. & aperuit Noe tectum arcæ, quam fecit: & vidit quòd defecit aqua à facie terræ. 13	13 ὅ ἐγένετο ἐν τῷ ἑνὶ ὅ ἑξακοσιοςῷ ἔτει, ἐν τῇ ζωῇ τȣ νῶε, τȣ πϱώτȣ μηνός ἐξέλιπε τὸ ὕδωϱ ἀπὸ πϱσώπȣ τῆς γῆς. ὅ ἀπεκάλυψε νῶε τὴν ςέγ ἰω τῆς κιβωτȣ, ἰω ἐποίησεν. ὅ εἶ- δεν, ὅτι ἐξέλιπε τὸ ὕδωϱ ἀπὸ πϱσώπȣ τῆς γῆς.
* In autem secundo mense, septima & decima die, arefacta est terra. & septima & vigesima mé- sis aperuit arcam. * Et ait Dominus Deus Noe, dicens: * Egredere de arca tu, & filij tui, & vxor tua, & vxores filiorum tuorum tecum: 14 15 16	14 ἐν δὲ τῷ δευτέϱω μηνὶ ἑπὰ ὅ δεκάτῃ ἡμέϱᾳ ἐξηϱάνθη 15 ἡ γῆ. ὅ ἐβδόμη ὅ εἰκάδι τȣ μηνὸς ἀνέωξε τὴν κιβωτόν. * ὅ 16 εἶπεν κύϱιΘ ὁ θεὸς τῷ νῶε, λέγων· * ἔξελθε ἐκ τῆς κιβωτȣ σὺ, ὅ οἱ ἱοί Ȣ, ὅ ἡ γυνή Ȣ, ὅ αἱ γυναῖκες τῶ ὑῶν Ȣ μῇ Ȣ·

CHALDAICAE PARAPHRASIS TRANSLATIO.

¹³ Et deleuit omnem substantiam quæ erat super faciem terræ, ab homine vsque ad iumentum, vsque ad reptile, & vsque ad volucres cæli: & deleta sunt de terra : & relictus est solummodo Noe, & qui cum eo erant in arca. ¹⁴ Et præualuerunt aquæ super terram centum & quinquaginta diebus.

CAP. VIII.

ET recordatus est Deus Noe, & omnium animalium & omnium iumentorum quæ erant cum eo in arca: & transire fecit Deus ventum super terram: & cessarunt aquæ. ² Et clausi sunt fontes abyssi, & fenestræ cæli : & prohibita est pluuia de cælo. ³ Et reuersæ sunt aquæ desuper terram, euntes & reuertentes : & diminutæ sunt aquæ post centum & quinquaginta dies. ⁴ Et quieuit arca in mense septimo, in decimaseptima die mensis, super montes Cardu. ⁵ Et aquæ ibant & diminuebantur. vsque ad decimum mensem: in prima die mensis decimi apparuerunt capita montium. ⁶ Et factum est in fine quadraginta dierum ; & aperuit Noe fenestram arcæ quam fecerat : ⁷ Et emisit coruum; & egrediebatur & reuertebatur, donec siccarentur aquæ desuper terram. ⁸ Et emisit columbam à se, vt videret si alleuiatæ fuissent aquæ desuper faciem terræ. ⁹ Et non inuenit columba requiem plantæ pedis sui: & re- uersa est ad eum in arcam: quoniam aquæ erant super faciem vniuersæ terræ: & extendit manum suam, & tulit eam; & induxit eam secum in arcam. ¹⁰ Et expectauit adhuc septem diebus aliis, & rursus emisit columbam ex arca. ¹¹ Et venit ad eum columba in tempore vespertino: & ecce fo- lium oliuæ quod decerpserat ore suo: & cognouit Noe quòd aquæ imminutæ erant desuper terram. ¹² Et expectauit vltra septem diebus a- liis; & emisit columbam; & nunquam est reuersa ad eum amplius. ¹³ Et factum est in sexcentesimo & vno anno, prima die mensis, siccatæ sunt aquæ desuper terram: & abstulit Noe tectum arcæ: & vidit; & ecce siccata erat facies terræ. ¹⁴ Et in mense secundo, vigesima septima die mensis, arefacta est terra. ¹⁵ Et locutus est Deus cum Noe, dicens: ¹⁶ Egredere de arca tu, & vxor tua, & filij tui, & vxores filiorum tuorum tecū.

21 And the people stood afarre off, and Moses drew neere vnto the thicke darkenes, where God was.

22 ¶And the LORD said vnto Moses, Thus thou shalt say vnto the children of Israel, Yee haue seene that I haue talked with you from heauen.

23 Ye shall not make with me gods of siluer, neither shall ye make vnto you gods of gold.

24 ¶An Altar of earth thou shalt make vnto me, and shalt sacrifice thereon thy burnt offerings, and thy peace offerings, thy sheepe, and thine oxen: In all places where I record my Name, I will come vnto thee, and I will blesse thee.

*Deut. 7. 5.iosh. 8. 31.
†Hebr.build them with hewing.

25 And * if thou wilt make mee an Altar of stone, thou shalt not † build it of hewen stone : for if thou lift vp thy toole vpon it,thou hast polluted it.

26 Neither shalt thou goe vp by steps vnto mine Altar, that thy nakednesse be not discouered thereon.

CHAP. XXI.

1 Lawes for men seruants. 5 For the seruant whose eare is boared. 7 For women seruants. 12 For manslaughter. 16 For stealers of men. 17 For cursers of parents. 18 For smiters. 22 For a hurt by chance. 28 For an oxe that goareth. 33 For him that is an occasion of harme.

*Leuit.25. 41.deut.15 12.iere. 34. 14.

NOw these are the Iudgements which thou shalt set before them.

2 *If thou buy an Hebrew seruant, sixe yeeres he shall serue,and in the seuenth he shall goe out free for nothing.

†Hebr.with his body.

3 If he came in † by himselfe,he shal goe out by himselfe: if he were married, then his wife shall goe out with him.

4 If his master haue giuen him a wife, and she haue borne him sonnes or daughters ; the wife and her children shall be her masters,and he shall go out by himselfe.

†Hebr.saying shall say.

5 And if the seruant † shall plainely say, I loue my master, my wife,and my children, I will not goe out free :

6 Then his master shall bring him vnto the Iudges, hee shall also bring him to the doore,or vnto the doore post, and his master shall boare his eare through with an aule,and he shall serue him for euer.

7 ¶And if a man sell his daughter

to be a mayd seruant, shee shall not goe out as the men seruants doe.

†Hebr. be euill in the eyes of,&c.

8 If she †please not her master, who hath betrothed her to himselfe , then shall he let her be redeemed: To sell her vnto a strange nation hee shall haue no power , seeing he hath dealt deceitfully with her.

9 And if he haue betrothed her vnto his sonne , he shall deale with her after the maner of daughters.

10 If he take him another wife, her food,her rayment,and her duety of mariage shall he not diminish.

11 And if he doe not these three vnto her, then shall she goe out free without money.

*Leuit.24. 17.

12 ¶*He that smiteth a man,so that he die, shalbe surely put to death.

*Deut. 19. 3.

13 And if a man lye not in wait, but God deliuer him into his hand, then *I will appoint thee a place whither hee shall flee :

14 But if a man come presumptuously vpon his neighbour to slay him with guile , thou shalt take him from mine Altar , that he may die.

15 ¶And he that smiteth his father, or his mother , shall bee surely put to death.

16 ¶And he that stealeth a man,and selleth him, or if he be found in his hand, he shall surely be put to death.

*Leuit. 20. 9.prou. 20. 20.math. 15.4.marke 7.10.
‖ Or,reuileth.
‖Or hic neighbour.

17 ¶And *hee that ‖ curseth his father or his mother ,shall surely bee put to death.

18 ¶And if men striue together, and one smite ‖ another with a stone , or with his fist,and he die not, but keepeth his bed :

†Hebr. ceasing.

19 If hee rise againe, and walke abroad vpon his staffe, then shall hee that smote him,be quit : onely he shall pay for † the losse of his time, and shall cause him to be throughly healed.

†Hebr. auenged.

20 ¶And if a man smite his seruant, or his mayd,with a rod,and hee die vnder his hand, hee shall bee surely † punished :

21 Notwithstanding, if he continue a day or two, hee shall not be punished, for he is his money.

22 ¶If men striue, and hurt a woman with child,so that her fruit depart from her, and yet no mischiefe follow, he shalbe surely punished, according as the womans husband will lay vpon him, and hee shall pay as the Iudges determine.

23 And

DE IMITATIONE CHRISTI
LIBER PRIMVS.

Admonitiones ad spiritualem vitam vtiles.

CAPVT I.

De imitatione Christi, & contemptu omnium vanitatum mundi.

QVI sequitur me, non ambulat in tenebris : dicit Dominus. Hæc sunt verba Christi, quibus admonemur, quatenus vitam

A

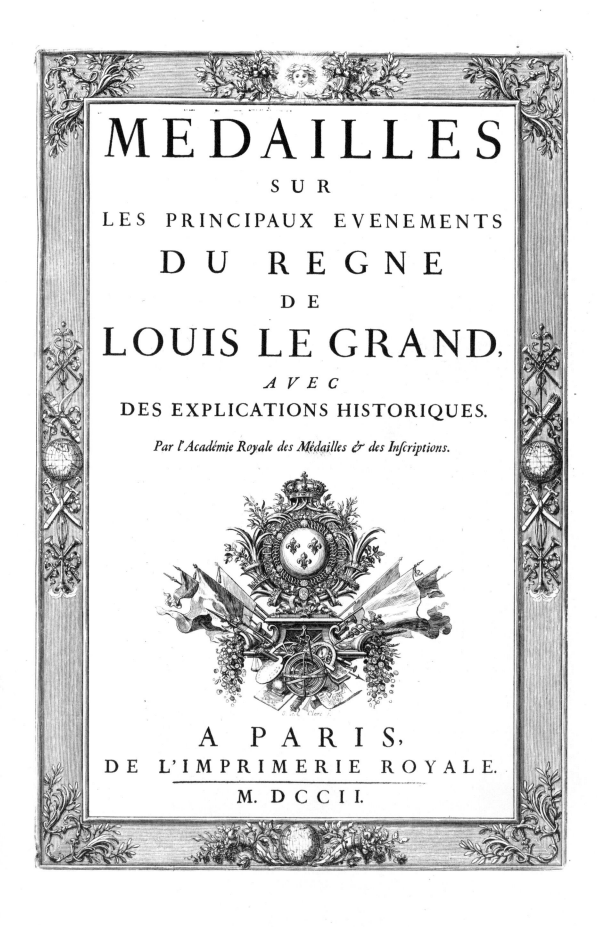

MEDAILLES

SUR

LES PRINCIPAUX EVENEMENTS

DU REGNE

DE

LOUIS LE GRAND,

AVEC

DES EXPLICATIONS HISTORIQUES.

Par l'Académie Royale des Médailles & des Inscriptions.

A PARIS,

DE L'IMPRIMERIE ROYALE.

M. DCCII.

68 IMPRIMERIE ROYALE, Paris, 1702

Médailles sur les Principaux Événements du Règne de Louis le Grand   12½ x 17¼

LA PAIX DE L'ITALIE,
PAR LA MEDIATION DU ROY.

LA guerre allumée entre le Pape Urbain VIII, & le Duc de Parme au sujet du Duché de Castro, dont le Pape s'estoit emparé, avoit donné occasion aux Princes d'Italie de prendre les armes pour leur propre seûreté. Les Vénitiens, le grand Duc de Toscane, & le Duc de Modéne firent une ligue entr'eux en faveur du Duc de Parme. On commit reciproquement diverses hostilitez, & l'on prit des Places de part & d'autre. Le Duc de Parme s'estoit avancé jusqu'aux portes de Rome, où il avoit jetté la terreur, & cette guerre pouvoit devenir funeste à toute l'Italie, lorsque le Roy interposa sa médiation. Le Cardinal Bichi, nommé Plénipotentiaire par Sa Majesté, fit divers voyages à Rome, à Florence, à Venise, & prés des Ducs de Parme, & de Modéne, & s'employa si efficacement dans cette négociation, qu'il conclut heureusement le Traité de Paix entre sa Sainteté, & les Princes liguez, avec l'entiere satisfaction de toutes les parties interessées. Le Pape rendit au Duc de Parme Castro & Montalto, & le grand Duc restitua au Pape plusieurs Places de l'Estat Ecclesiastique, qu'il avoit prises, ce qui restablit dans l'Italie une parfaite tranquillité.

C'est le sujet de cette Médaille. L'Italie avec ses attributs ordinaires y est representée assise. Les mots de la Légende, REX PACIS ARBITER, signifient, *le Roy arbitre de la Paix.* Ceux de l'Exergue, ITALIA PACATA. M.DC.XLIV. *la Paix rendüe à l'Italie. 1644.*

69 IMPRIMERIE ROYALE, Paris, 1702

Médailles sur les Principaux Événements du Règne de Louis le Grand   12½ x 17¼

THE

History of the Rebellion, &c.

BOOK II.

Pfal. LII. 2, 4.
*Thy Tongue devifeth Mifchiefs, like a fharp Rafour, working
deceitfully:*
Thou loveft all devouring words, O thou deceitful Tongue.

Pfal. LV. 21.
*The words of his Mouth were fmoother than Butter, but War
was in his Heart: his words were fofter than Oyl, yet were
they drawn Swords.*

Affairs in
Scotland *after
the King's re-
turn thence,
relating chiefly
to the compo-
fing a Liturgy
and Canons.*

IT was towards the end of the Year 1633, when the King return'd from *Scotland*, having left it to the Care of fome of the Bi- fhops there to provide fuch a Liturgy, and fuch a Book of Canons, as might beft fuit the nature and humour of the Better fort of that People; to which the reft would eafily fub- mit: and that, as faft as they made them ready, they fhould tranfmit them to the Arch-Bifhop of *Canterbury*, to whofe affi- ftance the King join'd the Bifhop of *London*, and Doctor *Wren*, who, by that time, was become Bifhop of *Norwich*; a man of a fevere fowr nature, but very Learned, and particularly verfed in the old Liturgies of the *Greek*, and *Latin* Churches. And after his Majefty fhould be this way certified of what was fo fent, he would recommend, and enjoyn the Practice, and Ufe of both to that his Native Kingdom. The Bifhops there had fomewhat to do, before they went about the preparing the Canons, and the Liturgy; what had pafs'd at the King's being there in Parliament, had left bitter Inclinations, and unruly Spirits in many of the moft popular Nobility; who watch'd only for an opportunity to Enflame the People, and were well-enough contented to fee Combuftible matter every day gather'd together, to contribute to that Fire.

THE promoting fo many Bifhops to be of the Privy-Council, and to fit in the Courts of Juftice, feem'd at firft wonderfully to facilitate all

L 2

that

70 OXFORD UNIVERSITY PRESS, Oxford, 1702–1704

Edward Hyde, Earl of Clarendon: *The History of the Rebellion
and Civil Wars in England*   10¾ x 17

C. JULII CÆSARIS

Ante Chr.
LVII.
U.C. *Varr.*
DCXCVII.

COMMENTARIORUM

DE

BELLO GALLICO

LIBER II.

UUM effet Cæfar in citeriore Gallia in hibernis, ita uti fupra demonftravimus; crebri ad eum rumores afferebantur, litterifque item Labieni certior fiebat, omnes Belgas, quam tertiam effe Galliæ partem dixeramus, contra populum R. conjurare; obfi-

§. 1.
Belgarum
omnium con-
tra P.R.con-
juratio.

defque inter fe dare: Conjurandi has effe cauffas: primum, quod vererentur, ne, omni pacata Gallia, ad eos exercitus nofter adduceretur: deinde, quod ab nonnullis Gallis follicitarentur; partim qui ut Germanos diutius in Gallia verfari noluerant, ita populi R. exercitum hiemare atque inveterafcere in Gallia molefte ferebant; partim qui mobilitate & levitate animi, novis imperiis ftudebant: ab nonnullis etiam, quod in Gal-

I 2   lia

QVINTI
HORATII FLACCI
OPERA.
VOL. I.

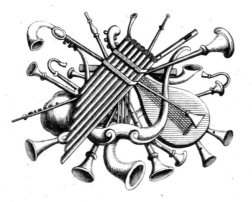

LONDINI
AENEIS TABVLIS INCIDIT
IOHANNES PINE
MDCCXXXIII.

72   JOHN PINE, London, 1733–1737

Horace: *Opera*   5¼ x 8¾

M. T. CICERO's
CATO MAJOR,
OR HIS
DISCOURSE
OF
OLD-AGE:

With Explanatory NOTES.

PHILADELPHIA:
Printed and Sold by B. FRANKLIN,
MDCCXLIV.

73 BENJAMIN FRANKLIN, Philadelphia, 1744
Cicero: *Cato Major* 6⅛ x 8½

FABLE II.

Le Corbeau et le Renard.

Maître Corbeau fur un arbre perché,
Tenoit en fon bec un fromage:
Maître Renard, par l'odeur alléché,
Lui tint à peu près ce langage.
Hé bon jour, Monfieur du Corbeau!
Que vous êtes joli! Que vous me femblez beau!
Sans mentir, fi votre ramage
Se rapporte à votre plumage,
Vous êtes le phénix des hôtes de ces bois.
A ces mots, le Corbeau ne fe fent pas de joie:
Et pour montrer fa belle voix,
Il ouvre un large bec, laiffe tomber fa proie.
Le Renard s'en faifit, & dit: mon bon Monfieur,
Apprenez que tout flatteur
Vit aux dépens de celui qui l'écoute:
Cette leçon vaut bien un fromage fans doute.
Le Corbeau honteux & confus
Jura, mais un peu tard, qu'on ne l'y prendroit plus.

LE CORBEAU ET LE RENARD, Fable II.

74 CHARLES ANTOINE JOMBERT
Paris, 1755–1759

Jean de La Fontaine: *Fables Choisies Mises en Vers*
11⅛ x 16

LE CALENDRIER
DES VIEILLARDS.
Nouvelle tirée de Bocace.

PLUS d'une fois je me suis étonné
Que ce qui fait la paix du mariage,
En est le point le moins confidéré.
Lorfque l'on met une fille en ménage,
Les pere & mere ont pour objet le bien ;
Tout le furplus, ils le comptent pour rien ;
Jeunes tendrons à vieillards apparient ;
Et cependant je vois qu'ils fe foucient
D'avoir chevaux à leur char attelés
De même taille, & mêmes chiens couplés.
Ainfi des bœufs, qui de force pareille
Sont toûjours pris : car ce feroit merveille
Si, fans cela, la charrue alloit bien.
Comment pourroit celle du mariage
Ne mal aller, étant un attelage
Qui bien fouvent ne fe rapporte en rien ?
J'en vas conter un exemple notable.
   ON fçait qui fut Richard de Quinzica,
Qui mainte fête à fa femme allégua,
Mainte Vigile, & maint jour fériable,

E iij

75   JOSEPH GÉRARD BARBOU, Amsterdam [Paris], 1762
Jean de La Fontaine: *Contes et Nouvelles en Vers*   4⅝ x 7¼

PUBLII VIRGILII

MARONIS

BUCOLICA,

GEORGICA,

ET

AENEIS.

BIRMINGHAMIAE:

Typis JOHANNIS BASKERVILLE.

MDCCLVII.

76 JOHN BASKERVILLE, Birmingham, 1757

Virgil: *Bucolica, Georgica, et Aeneis*   8¾ x 11 ⁵⁄₁₆

Jamque eadem fummis pariter, minimifque libido:
Nec melior pedibus filicem quæ conterit atrum;
Quam quæ longorum vehitur cervice Syrorum.
Ut fpectet ludos, conducit Ogulnia veftem,
Conducit comites, fellam, cervical, amicas,
Nutricem, et flavam, cui det mandata, puellam.
Hæc tamen argenti fupereft quodcumque paterni
Lævibus athletis, ac vafa noviffima donat.
Multis res angufta domi eft: fed nulla pudorem
Paupertatis habet; nec fe metitur ad illum,
Quem dedit hæc pofuitque modum. Tamen utile quid fit,
Profpiciunt aliquando viri; frigufque, famemque,
Formica tandem quidam expavere magiftra.
Prodiga non fentit pereuntem fœmina cenfum:
At velut exhaufta redivivus pullulet arca
Nummus, et e pleno femper tollatur acervo,
Non unquam reputat, quanti fibi gaudia conftent.
Sunt quas eunuchi imbelles, ac mollia femper
Ofcula delectent, et defperatio barbæ,
Et quod abortivo non eft opus. Illa voluptas
Summa tamen, quod jam calida et matura juventa
Inguina traduntur medicis, jam pectine nigro.

K   Ergo

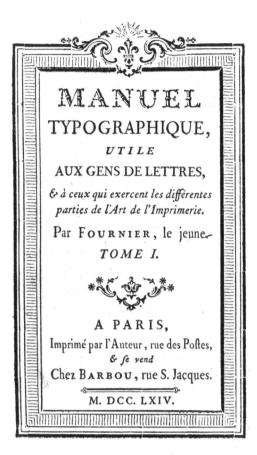

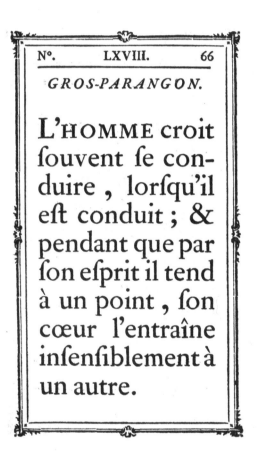

78 PIERRE SIMON FOURNIER, Paris, 1764
Pierre Simon Fournier: *Manuel Typographique*
4¼ x 6¾

PARADISE LOST,

A POEM.

THE AUTHOR

JOHN MILTON.

GLASGOW:

PRINTED BY ROBERT AND ANDREW FOULIS,
PRINTERS TO THE UNIVERSITY,
M.DCC.LXX.

79   ROBERT AND ANDREW FOULIS, Glasgow, 1770
John Milton: *Paradise Lost*   9¼ x 14¾

LES
BAISERS,
PRÉCÉDÉS
DU MOIS DE MAI,
POËME.

A LA HAYE,

Et se trouve à Paris,

Chez LAMBERT, Imprimeur, rue de la Harpe.

ET DELALAIN, rue de la Comédie Françoise.

M. DCC. LXX.

80 LAMBERT AND DELALAIN, The Hague [Paris], 1770

Claude-Joseph Dorat: *Les Baisers*   5½ x 9

LA GUERRA
DE JUGURTA
POR
CAYO SALUSTIO CRISPO.

IN causa alguna se quexan los hombres de que su naturaleza es flaca y de corta duracion ; y que se govierna mas por la suerte , que por su virtud. Porque si bien se mira , se hallarà por el contrario , que no hai en el mundo cosa mayor , ni mas excelente ; y que no la falta vigor ni tiempo , si solo aplicacion e industria. Es pues la guia y el govierno entero de nuestra vida el animo ; el qual , si se encamina a la gloria por el sendero de la virtud , harto

C. SALLUSTII CRISPI
IUGURTHA.

Falso queritur de natura sua genus humanum , quod imbecille , atque ævi brevis, sorte potius , quam virtute , regatur. Nam contra reputando , neque majus aliud , neque præstabilius invenias ; magisque naturæ industriam hominum , quam vim , aut tempus deesse. Sed dux , atque imperator vitæ mortalium , animus est : qui ubi ad gloriam virtutis via grassa-

N

Sallust: *La Conjuración de Catilina y la Guerra de Jugurta*   9⅞ x 13¾

LECTO VSI FVERINT: QVAM LI-
CENTIAM QVVM ET IPSE ANA-
·CREON MINIME RESPVERIT, VI-
TIO NE VERTENDVM ILLI ERIT,
SI EIVS DICTIO, SCRIBENDIQVE
RATIO CONSTANTER *IONICA* A-
LICVI NEQVAQVAM VISA SIT?

CAPVT IX.

HACTENVS DE GALLIS, GER-
MANIS, BATAVIS ANACREONTIS
INTERPRETIBVS, ATQVE ENAR-
RATORIBVS DIXI. NVNC AD BRI-
TANNOS VENIO, QVI QVEMAD-
MODVM IN VNIVERSAE NATV-
RAE INVESTIGATIONE, IN MA-

THEMATICIS DISCIPLINIS , IN
PHILOSOPHICIS MEDITATIONI-
BVS CAETERIS PLERVMQVE AN-
TESTARE VIDENTVR; SIC ETIAM
IN ANTIQVIS SCRIPTORIBVS IN-
GENIOSE, DISERTEQVE VERTEN-
DIS, ENVCLEANDISQVE SVM-
MAM, ET SINGVLAREM LAVDEM
OBTINVERVNT. PRIMVM, QVOD
ANGLICA TYPOGRAPHIA RERVM
ANACREONTICARVM SPECIMEN
EXHIBVIT, FVIT ODARIORVM E-
DITIO LONDINI CVRATA ANNO
MDCLVI AD FIDEM LAVDATI E-
XEMPLARIS H. STEPHANI. TVM
COMPTISSIMIS, ET SVAVISSIMIS
HISCE CARMINIBVS EXPLICAN-

Anacreon: Odes (Greek)   4¼ x 6¼

Q.

HORATII

FLACCI

OPERA

PARMAE

IN AEDIBVS PALATINIS

CIƆ IƆ CC LXXXXI.

TYPIS BODONIANIS.

83 GIAMBATTISTA BODONI, Parma, 1791

Horace: *Opera*   12 x 18¾₆

delle lettere; a dimostrar il quale se possono i doviziosi cercare sfoggiati volumi superbamente impressi, sarà ufficio dell'arte tipografica il somministrarne. Converralle adunque perciò trovar il bello nel grande, come abbiam veduto che per lo comodo ella dee trovarlo nel piccolo.

Ma il bello in che direm noi che consista? Forse più che in altro in due cose; nella convenienza, che la mente appaga, soddisfatta quando riflettendo ella scorge le parti tutte d'un'opera cospirare a uno stesso intento, e nella proporzione, che contenta gli sguardi, o più veramente la fantasia, la qual serba in sè certe immagini e figure, alle quali ciò che più conformasi più le piace. E la

Giambattista Bodoni: *Manuale Tipografico*   8⅜ x 11⅞

CORALE
3

Quousque tan-
dem abutêre, Ca-
tilina , patientiâ
nostrâ? quamdiu
etiam furor iste
tuus nos eludet ?
quem ad finem se-

COMACCHIO

85 GIAMBATTISTA BODONI (Widow of), Parma, 1818
Giambattista Bodoni: *Manuale Tipografico* 8⅜ x 11⅞

THE

DRAMATIC WORKS

OF

SHAKSPEARE

REVISED

BY GEORGE STEEVENS.

AS YOU LIKE IT.

LONDON

PRINTED BY W. BULMER & CO.

𝕾𝖍𝖆𝖐𝖘𝖕𝖊𝖆𝖗𝖊 𝕻𝖗𝖎𝖓𝖙𝖎𝖓𝖌-𝕺𝖋𝖋𝖎𝖈𝖊,

FOR JOHN AND JOSIAH BOYDELL, GEORGE AND W. NICOL:

FROM THE TYPES OF P. MARTIN.

MDCCCII.

86 WILLIAM BULMER (for J. Boydell), London, 1792–1802

Shakespeare: *The Dramatic Works* 12⅞ x 17

THE TRAVELLER.

Remote, unfriended, melancholy, slow,
Or by the lazy Scheld, or wandering Po;
Or onward, where the rude Carinthian boor
Against the houseless stranger shuts the door;
Or where Campania's plain forsaken lies,
A weary waste, expanding to the skies;
Where-e'er I roam, whatever realms to see,
My heart, untravell'd, fondly turns to thee:
Still to my Brother turns, with ceaseless pain,
And drags at each remove a lengthening chain.

87 WILLIAM BULMER, London, 1795
Poems by Goldsmith and Parnell   9⅜ x 11⅞

THE

SEASONS,

BY

James Thomſon.

ILLUSTRATED WITH

ENGRAVINGS

BY

F. BARTOLOZZI, R. A. AND *P. W. TOMKINS,*

Hiſtorical Engravers to Their Majeſties;

FROM

ORIGINAL PICTURES

PAINTED FOR THE WORK

BY

W. HAMILTON, R. A.

LONDON:

PRINTED FOR P. W. TOMKINS, NEW BOND-STREET.

THE LETTER-PRESS BY T. BENSLEY.

THE TYPES BY V. FIGGINS.

MDCCXCVII.

13

To naked waste; a dreary vale of tears:
The great magician's dead! thou poor pale piece
Of outcast earth—in darkness! what a change
From yesterday! thy darling hope so near,
Long-labour'd prize, O how ambition flush'd
Thy glowing cheek! ambition, truly great,
Of virtuous praise: death's subtle seed within,
Sly, treacherous miner! working in the dark,
Smiled at thy well-concerted scheme, and beckon'd
The worm to riot on that rose so red,
Unfaded ere it fell—one moment's prey!
  Man's foresight is conditionally wise;
Lorenzo! wisdom into folly turns
Oft, the first instant its idea fair
To lab'ring thought is born: how dim our eye!
* The present moment terminates our sight;
Clouds, thick as those on doomsday, drown the next;
We penetrate, we prophesy in vain:
Time is dealt out by particles; and each,
Ere mingled with the streaming sands of life,
By fate's inviolable oath is sworn
Deep silence, " where eternity begins."
  By nature's law, what may be, may be now;
There's no prerogative in human hours:
In human hearts what bolder thought can rise,
Than man's presumption on to-morrow's dawn?
Where is to-morrow?—in another world!
For numbers this is certain; the reverse
Is sure to none; and yet on this perhaps,
This peradventure—infamous for lies,

Pub.d June 27.th 1796. by R. Edwards. N.º 142 New Bond Street.

89   WILLIAM BLAKE (Illustrator), London, 1797
Edward Young: *Night Thoughts*   12¾ x 16⅜

CONTES

ET

NOUVELLES EN VERS.

PAR

JEAN DE LA FONTAINE.

TOME PREMIER.

A PARIS,

DE L'IMPRIMERIE DE P. DIDOT L'AÎNÉ.

L'AN III DE LA RÉPUBLIQUE.

M. DCC. XCV.

90   PIERRE DIDOT L'AÎNÉ, Paris, 1795

Jean de La Fontaine: *Contes et Nouvelles en Vers*   9¼ x 12¼

PUBLII

VIRGILII MARONIS

GEORGICA.

~~~~~~~~~~~~~~~~~~~~~~~~~~~~~~~~~~~~~

LIBER PRIMUS.

Quid faciat lætas segetes, quo sidere terram
Vertere, Mæcenas, ulmisque adjungere vites,
Conveniat; quæ cura boum, qui cultus habendo
Sit pecori; apibus quanta experientia parcis;
Hinc canere incipiam. Vos, o clarissima mundi
Lumina, labentem cœlo quæ ducitis annum,
Liber, et alma Ceres, vestro si munere tellus
Chaoniam pingui glandem mutavit arista,
Poculaque inventis Acheloïa miscuit uvis;
Et vos, agrestum præsentia numina, Fauni,
Ferte simul, Faunique, pedem, Dryadesque puellæ:
Munera vestra cano. Tuque o, cui prima frementem
Fudit equum magno tellus percussa tridenti,
Neptune; et cultor nemorum, cui pinguia Ceæ

7.

91 PIERRE DIDOT L'AÎNÉ, Paris, 1798

Virgil: *Bucolica, Georgica, et Aeneis* 13¼ x 18⅞

92　PIERRE DIDOT L'AÎNÉ, Paris, 1801

Jean Racine, *Oeuvres*　14 x 19¾

OEUVRES

DE

JEAN RACINE.

....

TOME PREMIER.

À PARIS,

DE L'IMPRIMERIE DE PIERRE DIDOT L'AÎNÉ,

AU PALAIS NATIONAL DES SCIENCES ET ARTS.

AN IX; M. DCCCI.

93 PIERRE DIDOT L'AÎNÉ, Paris, 1801

Jean Racine, *Oeuvres* 14 x 19¾

THE

Complete Angler

OR THE

CONTEMPLATIVE MAN'S RECREATION

BEING A DISCOURSE OF RIVERS FISH-PONDS

FISH AND FISHING WRITTEN BY

IZAAK WALTON

AND

INSTRUCTIONS HOW TO ANGLE FOR A TROUT OR

GRAYLING IN A CLEAR STREAM BY

CHARLES COTTON

WITH ORIGINAL MEMOIRS AND NOTES BY

SIR HARRIS NICOLAS

K.C.M.G.

LONDON

WILLIAM PICKERING

1836

94 WILLIAM PICKERING, London, 1836

Izaak Walton: *The Complete Angler*   7⅛ x 10⅝

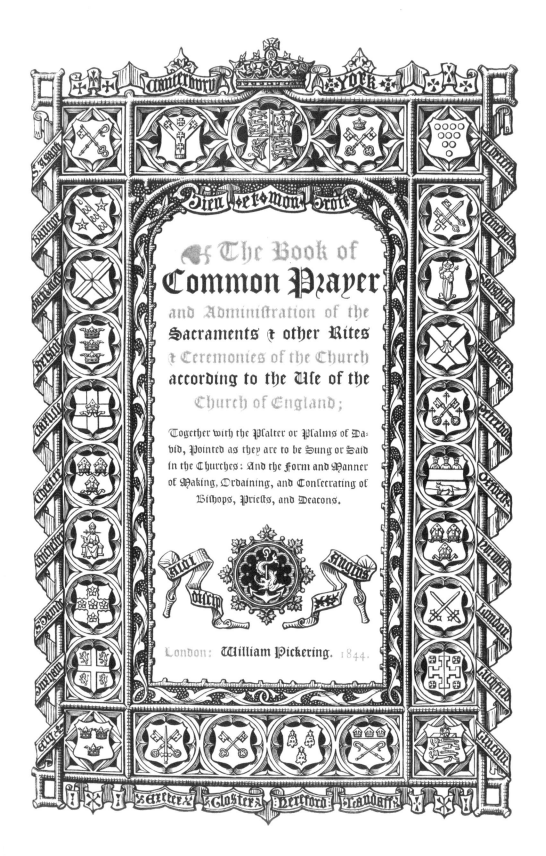

95 WILLIAM PICKERING, London, 1844

The Book of Common Prayer 9 x 13¾

de l'amitié, se réveillaient dans leur âme, une
religion pure, aidée par des mœurs chastes, les
dirigeaient vers une autre vie, comme la flamme
qui s'envole vers le ciel, lorsqu'elle n'a plus
d'aliment sur la terre.

es devoirs de la nature ajou-
taient encore au bonheur de
leur société. Leur amitié mu-
tuelle redoublait à la vue de
leurs enfants, fruit d'un amour
également infortuné. Elles prenaient plaisir à les
mettre ensemble dans le même bain et à les
coucher dans le même berceau. Souvent elles les
changeaient de lait. « Mon amie, disait madame
» de La Tour, chacune de nous aura deux enfants,
» et chacun de nos enfants aura deux mères. »
Comme deux bourgeons qui restent sur deux
arbres de la même espèce, dont la tempête a
brisé toutes les branches, viennent à produire
des fruits plus doux, si chacun d'eux, détaché
du tronc maternel, est greffé sur le tronc voi-
sin ; ainsi, ces deux petits enfants, privés de tous
leurs parents, se remplissaient de sentiments
plus tendres que ceux de fils et de fille, de
frère et de sœur, quand ils venaient à être chan-
gés de mamelles par les deux amies qui leur

LONDRES

De nombreux voyages en Angleterre, et des séjours fréquents et prolongés dans la capitale des Trois-Royaumes, nous ont fait pénétrer assez intimement dans la vie anglaise; nous en connaissons les contrastes, et nous en avons sondé les mystères; nous avons, à plusieurs reprises, étudié ses aspects divers, multiples et changeants. — Et pourtant, au moment de prendre la plume pour écrire la première page d'un livre qui s'appellera LONDRES, nous comprenons si bien la grandeur et la difficulté de notre tâche, que nous éprouvons un mouvement d'hésitation et de doute. L'impossibilité de tout dire et la certitude d'être incomplet se présentent à nous avec une évidence désespérante. Nous

1

97 GUSTAVE DORÉ (Illustrator), Paris, 1876
L. Enault: *Londres* 10¾ x 14⅝

WITH DECORATIONS BY CHARLES RICKETTS
LONDON MDCCCXCIV
ELKIN MATHEWS AND JOHN LANE . AT THE SIGN OF THE BODLEY HEAD.

IN A DIM CORNER OF MY ROOM FOR LONGER THAN MY FANCY THINKS
A BEAUTIFUL AND SILENT SPHINX HAS WATCHED ME THROUGH THE SHIFTING GLOOM.

INVIOLATE AND IMMOBILE SHE DOES NOT RISE SHE DOES NOT STIR
FOR SILVER MOONS ARE NAUGHT TO HER AND NAUGHT TO HER THE SUNS THAT REEL.

RED FOLLOWS GREY ACROSS THE AIR THE WAVES OF MOONLIGHT EBB AND FLOW
BUT WITH THE DAWN SHE DOES NOT GO AND IN THE NIGHT-TIME SHE IS THERE.

DAWN FOLLOWS DAWN AND NIGHTS GROW OLD AND ALL THE WHILE THIS CURIOUS CAT
LIES COUCHING ON THE CHINESE MAT WITH EYES OF SATIN RIMMED WITH GOLD.

UPON THE MAT SHE LIES AND LEERS AND ON THE TAWNY THROAT OF HER
FLUTTERS THE SOFT AND SILKY FUR OR RIPPLES TO HER POINTED EARS.

COME FORTH MY LOVELY SENESCHAL! SO SOMNOLENT, SO STATUESQUE!
COME FORTH YOU EXQUISITE GROTESQUE! HALF WOMAN AND HALF ANIMAL!

COME FORTH MY LOVELY LANGUOROUS SPHINX! AND PUT YOUR HEAD UPON MY KNEE!
AND LET ME STROKE YOUR THROAT AND SEE YOUR BODY SPOTTED LIKE THE LYNX!

AND LET ME TOUCH THOSE CURVING CLAWS OF YELLOW IVORY AND GRASP
THE TAIL THAT LIKE A MONSTROUS ASP COILS ROUND YOUR HEAVY VELVET PAWS!

A THOUSAND

98   CHARLES RICKETTS (Designer and Illustrator), London, 1894
Oscar Wilde: *The Sphinx*   6¾ x 8⅝

They shift the moving Toyshop of their Heart ;   100
Where Wigs with Wigs, with Sword-knots Sword-knots
     strive,
Beaux banish Beaux, and Coaches Coaches drive.
This erring Mortals Levity may call,
Oh blind to Truth ! the *Sylphs* contrive it all.

    Of these am I, who thy Protection claim,   105
A watchful Sprite, and *Ariel* is my Name.
Late, as I rang'd the crystal Wilds of Air,
In the clear Mirror of thy ruling *Star*
I saw, alas ! some dread Event impend,
Ere to the Main this morning's Sun descend,   110
But Heav'n reveals not what, or how, or where :
Warn'd by thy *Sylph*, oh pious Maid beware !
This to disclose is all thy Guardian can.
Beware of all, but most beware of Man !

    He said : when *Shock*, who thought she slept too long,
Leap'd up, and wak'd his Mistress with his Tongue.   116
'Twas then, *Belinda !* if Report say true,
Thy Eyes first open'd on a *Billet-doux ;*
Wounds, Charms, and *Ardors,* were no sooner read,
But all the Vision vanish'd from thy Head.   120

    And now, unveil'd, the *Toilet* stands display'd,
Each Silver Vase in mystic Order laid.

99   AUBREY BEARDSLEY (Illustrator)
CHISWICK PRESS, London, 1896

Alexander Pope: *The Rape of the Lock*   8 x 10

And they are gone: aye, ages long ago
These lovers fled away into the storm.
That night the Baron dreamt of many a woe,
And all his warrior-guests, with shade and form
Of witch, and demon, and large coffin-worm,
Were long be-nightmar'd. Angela the old
Died palsy-twitch'd, with meagre face deform;
The Beadsman, after thousand aves told,
For aye unsought-for slept among his ashes cold.

HYPERION. A Fragment.

BOOK I.

EEP in the shady
sadness of a vale
Far sunken from the
healthy breath of morn,
Far from the fiery noon,
and eve's one star,
Sat gray-hair'd Saturn,
quiet as a stone,
Still as the silence round
about his lair;
Forest on forest hung about his head
Like cloud on cloud. No stir of air was there,
Not so much life as on a summer's day
Robs not one light seed from the feather'd grass,
But where the dead leaf fell, there did it rest.
A stream went voiceless by, still deadened more

205

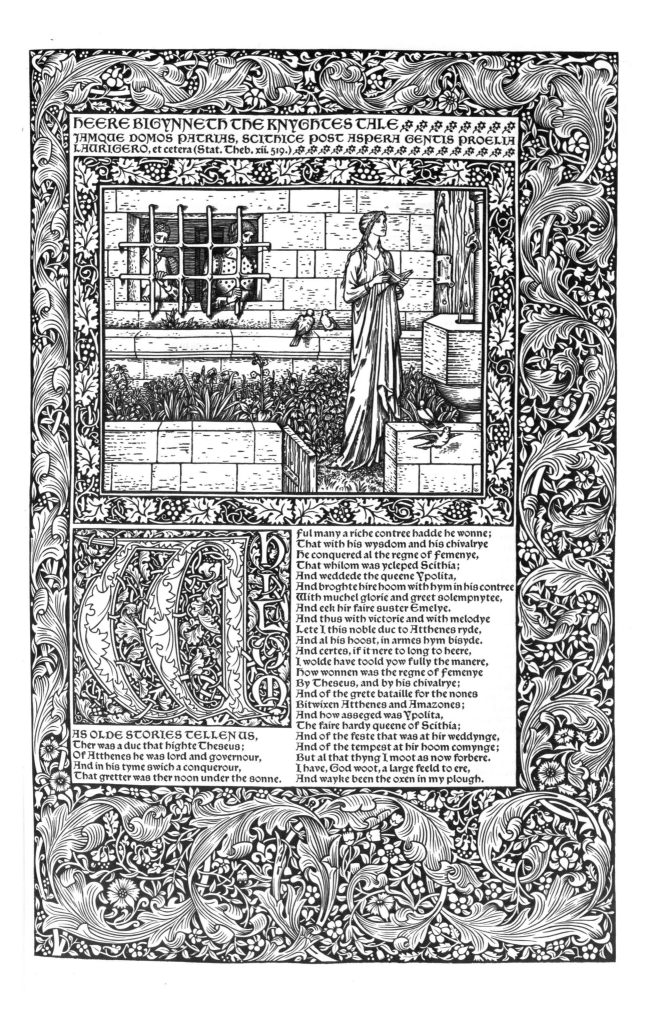

KELMSCOTT PRESS, Hammersmith, 1896

Geoffrey Chaucer: *Works*   11 x 16½

PRÉFACE
DU TRADUCTEUR

———

*La version faite par Amyot des Pastorales de
Longus, bien que remplie d'agrément, comme tout le
monde sait, est incomplète et inexacte; non qu'il ait
eu dessein de s'écarter en rien du texte de l'auteur,
mais c'est que d'abord il n'eut point l'ouvrage grec
entier, dont il n'y avoit en ce temps-là que des copies
fort mutilées. Car tous les anciens manuscrits de
Longus ont des lacunes et des fautes considérables,
et ce n'est que depuis peu qu'en en comparant plusieurs, on est parvenu à suppléer l'un par l'autre et*

B.

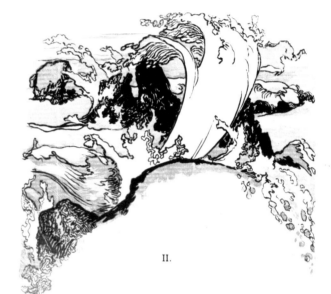

soutenu et comme échauffé par les oranges qui se maintinrent, à leur tour, sans s'adultérer, appuyés et, en quelque sorte, attisés qu'ils furent par le souffle pressant des bleus.

En fait de meubles, des Esseintes n'eut pas de longues recherches à opérer, le seul luxe de cette pièce devant consister en des livres et des fleurs rares ; il se borna, se réservant d'orner plus tard, de quelques dessins ou de quelques tableaux, les cloisons demeurées nues, à établir sur la majeure partie de ses murs des rayons et des casiers de bibliothèque en bois d'ébène, à joncher le parquet de peaux de bêtes fauves et de fourrures de renards bleus, à installer près d'une massive table de changeur du xvᵐᵉ siècle, de profonds fauteuils à oreillettes et un vieux pupitre de chapelle, en fer forgé, un de ces antiques lutrins sur lesquels le diacre plaçait jadis l'antiphonaire et qui supportait maintenant l'un des pesants in-folios du Glossarium mediæ et infimæ latinitatis de du Cange.

Les croisées dont les vitres, craquelées, bleuâtres, parsemées de culs de bouteille aux bosses piquetées d'or, interceptaient la vue de la campagne et ne laissaient pénétrer qu'une lumière feinte, se vêtirent, à leur tour, de rideaux taillés dans de vieilles étoles, dont l'or assombri et quasi sauré, s'éteignait dans la trame d'un roux presque mort.

Enfin, sur la cheminée dont la robe fut, elle aussi, découpée dans la somptueuse étoffe d'une dalmatique florentine, entre deux ostensoirs, en cuivre doré, de style byzantin, provenant de l'ancienne Abbaye-au-Bois de Bièvre, un merveilleux canon d'église, aux trois compartiments séparés, ouvragés comme une dentelle, contint, sous le verre de son cadre, copiées sur un authentique vélin, avec d'admirables lettres de missel et de splendides enluminures, trois pièces de Baudelaire : à droite et à gauche, les sonnets portant ces titres « La Mort des Amants » — «L'Ennemi» ; — au milieu, le poème en prose intitulé : « Any where out of the world — N'importe où, hors du monde ».

II.

APRÈS la vente de ses biens, des Esseintes garda les deux vieux domestiques qui avaient soigné sa mère et rempli tout à la fois l'office de régisseurs et de concierges du château de Lourps, demeuré jusqu'à l'époque de sa mise en adjudication inhabité et vide.

Il fit venir à Fontenay ce ménage habitué à un emploi de garde-malade, à une régularité d'infirmiers distribuant, d'heure en heure, des cuillerées de potion et de tisane, à un rigide silence de moines claustrés, sans communication avec le dehors, dans des pièces aux fenêtres et aux portes closes.

Le mari fut chargé de nettoyer les chambres et d'aller aux provisions, la femme, de préparer la cuisine. Il leur céda le premier étage de la maison, les obligea à porter d'épais chaussons de feutre,

103   AUGUSTE LEPÈRE (Illustrator), *Les Cents Bibliophiles*, Paris, 1903
   J. K. Huysmans: *À Rebours*   6¾ x 10⅛

IN THE BEGINNING

GOD CREATED THE HEAVEN AND THE EARTH. ⟨AND THE EARTH WAS WITHOUT FORM, AND VOID; AND DARKNESS WAS UPON THE FACE OF THE DEEP, & THE SPIRIT OF GOD MOVED UPON THE FACE OF THE WATERS. ⟨And God said, Let there be light: & there was light. And God saw the light, that it was good: & God divided the light from the darkness. And God called the light Day, and the darkness he called Night. And the evening and the morning were the first day. ⟨And God said, Let there be a firmament in the midst of the waters, & let it divide the waters from the waters. And God made the firmament, and divided the waters which were under the firmament from the waters which were above the firmament: & it was so. And God called the firmament Heaven. And the evening & the morning were the second day. ⟨And God said, Let the waters under the heaven be gathered together unto one place, and let the dry land appear: and it was so. And God called the dry land Earth; and the gathering together of the waters called he Seas: and God saw that it was good. And God said, Let the earth bring forth grass, the herb yielding seed, and the fruit tree yielding fruit after his kind, whose seed is in itself, upon the earth: & it was so. And the earth brought forth grass, & herb yielding seed after his kind, & the tree yielding fruit, whose seed was in itself, after his kind: and God saw that it was good. And the evening & the morning were the third day. ⟨And God said, Let there be lights in the firmament of the heaven to divide the day from the night; and let them be for signs, and for seasons, and for days, & years: and let them be for lights in the firmament of the heaven to give light upon the earth: & it was so. And God made two great lights; the greater light to rule the day, and the lesser light to rule the night: he made the stars also. And God set them in the firmament of the heaven to give light upon the earth, and to rule over the day and over the night, & to divide the light from the darkness: and God saw that it was good. And the evening and the morning were the fourth day. ⟨And God said, Let the waters bring forth abundantly the moving creature that hath life, and fowl that may fly above the earth in the open firmament of heaven. And God created great whales, & every living creature that moveth, which the waters brought forth abundantly, after their kind, & every winged fowl after his kind: & God saw that it was good. And God blessed them, saying, Be fruitful, & multiply, and fill the waters in the seas, and let fowl multiply in the earth. And the evening & the morning were the fifth day. ⟨And God said, Let the earth bring forth the living creature after his kind, cattle, and creeping thing, and beast of the earth after his kind: and it was so. And God made the beast of the earth after his kind, and cattle after their kind, and every thing that creepeth upon the

27

104   DOVES PRESS, Hammersmith, 1903–1905

The English Bible   9¼ x 13¼

SCÈNE PREMIÈRE.
ÉLIANTE, PHILINTE.

PHILINTE.

Non, l'on n'a point vu d'âme à manier si dure,
Ni d'accommodement plus pénible à conclure :
En vain de tous côtés on l'a voulu tourner,
Hors de son sentiment on n'a pu l'entraîner;
Et jamais différend si bizarre, je pense,
N'avoit de ces Messieurs occupé la prudence.
« Non, Messieurs, disoit-il, je ne me dédis point,
Et tomberai d'accord de tout, hors de ce point.
De quoi s'offense-t-il? et que veut-il me dire?

11.

walt, ihr Werthſchäßenden: und dieß iſt eure verborgene Liebe und eurer Seele Glänzen, Zittern und Überwallen. Aber eine ſtärkere Gewalt wächſt aus euren Werthen und eine neue Überwindung: an der zerbricht Ei und Eierſchale. Und wer ein Schöpfer ſein muß im Guten und Böſen: wahrlich, der muß ein Vernichter erſt ſein und Werthe zerbrechen. Alſo gehört das höchſte Böſe zur höchſten Güte: dieſe aber iſt die ſchöpferiſche. – Reden wir nur davon, ihr Weiſeſten, ob es gleich ſchlimm iſt. Schweigen iſt ſchlimmer; alle verſchwiegenen Wahrheiten werden giftig. Und mag doch Alles zerbrechen, was an unſeren Wahrheiten zerbrechen – kann! Manches Haus giebt es noch zu bauen! –

ALSO SPRACH ZARATHUSTRA.

VON DEN ERHABENEN

STILL iſt der Grund meines Meeres: wer erriethe wohl, daß er ſcherz-hafte Ungeheuer birgt! Unerſchütterlich iſt meine Tiefe: aber ſie glänzt von ſchwimmenden Räthſeln und Gelächtern. Einen Erhabenen ſah ich heute, einen Feierlichen, einen Büßer des Geiſtes: oh wie lachte meine Seele ob ſeiner Häßlichkeit! Mit erhobener Bruſt und Denen gleich, welche den Athem an ſich ziehn: alſo ſtand er da, der Erhabene, und ſchweig-ſam: Behängt mit häßlichen Wahrheiten, ſeiner Jagdbeute, und reich an zerriſſenen Kleidern; auch viele Dornen hiengen an ihm – aber noch ſah ich keine Roſe. Noch lernte er das Lachen nicht und die Schönheit. Finſter kam dieſer Jäger zurück aus dem Walde der Erkenntniß. Vom Kampfe kehrte er heim mit wilden Thieren: aber aus ſeinem Ernſte blickt auch noch ein wildes Thier – ein unüberwundenes! Wie ein Tiger ſteht er immer noch da, der ſpringen will; aber ich mag dieſe geſpannten Seelen nicht, unhold iſt mein Geſchmack allen dieſen Zurückgezognen. Und ihr ſagt mir, Freunde, daß nicht zu ſtreiten ſei über Geſchmack und Schmecken? Aber alles Leben iſt Streit um Geſchmack und Schmecken! Geſchmack: das iſt Gewicht zugleich und Wagſchale und Wägender; und wehe allem Lebendigen, das ohne Streit um Gewicht und Wagſchale und Wägende leben wollte! Wenn er ſeiner Erhabenheit müde würde, dieſer Erha-bene: dann erſt würde ſeine Schönheit anheben, – und dann erſt will ich ihn ſchmecken und ſchmackhaft finden. Und erſt, wenn er ſich von ſich ſel-ber abwendet, wird er über ſeinen eignen Schatten ſpringen – und, wahrlich! hinein in ſeine Sonne. Allzulange ſaß er im Schatten, die Wangen bleich-ten dem Büßer des Geiſtes; faſt verhungerte er an ſeinen Erwartungen. Verachtung iſt noch in ſeinem Auge; und Ekel birgt ſich an ſeinem Munde. Zwar ruht er jeßt, aber ſeine Ruhe hat ſich noch nicht in die Sonne gelegt. Dem Stiere gleich ſollte er thun; und ſein Glück ſollte nach Erde riechen, und nicht nach Verachtung der Erde. Als weißen Stier möchte ich ihn ſehn, wie er ſchnaubend und brüllend der Pflugſchar vorangeht: und ſein Gebrüll ſollte noch alles Irdiſche preiſen! Dunkel noch iſt ſein Antliß; der Hand Schatten ſpielt auf ihm. Verſchattet iſt noch der Sinn ſeines Auges. Seine That ſelber iſt noch der Schatten auf ihm: die Hand verdunkelt den Handelnden. Noch hat er ſeine That nicht überwunden. Wohl liebe ich an ihm den Nacken des Stiers: aber nun will ich auch noch das Auge des Engels ſehn. Auch ſeinen Helden-Willen muß er noch verlernen: ein Gehobener ſoll er mir ſein und nicht nur ein Erhabener: – der Äther ſelber ſollte ihn heben, den Willenloſen! Er bezwang Unthiere, er löſte Räthſel: aber erlöſen ſollte er auch noch ſeine Unthiere und Räthſel, zu himmliſchen Kindern ſollte er ſie noch verwandeln. Noch hat ſeine Erkenntniß nicht

58

106 HENRY VAN DE VELDE (Designer), W. Drugulin, Leipzig, 1908

Friedrich Nietzsche: *Also sprach Zarathustra*   9³⁄₄ x 14⁵⁄₈

IN QUELLA PARTE del libro della mia memoria, dinanzi alla quale poco si potrebbe leggere, si trova una rubrica, la quale dice: Incipit Vita Nova. Sotto la quale rubrica io trovo scritte le parole, le quali è mio intendimento d'assemprare in questo libello, e se non tutte, almeno la loro sentenza. Nove fiate già, appresso al mio nascimento, era tornato lo cielo della luce quasi ad un medesimo punto, quanto alla sua propria girazione, quando alli miei occhi apparve prima la gloriosa donna della mia mente, la quale fu chiamata da molti Beatrice, i quali non sapeano che si chiamare. Ella era già in questa vita stata tanto, che nel suo tempo lo cielo stellato era mosso verso la parte d'oriente delle dodici parti l'una d'un grado: sì che quasi dal principio del suo anno nono apparve a me, ed io la vidi quasi alla fine del mio nono anno. Ella apparvemi vestita di nobilissimo colore, umile ed onesto, sanguigno, cinta ed ornata alla guisa che alla sua giovanissima etade si convenia. In quel punto dico veracemente che lo spirito della vita, lo quale dimora nella segretissima camera del cuore, cominciò a tremare sì fortemente, che appariva ne' menomi polsi orribilmente; & tremando disse queste parole: Ecce Deus for-

b1

tior me, qui veniens dominabitur mihi. In quel punto lo spirito animale, il quale dimora nell' alta camera, nella quale tutti li spiriti sensitivi portano le loro percezioni, si cominciò a maravigliare molto, & parlando spezialmente allo spirito del viso, disse queste parole: Apparuit iam beatitudo vestra. In quel punto lo spirito naturale, il quale dimora in quella parte, ove si ministra lo nutrimento nostro, cominciò a piangere, & piangendo disse queste parole: Heu miser! quia frequenter impeditus ero deinceps. D'allora innanzi dico ch'Amore signoreggiò l'anima mia, la quale fu sì tosto a lui disposta, e cominciò a prendere sopra me tanta sicurtade e tanta signoria, per la virtù che gli dava la mia imaginazione, che mi convenia fare compiutamente tutti i suoi piaceri. Egli mi comandava molte volte, che io cercassi per vedere quest'angiola giovanissima: ond'io nella mia puerizia molte fiate l'andai cercando; e vedeala di sì nobili e laudabili portamenti, che certo di lei si potea dire quella parola del poeta Omero: Ella non pare figliuola d'uomo mortale, ma di Dio. Ed avvegna che la sua immagine, la quale continuamente meco stava, fosse baldanza d'amore a signoreggiarmi, tuttavia era di sì nobile virtù, che nulla volta sofferse, che Amore mi reggesse senza il fedele consiglio della ragione in quelle cose, là dove cotal consiglio fosse utile a udire. E però che soprastare

1

107 ASHENDENE PRESS, Chelsea, 1909

Dante: *Opera*   10⅞ x 16

μηρούς τε κνήμας τε καὶ ἄμφω χεῖρας ὕπερθεν
αὐχένα τε στιβαρὸν μέγα τε σθένος, οὐδέ τι ἥβης
δεύεται, ἀλλὰ κακοῖσι συνέρρηκται πολέεσσιν.
οὐ γὰρ ἐγώ γέ τί φημι κακώτερον ἄλλο θαλάσσης
ἄνδρα γε συγχεῦαι, εἰ καὶ μάλα καρτερὸς εἴη.
Τὸν δ' αὖτ' Εὐρύαλος ἀπαμείβετο φώνησέν τε·
(Λαοδάμαν, μάλα τοῦτο ἔπος κατὰ μοῖραν ἔειπες.)
αὐτὸς νῦν προκάλεσσαι ἰὼν καὶ πέφραδε μῦθον.
Αὐτὰρ ἐπεὶ τό γ' ἄκους' ἀγαθὸς πάις Ἀλκινόοιο,
στῆ ῥ' ἐς μέσσον ἰὼν καὶ Ὀδυσσῆα προσέειπε·
Δεῦρ' ἄγε καὶ σύ, ξεῖνε πάτερ, πείρησαι ἀέθλων
εἴ τινά που δεδάηκας, ἔοικε δὲ ἴδμεν ἀέθλους.
οὐ μὲν γὰρ μεῖζον κλέος ἀνέρος, ὄφρα κ' ἔηισιν,
ἢ ὅ τι ποσσίν τε ῥέξει καὶ χερσὶν ἔηισιν.
ἀλλ' ἄγε πείρησαι, σκέδασον δ' ἀπὸ κήδεα θυμοῦ.
(σοὶ δ' ὁδὸς οὐκέτι δηρὸν ἀπέσσεται, ἀλλά τοι ἤδη
νηῦς τε κατείρυσται καὶ ἐπαρτέες εἰσὶν ἑταῖροι.)
Τὸν δ' ἀπαμειβόμενος προσέφη πολύμητις Ὀδυσσεύς·
Λαοδάμαν, τί με ταῦτα κελεύετε κερτομέοντες;
κήδεά μοι καὶ μᾶλλον ἐνὶ φρεσὶν ἤ περ ἄεθλοι,
ὃς πρὶν μὲν μάλα πολλὰ πάθον καὶ πολλὰ μόγησα,
νῦν δὲ μεθ' ὑμετέρηι ἀγορῆι νόστοιο χατίζων
ἧμαι, λισσόμενος βασιλῆά τε πάντα τε δῆμον.
Τὸν δ' αὖτ' Εὐρύαλος ἀπαμείβετο νείκεσέ τ' ἄντην·
Οὐ γάρ σ' οὐδέ, ξεῖνε, δαήμονι φωτὶ ἐίσκω
(ἄθλων οἷά τε πολλὰ μετ' ἀνθρώποισι πέλονται),
ἀλλὰ τῶι ὅς θ' ἅμα νηὶ πολυκληῖδι θαμίζων,
ἀρχὸς ναυτάων οἵ τε πρηκτῆρες ἔασι,
φόρτου τε μνήμων καὶ ἐπίσκοπος εἰσιν ὁδαίων
(κερδέων θ' ἁρπαλέων, οὐδ' ἀθλητῆρι ἔοικας).
Τὸν δ' ἄρ' ὑπόδρα ἰδὼν προσέφη πολύμητις Ὀδυσσεύς·
Ξεῖν', οὐ καλὸν ἔειπες· ἀτασθάλωι ἀνδρὶ ἔοικας.
οὕτως οὐ πάνθ' ὅσσα θεοὶ χαρίεντα διδοῦσιν
ἀνδράσιν, οὔτε φυὴν οὔτ' ἄρ φρένας οὔτ' ἀγορητύν.

θ 135-168

Knecht sein. Denn auch des Menschen Sohn ist 45
nicht gekommen, daß er sich dienen lasse, sondern
daß er diene und gebe sein Leben zur Bezah=
lung für viele.

+ Und sie kamen gen Jericho. Und da er aus Je= 46
richo ging, er und seine Jünger und ein großes
Volk, da saß ein Blinder, Bartimäus, des Timäus
Sohn, am Wege und bettelte. Und da er hörte, 47
daß es Jesus von Nazareth war, fing er an, zu
schreien und zu sagen: Jesu, du Sohn Davids,
erbarme dich mein! Und viele bedrohten ihn, er 48
sollte stillschweigen. Er aber schrie viel mehr: Du
Sohn Davids, erbarme dich mein! Und Jesus 49
stand still und ließ ihn rufen. Und sie riefen den
Blinden und sprachen zu ihm: Sei getrost! stehe
auf, er ruft dich! Und er warf sein Kleid von sich, 50
stand auf und kam zu Jesu. Und Jesus antwor= 51
tete und sprach zu ihm: Was willst du, daß ich
dir tun soll? Der Blinde sprach zu ihm: Rabbu=
ni, daß ich sehend werde. Jesus aber sprach zu 52
ihm: Gehe hin; dein Glaube hat dir geholfen.

Und alsbald ward er sehend und folgte ihm
nach auf dem Wege.

1 + Und da sie nahe an Jerusalem kamen, gen Beth=
phage und Bethanien, an den Ölberg, sandte
2 er seiner Jünger zwei und sprach zu ihnen: Ge=
het hin in den Flecken, der vor euch liegt. Und
alsbald, wenn ihr hineinkommt, werdet ihr fin=
den ein Füllen angebunden, auf welchem nie ein
Mensch gesessen hat; löset es ab und führet es
3 her! Und so jemand zu euch sagen wird: Warum
tut ihr das? so sprechet: Der Herr bedarf sein; so
4 wird ers alsbald hersenden. Sie gingen hin und
fanden das Füllen gebunden an die Tür, außen
5 auf der Wegscheide, und lösten es ab. Und etliche,
die dastanden, sprachen zu ihnen: Was macht
6 ihr, daß ihr das Füllen ablöset? Sie sagten aber
zu ihnen, wie ihnen Jesus geboten hatte, und die
7 ließens zu. Und sie führten das Füllen zu Jesu
und legten ihre Kleider darauf, und er setzte sich
8 darauf. Viele aber breiteten ihre Kleider auf den
Weg; etliche hieben Maien von den Bäumen und

109   RUDOLF KOCH, Offenbach-am-Main, 1926

Die vier Evangelien   4¾ x 6½

(DIE ECLOGEN VERGILS

IN DER URSPRACHE UND DEUTSCH
ÜBERSETZT VON RUDOLF ALEXANDER
SCHROEDER : MIT ILLUSTRATIONEN

GEZEICHNET UND GESCHNITTEN
VON ARISTIDE MAILLOL

110   CRANACH PRESSE, Weimar, 1926

Virgil: *Eclogues* (Latin and German)   10 x 12⅞

¶ ELEGY ON HIS MISTRESS

BY *our first strange and fatal interview,*
By all desires which thereof did ensue,
By our long starving hopes, by that remorse
Which my words' masculine persuasive force
Begot in thee, and by the memory
Of hurts, which spies and rivals threatened me,
I calmly beg. But by thy father's wrath,
By all pains, which want and divorcement hath,
I conjure thee, and all the oaths which I
And thou have sworn to seal joint constancy,
Here I unswear, and overswear them thus;
Thou shalt not love by ways so dangerous.
Temper, O fair love, love's impetuous rage;
Be my true mistress still, not my feigned page.
I'll go, and, by thy kind leave, leave behind
Thee, only worthy to nurse in my mind
Thirst to come back; oh! if thou die before,
My soul from other lands to thee shall soar.
Thy, else almighty, beauty cannot move
Rage from the seas, nor thy love teach them love,
Nor tame wild Boreas' harshness; thou hast read
How roughly he in pieces shivered
Fair Orithea, whom he swore he loved.
Fall ill or good, 'tis madness to have proved
Dangers unurged; feed on this flattery,
That absent lovers one in the other be.
Dissemble nothing, not a boy, nor change
Thy body's habit, nor mind's; be not strange
To thyself only. All will spy in thy face
A blushing womanly discovering grace.
Richly clothed apes are called apes, and as soon
Eclipsed as bright, we call the moon the moon.

31

III NONESUCH PRESS, London, 1923

The Love Poems of John Donne   6½ x 10¼

LA DIVINA COMMEDIA
OR THE DIVINE VISION OF
DANTE ALIGHIERI
IN ITALIAN &
ENGLISH

The Italian text edited by Mario Casella of the
University of Florence with the English version
of H. F. Cary and 42 illustrations after
the drawings by Sandro Botticelli.
The Nonesuch Press
1928

112 NONESUCH PRESS, London, 1928

Dante: *La Divina Commedia* (Italian and English)   8 x 12⅛

Ready to drop upon me, that when I wak'd
I cri'de to dreame againe.
  Ste. This will prove a brave kingdome to me,
Where I shall have my Musicke for nothing.
  Cal. When *Prospero* is destroy'd.
  Ste. That shall be by and by:
I remember the storie.
  Trin. The sound is going away,
Lets follow it, and after do our worke.
  Ste. Leade Monster,
Wee'l follow: I would I could see this Taborer,
He layes it on.
  Trin. Wilt come?
Ile follow *Stephano.*   *Exeunt.*

Scena Tertia.

                                                  (Another part of the island.)

*Enter Alonso, Sebastian, Anthonio, Gonʒallo,
Adrian, Francisco, &c.*

  Gon. By'r lakin, I can goe no further, Sir,
My old bones akes: here's a maze trod indeede
Through fourth rights, & Meanders: by your patience,
I needes must rest me.
  Al. Old Lord, I cannot blame thee,
Who, am my selfe attach'd with wearinesse
To th' dulling of my spirits: Sit downe, and rest:
Even here I will put off my hope, and keepe it
No longer for my Flatterer: he is droun'd
Whom thus we stray to finde, and the Sea mocks
Our frustrate search on land: well, let him goe.
  Ant. I am right glad, that he's so out of hope: *(Aside to Seb.)*
Doe not for one repulse forgoe the purpose
That you resolv'd t'effeɐt.

4-2

CAPITULUM II. OF THE CROSSE AND THE CROUNE OF OURE LORD JESU CRIST.

T Costantynoble is the Cros of our Lord Jesu Crist, and his Cote withouten Semes, that is clept Tunica inconsutilis, and the Spounge, and the Reed, of the whiche the Jewes zauen oure Lord Eyselle and Galle, in the Cros. And there is on of the Nayles, that Crist was naylled with on the Cros. And some Men trowen, that half the Cros, that Crist was don on, be in Cipres, in an Abbey of Monkes, that Men callen the hille of the holy Cros; but it is not so: For that Cros, that is in Cypre, is the Cros, in the whiche Dysmas the gode Theef was honged onne. But alle Men knowen not that; and that is evylle y don. For for profyt of the Offrynge, thei seye, that it is the Cros of oure Lord Jesu Crist. And zee schulle undrestonde, that the Cros of oure Lord was made of 4 manere of Trees, as it is conteyned in this Vers, In Cruce fit Palma, Cedrus, Cypressus, Oliva, For that pece, that wente upright fro the Erthe to the heved, was of Cypresse; and the pece, that wente overthwart, to the whiche his hondes weren nayled, was of Palme; and the Stock, that stode within the Erthe, in the whiche was made the Morteys, was of Cedre; and the Table aboven his heved, that was a Fote and an half long, on the whiche the Title was writen, in Ebreu, Grece and Latyn, that was Olyve. And the Jewes maden the Cros of theise 4 manere of Trees: For thei trowed that oure Lord Jesu Crist scholde han honged on the Cros, als longe as the Cros myghten laste. And therfore made thei the Foot of the Cros of Cedre. For Cedre may not, in Erthe ne in Watre, rote. And therfore thei wolde, that it scholde have lasted longe. For thei trowed, that the Body of Crist scholde have stonken; therfore thei made that pece, that went from the Erthe upward, of Cypres: For it is welle smellynge; so that the smelle of his Body scholde not greve Men, that wenten forby. And the overthwart pece was of Palme: For in the Olde Testament, it was ordyned, that whan on overcomen, he scholde be crowned with Palme: And for thei trowed, that thei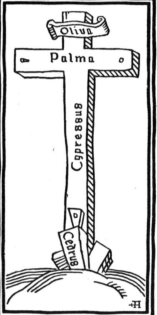 hadden the Victorye of Crist Jesus, therfore made thei the overthwart pece of Palme. And the Table of the Tytle, thei maden of Olyve; for Olyve

6

114 GRABHORN PRESS, San Francisco, 1928

The Voiage and Travaile of Sir John Maundevile, Kt. 9½ x 14¼

disgusted with everything he possesses? Plato said long ago that the best stomachs are not those which refuse all food." "But,"said Candide,"is there not pleasure in criticising, in finding faults where other men think they see beauty?" "That is to say,"answered Martin,"that there is pleasure in not being pleased.""Oh! Well,"said Candide,"then there is no one happy except me—when I see Mademoiselle Cunegonde again.""It is always good to hope,"said Martin. However, the days and weeks went by; Cacambo did not return and Candide was so much plunged in grief that he did not even notice that Paquette and Friar Giroflée had not once come to thank him.

HOW CANDIDE AND MARTIN SUPPED WITH SIX STRANGERS AND WHO THEY WERE

CHAPTER XXVI

ONE evening when Candide and Martin were going to sit down to table with the strangers who lodged in the same hotel, a man with a face the colour of soot came up to him from behind and, taking him by the arm, said: "Get ready to come with us, and do not fail." He turned round and saw Cacambo. Only the sight of Cunegonde could have surprised and pleased him more. He was almost wild with joy. He embraced his dear friend. "Cunegonde is here, of course? Where is she? Take me to her, let me die of joy with her." "Cunegonde is not here," said Cacambo. "She is in Constantinople." "Heavens! In Constantinople! But, were she in China, I would fly to her; let us start at once." "We will start after supper," replied Cacambo. "I cannot tell you any more; I am a slave, and my master is waiting for me; I must go and serve him at table! Do not say anything; eat your supper, and be in readiness." Candide, torn between joy and grief, charmed to see his faithful agent again, amazed to see him a slave, filled with the idea of seeing his mistress again, with turmoil in his heart,

LINES 31-33
The Apennines, interrupted by the strait of Messina, are continued in Sicily by the range anciently called Pelorus. The region of Falterona and Casentino, then well wooded and well watered, has become, owing to deforestation, rather dry. Heavy rains, like that described in Canto v, were then more common.

LINE 43
Porciano.

LINE 46
Arezzo.

LINE 50
Florence. The Florentines are again called wolves in Paradiso xxv, 6.

LINE 53
Pisa.

LINES 58-66
The ferocious Podestà (chief magistrate) of Florence in the first year of Dante's exile. Here of course the language is wholly figurative. Since the Florentines are wolves, the city itself becomes a grim wood containing their dens.

31 For from its fountain,—where the waters pour
   so amply from that rugged mountain chain
   torn from Pelorus, seldom teeming more,

34 As far as where it renders up again
   that which the heaven absorbs from out the flood,
   wherefrom the rivers have their flowing train,—

37 Virtue is driven like a serpent brood,
   the enemy of all, or through mischance
   of place, or scourge of evil habitude.

40 Whence so disnatured are the habitants
   of that unhappy vale, it would appear
   that Circe had them in her maintenance.

43 Among foul hogs, of acorns worthier
   than other viands made for use of men,
   it first directs its puny thoroughfare;

46 Curs it encounters, coming downward then,
   more snarling than their power gives warranty,
   and turns from them its muzzle in disdain;

49 The more it flows on downward swellingly,
   the more the dogs grown wolves are found by this
   accursed ditch of evil destiny,

52 Which then, descending many a deep abyss,
   finds fraudful foxes such as do not fear
   to be entrapt by any artifice.

55 Nor do I curb my tongue lest others hear:
   and good for this man to remember well
   the things true prophecy is making clear.

58 I see thy grandson, who becomes a fell
   hunter of those wolf-creatures, terror giving
   to all who by the cruel river dwell.

61 He traffics in their flesh while it is living,
   then slaughters them as would a wild-beast hoar;
   many of life, himself of praise bereaving.

116 JOHN HENRY NASH, San Francisco, 1929

Dante: *The Divine Comedy*   9 x 13⁷⁄₈

THE BOOK OF
COMMON PRAYER

and Administration of the Sacraments
and Other Rites and Ceremonies
of the Church

ACCORDING TO THE USE OF THE
PROTESTANT EPISCOPAL CHURCH
IN THE UNITED STATES OF AMERICA

❧

Together with The Psalter
or Psalms of David

PRINTED FOR THE COMMISSION
A. D. MDCCCCXXVIII

117   DANIEL BERKELEY UPDIKE, Boston, 1930

The Book of Common Prayer   9½ x 13⅜

beheld the linen clothes laid by themselves, and departed, wondering in himself at that which was come to pass.

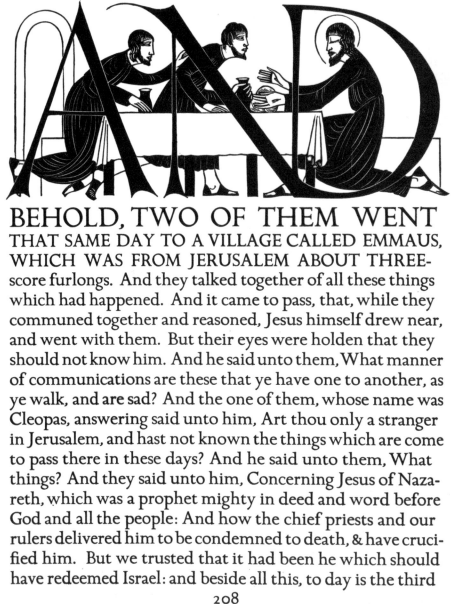

BEHOLD, TWO OF THEM WENT THAT SAME DAY TO A VILLAGE CALLED EMMAUS, WHICH WAS FROM JERUSALEM ABOUT THREE-score furlongs. And they talked together of all these things which had happened. And it came to pass, that, while they communed together and reasoned, Jesus himself drew near, and went with them. But their eyes were holden that they should not know him. And he said unto them, What manner of communications are these that ye have one to another, as ye walk, and are sad? And the one of them, whose name was Cleopas, answering said unto him, Art thou only a stranger in Jerusalem, and hast not known the things which are come to pass there in these days? And he said unto them, What things? And they said unto him, Concerning Jesus of Naza-reth, which was a prophet mighty in deed and word before God and all the people: And how the chief priests and our rulers delivered him to be condemned to death, & have cruci-fied him. But we trusted that it had been he which should have redeemed Israel: and beside all this, to day is the third

208

BOOK I

By now the other warriors, those that had escaped headlong ruin by sea or in battle, were safely home. Only Odysseus tarried, shut up by Lady Calypso, a nymph and very Goddess, in her hewn-out caves. She craved him for her bed-mate : while he was longing for his house and his wife. Of a truth the rolling seasons had at last brought up the year marked by the Gods for his return to Ithaca; but not even there among his loved things would he escape further conflict. Yet had all the Gods with lapse of time grown compassionate towards Odysseus—all but Poseidon, whose enmity flamed ever against him till he had reached his home. Poseidon, however, was for the moment far away among the Aethiopians, that last race of men, whose dispersion across the world's end is so broad that some of them can see the Sun-God rise while others see him set.

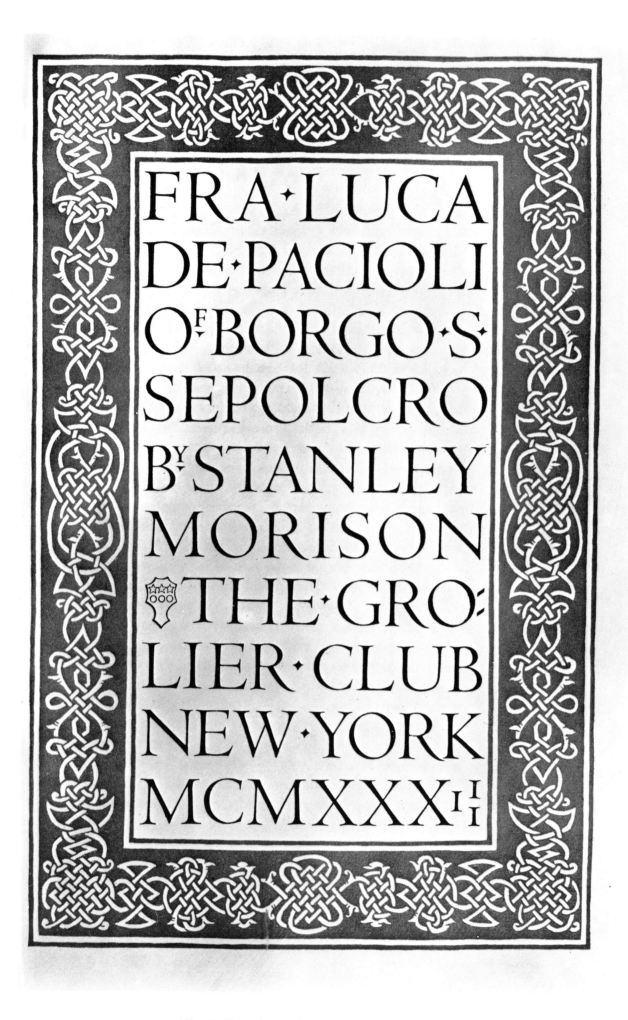

120   BRUCE ROGERS (Cambridge University Press), Cambridge, 1933
Stanley Morison: *Fra Luca de Pacioli*   8⅜ x 12⅜

THE

HOLY BIBLE

Containing the Old and New
Testaments : Translated out
of the Original Tongues and
with the former Translations
diligently compared and revised by His Majesty's special
Command

Appointed to be read in Churches

OXFORD

Printed at the University Press

1935

121   BRUCE ROGERS (Oxford University Press), Oxford, 1935
The Holy Bible   12¼ x 17¾

The First Book of Moses, called
GENESIS

CHAPTER I

IN THE BEGINNING GOD CREATED THE HEAVEN AND THE EARTH. ❡2 And the earth was without form, and void; and darkness was upon the face of the deep. And the Spirit of God moved upon the face of the waters. ❡3 And God said, Let there be light: and there was light. ❡4 And God saw the light, that it was good: and God divided the light from the darkness. ❡5 And God called the light Day, and the darkness he called Night. And the evening and the morning were the first day.

❡6 And God said, Let there be a firmament in the midst of the waters, and let it divide the waters from the waters. ❡7 And God made the firmament, and divided the waters which were under the firmament from the waters which were above the firmament: and it was so. ❡8 And God called the firmament Heaven. And the evening and the morning were the second day.

❡9 And God said, Let the waters under the heaven be gathered together unto one place, and let the dry land appear: and it was so. ❡10 And God called the dry land Earth; and the gathering together of the waters called he Seas: and God saw that it was good. ❡11 And God said, Let the earth bring forth grass, the herb yielding seed, and the fruit tree yielding fruit after his kind, whose seed is in itself, upon the earth: and it was so. ❡12 And the earth brought forth grass, and herb yielding seed after his kind, and the tree yielding fruit, whose seed was in itself, after his kind: and God saw that it was good. ❡13 And the evening and the morning were the third day.

❡14 And God said, Let there be lights in the firmament of the heaven to divide the day from the night; and let them be for signs, and for seasons, and for days, and years: ❡15 And let them be for lights in the firmament of the heaven to give light upon the earth: and it was so. ❡16 And God made two great lights; the greater light to rule the day, and the lesser light to rule the night: he made the stars also. ❡17 And God set them in the firmament of the heaven to give light upon the earth, ❡18 And to rule over the day and over the night, and to divide the light from the darkness: and God saw that it was good. ❡19 And the evening and the morning were the fourth day. ❡20 And God said, Let the waters bring forth abundantly the moving creature that hath life, and fowl that may fly above the earth in the open firmament of heaven. ❡21 And God created great whales, and every living creature that moveth, which the waters brought forth abundantly, after their kind, and every winged fowl after his kind: and God saw that it was good. ❡22 And God blessed them, saying, Be fruitful, and multiply, and fill the waters in the seas, and let fowl multiply in the earth. ❡23 And the evening and the morning were the fifth day.

❡24 And God said, Let the earth bring forth the living creature after his kind, cattle, and creeping thing, and beast of the earth after his kind: and it was so. ❡25 And God made the beast of the earth after his kind, and cattle after their kind, and every thing that creepeth upon the earth after his kind: and God saw that it was good.

❡26 And God said, Let us make man in our image, after our likeness: and let them have dominion over the fish of the sea, and over the fowl of the air, and over the cattle, and over all the earth, and over every creeping thing that creepeth upon the earth. ❡27 So God created man in his own image, in the image of God created he him; male and female created he them. ❡28 And God blessed them, and God said unto them, Be fruitful, and multiply, and replenish the earth, and subdue it: and have dominion over the fish of the sea, and over the fowl of the air, and over every living thing that moveth upon the earth.

❡29 And God said, Behold, I have given you every herb bearing seed, which is upon the face of all the earth, and every tree, in the which is the fruit of a tree yielding seed; to you it shall be for meat. ❡30 And to every beast of the earth,

122   BRUCE ROGERS (Oxford University Press), Oxford, 1935
The Holy Bible   12¼ x 17¾

PAPERMAKING BY HAND IN AMERICA

DARD HUNTER

CHILLICOTHE, OHIO
UNITED STATES OF AMERICA
MOUNTAIN HOUSE PRESS
Anno Domini 1950

123   DARD HUNTER, Chillicothe, Ohio, 1950

Dard Hunter: *Papermaking by Hand in America*   11½ x 16½

Lieblich tönt die gehämmerte Sens' und die Stimme des
                                    Landmanns/
  Der heimkehrend dem Stier gerne die Schritte gebeut/
Lieblich der Mutter Gesang/
                          die im Grase sitzt mit dem Söhnlein;
  Satt vom Sehen entschließ/aber die Wolken sind rot/
Und am glänzenden See/wo der Hain das offene Hoftor
  Übergrünt und das Licht golden die Fenster umspielt/
Dort empfängt mich das Haus
                          und des Gartens heimliches Dunkel/
  Wo mit den Pflanzen mich einst liebend der Vater erzog;
Wo ich frei/wie Geflügelte/spielt auf lustigen Ästen/
  Oder ins treue Blau blickte vom Gipfel des Hains.
Treu auch bist du von je/treu auch dem Flüchtlinge blieben/
  Freundlich nimmst du/wie einst/
                          Himmel der Heimat/mich auf.
Noch gedeihen die Pfirsiche mir/mich wundern die Blüten/
  Fast/wie die Bäume/steht herrlich mit Rosen der Strauch.
Schwer ist worden indes
                          von Früchten dunkel mein Kirschbaum/
  Und der pflückenden Hand reichen die Zweige sich selbst.
Auch zum Walde zieht mich/wie sonst/in die freiere Laube
  Aus dem Garten der Pfad oder hinab an den Bach/
Wo ich lag/und den Mut erfreut' am Ruhme der Männer/
  Ahnender Schiffer; und das konnten die Sagen von euch/
Dass in die Meer' ich fort/in die Wüsten musst/
                          ihr Gewaltgen!
  Ach/indes mich umsonst Vater und Mutter gesucht.
Aber wo sind sie?
                  du schweigst? du zögerst? Hüter des Hauses!
  Hab ich gezögert doch auch! habe die Schritte gezählt/
Da ich nahet'/und bin/gleich Pilgern/stille gestanden.
  Aber gehe hinein/melde den Fremden/den Sohn/
Dass sich öffnen die Arm' und mir ihr Segen begegne/
  Dass ich geweiht/und gegönnt wieder die Schwelle mir sei!
Aber ich ahnd es schon/in heilige Fremde dahin sind
  Nun auch sie mir/und nie kehret ihr Lieben zurück.

108

124 VICTOR HAMMER (Stamperia del Santuccio), Lexington, Kentucky, 1949
    J. C. F. Hölderlin: *Gedichte* 9 x 13

THE NYMPHS OF FIESOLE

BY GIOVANNI BOCCACCIO WITH THE WOODCUTS
MADE BY BARTOLOMMEO DI GIOVANNI FOR A LOST
QUATTROCENTO EDITION, WHICH WERE
USED TO ILLUSTRATE VARIOUS LATER
TEXTS AND HAVE NOW BEEN
REASSEMBLED AND
RECUT

EDITIONES OFFICINAE BODONI · VERONA
MDCCCCLII

125 GIOVANNI MARDERSTEIG (Officina Bodoni), Verona, 1952
Boccaccio: *The Nymphs of Fiesole*   7⅜ x 11⅛

SELECTIVE BIBLIOGRAPHY

Elizabeth Armstrong. *Robert Estienne, Royal Printer*. The University Press. Cambridge. 1954.

Nicolas Barker. *Stanley Morison*. Harvard University Press. Cambridge, Mass. 1972.

Roland Baugham and Robert O. Schad. *Great Books in Great Editions*. The Huntington Library. San Marino, Calif. 1954.

David Bland. *A History of Book Illustration*. The World Publishing Company. Cleveland and New York. 1958.

Joseph Blumenthal. *An Address at the Opening of the Bruce Rogers Centenary Exhibition, 15 April 1970, at The Grolier Club*. Printed in the *Gazette of The Grolier Club*, no. 14. New York. 1970.

Wilfred Blunt. *Cockerell*. Hamish Hamilton. London. 1964.

Book Typography 1815–1965 in Europe and the United States of America. Edited with an Introduction by Kenneth Day. The University of Chicago Press. 1966. First published in the Netherlands by NV Drukkerij G. J. Thieme. 1965.

Jacques Boussard. *The Civilisation of Charlemagne*. Weidenfeld and Nicolson. London. 1968.

Curt F. Bühler. *The Fifteenth-Century Book*. University of Pennsylvania Press. Philadelphia. 1960.

Curt F. Bühler. *Early Books and Manuscripts. Forty Years of Research*. The Grolier Club and The Pierpont Morgan Library. New York. 1973.

Warren Chappell. *A Short History of the Printed Word*. Alfred A. Knopf. New York. 1970.

Colin Clair. *A History of Printing in Britain*. Oxford University Press. New York. 1966.

Colin Clair. *Christopher Plantin*. Cassell and Co. London. 1960.

A. G. Dickens. *Reformation and Society in Sixteenth-Century Europe*. Harcourt, Brace & World, Inc. New York. 1970.

John Dreyfus. *Giovanni Mardersteig. An Account of His Work*. Keepsake for Gallery 303. New York. 1966.

Otto W. Fuhrmann. *Gutenberg and the Strasbourg Documents of 1439*. Press of the Woolly Whale. New York. 1940.

Philip Gaskell. *A New Introduction to Bibliography*. Oxford University Press. New York & Oxford. 1972.

David Greenhood and Helen Gentry. *Chronology of Books & Printing*. The Macmillan Company. New York. 1936.

Benton L. Hatch, Editor. *A Check List of the Publications of Thomas Bird Mosher of Portland Maine*. With a Biographical Essay by Ray Nash. The University of Massachusetts Press. Amherst. 1966.

Heritage of the Graphic Arts. Edited by Chandler B. Grannis. R. R. Bowker Company. New York and London. 1972.

Philip Hofer. *The Artist & the Book 1860–1960, in Western Europe and the United States*. Museum of Fine Arts, Boston. Harvard College Library. 1961.

Dard Hunter. *Papermaking: The History and Technique of an Ancient Craft*. Alfred A. Knopf. New York. 1947.

Dard Hunter. *My Life with Paper*. Alfred A. Knopf. New York. 1958.

A. F. Johnson. *Selected Essays on Books and Printing*. Edited by Percy H. Muir. Van Gendt & Co., Amsterdam. Abner Schram. New York. 1970.

Geoffrey Keynes. *William Pickering, Publisher*. The Fleuron. London. 1924.

Hellmut Lehmann-Haupt. *Gutenberg and the Master of the Playing Cards*. Yale University Press. New Haven and London. 1966.

Hellmut Lehmann-Haupt. *Peter Schoeffer of Gernsheim and Mainz*. The Printing House of Leo Hart. Rochester, N.Y. 1950.

Hellmut Lehmann-Haupt. With Laurence C. Wroth and Rollo G. Silver. *The Book in America*. R. R. Bowker Company. New York. 1951.

Norma Levarie. *The Art & History of Books*. James H. Heineman, Inc. New York. 1968.

John Lewis. *Anatomy of Printing*. Watson-Guptill Publications. New York. 1970.

A. Hyatt Mayor. *Prints and People*. The Metropolitan Museum of Art. New York. 1971.

Ruari McLean. *Victorian Book Design and Colour Printing*. Second edition. Faber and Faber. London. 1972.

Douglas C. McMurtrie. *The Book: The Story of Printing & Bookmaking*. Third edition. Oxford University Press. New York. 1943.

Francis Meynell. *English Printed Books*. Collins. London. 1946.

Francis Meynell. *My Lives*. Random House. New York. 1971.

James Moran. *Stanley Morison: His Typographic Achievement*. Hastings House. New York. 1971.

Stanley Morison and Kenneth Day. *The Typographic Book 1450–1935. A Study of Fine Typography Through Five Centuries*. The University of Chicago Press. 1963.

Stanley Morison. *John Bell*. Cambridge University Press. 1931.

Stanley Morison. *Politics and Script*. At the Clarendon Press. Oxford. 1972.

Ruth Mortimer, Compiler. *French Sixteenth Century Books*. Harvard University Press. Cambridge, Mass. 1964.

The Nonesuch Century. An Appraisal, a Personal Note and a Bibliography of the first hundred books issued by the Press, 1923–1934. The Nonesuch Press. London. 1936.

Alfred W. Pollard. *Fine Books*. Methuen and Co., Ltd. London. 1912.

Printing and the Mind of Man. Catalogue of the exhibitions at the British Museum and at Earls Court, London, July, 1963. Copies obtainable from the British Museum.

Printing and the Mind of Man. A Descriptive Catalogue Illustrating the Impact of Print on the Evolution of Western Civilization During Five Centuries. Compiled and edited by John Carter and Percy H. Muir. Cassell and Company. London. Holt, Rinehart and Winston. New York. 1967.

Quarto-millenary—The First 250 Publications and the First 25 Years of The Limited Editions Club. The Limited Editions Club. New York. 1959.

Will Ransom. *Private Presses and Their Books*. R. R. Bowker and Co. New York. 1929.

Bruce Rogers, with James Hendrickson. *Paragraphs on Printing*. William E. Rudge's Sons. New York. 1943.

Bruce Rogers. *Report on the Typography of the Cambridge University Press*. Printed at Christmas 1950 by Brooke Crutchley, University Printer. Cambridge.

Victor Scholderer. *Fifty Essays in Fifteenth- and Sixteenth-Century Bibliography*. Edited by Dennis Rhodes. Menno Hertzberger & Co. Amsterdam. 1966.

Clifford K. Shipton. *Isaiah Thomas. Printer, Patriot and Philanthropist*. The Printing House of Leo Hart. Rochester, N.Y. 1948.

Rollo G. Silver. *The American Printer, 1787–1825*. The Bibliographical Society of the University of Virginia. 1967.

Oliver Simon. *Printer and Playground. An Autobiography*. Faber and Faber. London. 1956.

H. Halliday Sparling. *The Kelmscott Press and William Morris, Master Craftsman*. Macmillan and Co., Limited. London. 1924.

S. H. Steinberg. *Five Hundred Years of Printing*. Penguin Books. Baltimore, Md. 1961.

Norman H. Strouse. [*Thomas Bird Mosher*] *The Passionate Pirate*. Bird and Bull Press. North Hills, Pa. 1964.

Paul Thompson. *The Work of William Morris*. The Viking Press. New York. 1967.

Geofroy Tory. *Champ Fleury*. Translated into English and Annotated by George B. Ives. The Grolier Club. New York. 1927.

Daniel Berkeley Updike. *In the Day's Work*. Harvard University Press. Cambridge, Mass. 1924.

Daniel Berkeley Updike. *Printing Types, their History, Forms and Use*. Third edition. The Belknap Press of Harvard University. Cambridge, Mass. 1962.

Updike: American Printer and His Merrymount Press. Notes on the Press and Its Work by Daniel Berkeley Updike. With a Gathering of Essays by Stanley Morison, Gregg Anderson, T. M. Cleland, M. A. De Wolfe Howe, George Parker Winship, Rudolph Ruzicka, David T. Pottinger, Carl P. Rollins. The American Institute of Graphic Arts. New York. 1947.

Hendrick D. L. Vervliet, Editor. *The Book through Five Thousand Years*. Phaidon Press. London and New York. 1972.

Frederic Warde. *Bruce Rogers. Designer of Books*. Harvard University Press. Cambridge, Mass. 1925.

James Wardrop. *The Script of Humanism*. At the Clarendon Press. Oxford. 1963.

Monroe Wheeler. *Modern Painters and Sculptors as Illustrators*. The Museum of Modern Art. New York. 1936.

Philippe Wolff. *The Awakening of Europe*. Penguin Books. Baltimore, Md. 1968.

Lawrence C. Wroth, Editor. *A History of the Printed Book. Number 3 of The Dolphin: A Journal of The Making of Books*. The Limited Editions Club. New York. 1938.

Lawrence C. Wroth. *The Colonial Printer*. Second edition. The Southworth-Anthoenson Press. Portland, Me. 1938.

INDEX

Letterpress composition and printing in the Baskerville type for text,

with Bulmer headings, and Perpetua for title display, by

THE STINEHOUR PRESS · LUNENBURG · VERMONT

Plates made and printed by the

MERIDEN GRAVURE COMPANY · MERIDEN · CONNECTICUT

*

TYPOGRAPHY BY JOSEPH BLUMENTHAL